PARIS CHIC

THE PARISIAN'S OWN INSIDER SHOPPING GUIDE

DOMINIQUE BRABEC and ÉGLÉ SALVY

Illustrations by
PASCALE LAURENT

THAMES AND HUDSON

PREFACE

We have been journalists for 25 years – working in tandem for 20 – with responsibility for women's pages such as *Madame-Express*. An experience that has inevitably left its mark – and a fat notebook bulging with addresses. From amongst these we have selected the *crème de la crème*. Some are obvious ones and we simply explain wherein their excellence lies. Others are less well known and we tell you why we like them. Adding, in some cases, a heart symbol to indicate a special preference, or a club to indicate a price range that strikes us as particularly reasonable. Because 'chic' doesn't always have to imply 'expensive'.

Make no mistake: this book is a guide, not a catalogue. There are plenty of shops that you won't find here: we have our prejudices and are ready to defend them. From the latest in hip trends to classical lines, from high-tech to Italian veneer, from brand-new collections to traditional craftsmen, our curiosity is insatiable. To our friends, just as to our Editors in Chief, we have always declared our love of 'walking the streets'. And we rarely ever return empty-handed.

We have included some maps among the illustrations to show our favourite areas, areas we have scoured innumerable times, and where the concentration of good shops seems to increase with every visit. We keep saying 'we' because, though one of us (Dominique Brabec) is more of a specialist in fashion and the other (Eglé Salvy) is more of an interior design person, we have both observed that more and more shops these days are selling a whole variety of very different items – boldly juggling under one roof skirts and chairs, jams and watches, tablecloths and nightgowns. Some of the big couturiers have been setting a precedent in this area for years, first creating accessories, then following them with household items, carpets, linen, and so on. After all, clothes and décor are closely linked in the course of our daily lives, so why separate them arbitrarily? (That said, however, this is precisely what we have done at the end of the guide in deciding to divide the shops into two separate indexes, feeling that a single one would have proved indigestible.) In 'The Art of Fashion' couturiers rub shoulders with designers, both established and avant-garde, and we make special mention of women designers who design for women. We have followed this chapter with 'The Parisian Woman's Wardrobe', classifying the clothes by type (tops, party dresses, etc.), and concluded this first section with 'Fashion Accessories' and 'The Art of Beauty'. In 'Large and Spacious Stores' we have given, in addition to a section on department stores, one on that new generation of shop which, by virtue of its size and its plethora of choice could just as well be called a 'small large shop' (we prefer the term 'megastore'). Under the heading 'The Classics' we tell the story of 41 cult objects which have acquired almost mythical status (and where to find them). 'In the Know' lets the cat out of the bag about the addresses that some women are reluctant to reveal even to their best friend!

There follow three chapters devoted to 'Household Arts' (including decorators, designers, antique and second-hand dealers), to 'Household Basics' and to the 'Household Accessories' essential to stylish living. Then, since Paris is a highly cosmopolitan city, we have gathered a number of shops together under the flag of their country of origin. And finally, since no one can live on shopping and fresh air alone, we have listed all those places where we like to stop for a drink or a bite to eat.

'Where can I find . . .?' is a question we have heard so many times. In response we have put together here a list of well over 1,000 addresses approved by both of us. The only thing we disagree about – and have done for 20 years – is where to buy macaroons. We each have our pet haunt: one of us particularly likes Dalloyau, the other Ladurée. We frequently make a special detour – for a treat, and in an attempt to win the other over. But it never works.

D.B. and E.S.

CONTENTS

THE ART OF FASHION

THE COUTURIERS

*Don't be put off by the uniformed porter, often employed to guard
the entrance. Or the saleswomen, who can be rather stuck-up.
Anyone is entitled to look round the couturiers' boutiques.
Frequently nestled into the ground floor of the couture house itself,
they are the showpiece of every collection. The décor is a treat in
itself – and you may even be able to afford the odd item – so don't
hesitate to seek them out.*

PIERRE BALMAIN The large glass door slides silently open.
You enter a small hallway, decorated entirely in Burgundian
stone, ivory columns and palmwood. It takes a certain amount of
courage to climb the staircase and enter the boutique, which is
like an elegant drawing-room with white upholstered sofas. The
top-of-the-range ready-to-wear collection under the 'Ivoire' label
is, actually, closer to a full-blown haute couture collection.
Smart outfits, elegant dresses, very 'city chic'. Almost a couture
department complete with fitting-rooms.

PIERRE BALMAIN   44, RUE FRANÇOIS-Iᵉʳ VIII – 47 20 35 34

CHRISTIAN LACROIX opened his boutique in the entrance
hall of his private town house. The interior – terracotta floor tiles,
padded chairs and distressed walls – was designed in the same
style as the couture salons by the duo Elisabeth Garouste and
Mattia Bonetti. Here you will find crêpe pyjamas, colourful suits,
sarongs and exquisite foulard tops with ribbed-silk collars and
sleeves. There are the essential Lacroix accessories inspired by
Provence and the bullring, and also Byzantine touches: hearts,
crosses, suns, studded belts, straw hats. There's an affordable
little line of dresses at around 2,000 francs.

♡   **CHRISTIAN LACROIX   73, RUE DU FAUBOURG SAINT-HONORÉ VIII –
42 65 79 08**

You can tell immediately that Christian Lacroix is a child of the sun. In his space in the Avenue Montaigne, the ceiling is the colour of a blue, cloudless sky, the floor is covered in red hexagonal tiles, Spanish-Mexican-style furniture, chairs lined with roses like stained-glass windows or shining with crosses, hearts, the initials 'C' and 'L' that you can buy at 500 francs a pair and use as 'designer labels'. On hangers you'll find the whole ready-to-wear collection and the cruise collection.

♡   **CHRISTIAN LACROIX   26, AVENUE MONTAIGNE VIII – 47 20 68 95**

LECOANET HÉMANT Didier Lecoanet and Hémant Sagar are the youngest of the Parisian couturiers. These two friends, the one from Chomont and the other from Delhi, showed their first collection in September 1982. Nowadays, they have set themselves up in a section of the former Alençon building in the Marais. In ivory-coloured salons with ebony and gold chairs, the collections and the accessories are exhibited after fashion shows.

LECOANET HÉMANT   24, RUE VIEILLE-DU-TEMPLE IV – 42 72 45 16; 84, RUE DU FAUBOURG SAINT-HONORÉ VIII – 42 65 43 37

HANAË MORI is the only Japanese woman in the world of Parisian haute couture. Her first shop is hidden away in a cul-de-sac opposite the artistes' entrance of the Théâtre des Champs-Elysées. Her second premises, the beacon of her trademark, are decorated in natural oak and untreated marble, with typically Japanese purity of design. They play a starring role in the Rue du Faubourg Saint-Honoré. Elegant women will be able to discover her wonderful dinner dresses and evening gowns in crushed velvet, with their highly detailed embroidery. She also has accessories at reasonable prices.

HANAË MORI   9, RUE DU FAUBOURG SAINT-HONORÉ VIII – 42 65 14 38; 17–19, AVENUE MONTAIGNE VIII – 47 23 52 03

PACO RABANNE The stainless-steel sorcerer, who dressed Brigitte Bardot, Audrey Hepburn, Jane Fonda in *Barbarella* and Françoise Hardy on stage, is just as adept with fabric as he is with metal. His wonderful boutique, designed by the architect Eric Raffy, has the feel of a cave: the walls have no angles and the light has an almost liquid quality. All his creations can be found here, from that miracle of lightness, his evening bag, with small hand-applied aluminium plates, to quasi-classical suits and hipster belts.

PACO RABANNE   7, RUE DU CHERCHE-MIDI VI – 40 49 08 53

PIERRE CARDIN himself formed the concept behind his boutique, aglow with light and colour. This independent designer, who never stops pushing himself to the limits of his abilities, wanted to gather his whole universe together on two floors and in several well-defined spaces which, at the same time, all interconnect. There are hyper-realistic backdrops, pieces of polished wood sculpture-furniture in pure geometric shapes which open up to reveal a conjurer's hat of surprises, and deep sofas in which to sit and watch videos of fashion shows. Tremendously well-cut coats, men's suits, structured dresses – all these are on offer as well as perfumes, including the most recent addition: 'Rose Cardin'.

PIERRE CARDIN   27, AVENUE DE MARIGNY VIII – 42 66 92 25

CHANEL In the 20s she was the first to strip her gilded walls and decorate her screens instead with crushed suede. She dyed her carpets beige to simulate sun-dried earth. Christian Gaillon, the architect, knew exactly how to use black-and-white, pure, linear décor and immense mirrors and still keep within the spirit of the establishment. Still irresistible are the famous Chanel suit, the padded handbag, the pigeon's-nest earrings and the range of perfumes from 'No. 5' to 'Egoïste'.

♡   **CHANEL   31, RUE CAMBON I – 42 61 54 55; 40–42, AVENUE MONTAIGNE VIII – 47 23 74 12**

CHRISTIAN DIOR What a long time ago February 1947 seems, when Dior opened the doors of his first boutique and, with it, presented his 'New Look'. Hung with toile de Jouy (an idea of Christian Bérard's) in pearl grey (Dior's favourite colour), it would appear to be old-fashioned in the face of 1,600 square metres decorated entirely by Roland De Leu. The 16th-century theme remains intact but, now, in a neo-classical kind of way, complete with columns, an antique rotunda and Roman paving, all harmonizing in grey. You can be clothed there from the day of your birth. A small department store, in fact, in which every item carries the Dior label from the guest towels to the luggage, via the ready-to-wear women's collection designed by Gianfranco Ferré and the men's designed by Patrick Lavoix, a refugee from the House of Lanvin. Five assistants are entrusted with the task of making up white packets, tied with grey ribbon and stamped with the initials CD. In the gift department you will find an impressive selection from as little as 150 francs.

♡   **CHRISTIAN DIOR   32, AVENUE MONTAIGNE VIII – 40 73 54 44**

EMANUEL UNGARO entrusted Christian de Portzamparc with the task of decorating his space in the Avenue Montaigne. You go from one shop to the next pushing open splendid antique white-leaded and sculpted wooden doors. The entire ready-to-wear collection is gathered together in the shop, from the sublime, draped dresses to the jersey wool suits, from the

'Parallèle' range to the more affordable 'Solo Donna'. There is an alcove reserved exclusively for the two perfumes 'Diva' and 'Senso'. You'll find fashion on the first floor.

♡ **EMANUEL UNGARO**   2, AVENUE MONTAIGNE VIII – 47 23 61 94

GUY LAROCHE is a friendly shop which offers the best ratio of quality to price range of all the haute couture designers. It's not avant-garde but it has fashionable elegance. There are also hats designed by the stylist Guy Douvier who formerly worked very closely with Mlle Chanel and subsequently at Dior. Best-selling items: the suits.

♧ **GUY LAROCHE**   29, AVENUE MONTAIGNE VIII – 47 23 78 72

NINA RICCI is one of the biggest and most beautiful of the designer boutiques. The entrance is guarded deferentially by a porter. On the ground floor you will find the boutique areas, one of which contains the cashmeres including the famous square-patterned cloaks, another the highly sophisticated leatherware and, at very reasonable prices, an area with a very good range of presents for new-born babies (from around 150 francs). Gifts like imitation antique bibs, hand-knitted bootees, babies' travelling bags, and household objects. There is a very beautiful but expensive lingerie department, and a collection of gold and diamond jewelry specially created for Ricci by Gianmaria Buccellati, which may be gazed upon and admired but certainly not purchased. The shop selling off the old catwalk creations is no longer in the basement, but can now be found at 19, RUE FRANÇOIS-Ier VIII. The large shop remains:

NINA RICCI   39, AVENUE MONTAIGNE VIII – 47 23 78 88

JEAN PATOU The shop is, once again, on the ground floor, which is now exclusively devoted to the perfumes from 'Joy' to 'Mille', to all the scents in the 'Ma Collection' range, and to the accessories like the scarves, the shawls (from around 800 francs), the small leather-goods department, the jewelry, and, particularly, the earrings (from around 250 francs).

JEAN PATOU   7, RUE SAINT-FLORENTIN VIII – 44 77 33 00

CARVEN In 1945 Madame Carven set up shop at the round-about known as the Rond Point des Champs-Elysées. On display she has a young, modern range, dedicated to petite women, like herself. She also specializes in uniforms. In her salon-boutique, the pretty little princess dresses and outfits for tiny figures are set off by huge mirrors and quilted damask curtains.

CARVEN   6, ROND-POINT DES CHAMPS-ÉLYSÉES VIII – 42 25 66 52

TORRENTE Rosette Mett Torrente set up in business in the premises which once sheltered Robert Piguet and from where

Christian Dior began his career. Three shops open on to each other. The felt-covered, immaculate interior has been fitted out by Yves Taralon. There are walls draped in white, doors covered in small ceramic tiles, furniture made of white-leaded oak, and there are reflecting screens. In this shop the soft woollen cardigans, the little pullovers and the shirts are all perfect and sophisticated, a fact that a lot of people don't know. Miss Torrente is the more affordable range (from 1,500 francs).

TORRENTE   3, ROND-POINT DES CHAMPS-ÉLYSÉES VIII – 42 56 14 14

GIVENCHY A large glass door covered in tiles, a wide stone staircase, a floor covered in black and white – all this goes to make up the shop of Audrey Hepburn's favourite designer, which looks like the hall of an upmarket town house. Of course, you will find the beautiful, elegant suits, the pretty dresses with their short sleeves and the shirts that suited the beautiful actress so very well. You will also find all the accessories, shawls and T-shirts. Regulars know that what you find here, and only either here or in the couture salons, is the jewelry created to go with the collection.

GIVENCHY   3, AVENUE GEORGE-V VIII – 47 23 81 31

LOUIS FÉRAUD is a couturier, but he's also a painter. Between painting and designing there is but a very small gap, which Louis Féraud has bridged. He gets the inspiration for the prints on his ready-to-wear clothes, his shirts and his scarves from his own paintings, and they should be seen in their full technicolour range.

LOUIS FÉRAUD   88–90, RUE DU FAUBOURG SAINT-HONORÉ VIII – 42 65 27 29

YVES SAINT LAURENT The entrance to the shop is also that of the haute couture establishment. You have to climb a handsome red-carpeted staircase to reach the receptionist. On the right are the fashion-show salons and on the left is the pretty area in Napoleon III style (1860s) where you will find the necklaces which are accessories to the couture collections, as well as the cashmere pullovers and the shawls.

♡   YVES SAINT LAURENT   5, AVENUE MARCEAU XVI – 47 23 72 71

GRÈS The High Priestess of the draped dress, she has now allowed a Japanese consortium to open up a boutique using her name. It has the feel of a 'maison de haute couture' with its two storeys, its light-coloured wood, padded lifts and the sophisticated atmosphere in which you will find a collection that has been carefully thought through by a team of five. The shop's strong point is the classically styled evening gowns.

GRÈS   422, RUE SAINT-HONORÉ VIII – 42 60 72 00

And also:

LANVIN 22, FAUBOURG SAINT-HONORÉ VIII – 44 71 33 33
PER SPOOK 18, AVENUE GEORGE-V VIII – 47 23 00 19
BALENCIAGA 10, AVENUE GEORGE-V VIII – 47 20 21 11
TED LAPIDUS 35, RUE FRANÇOIS-Iᵉʳ VIII – 47 20 56 14
COURRÈGES 40, RUE FRANÇOIS-Iᵉʳ VIII – 47 20 70 44

THE CREATORS OF FASHION

The creators of fashion want to show their collections to advantage. From the most celebrated to the latest on the scene, they simply have to have a shop in Paris and, with it, a way of displaying their goods. But it's also a way of constantly testing women's reactions to their clothes.

CHANTAL THOMASS is not only the queen of the sexy undergarment, she can also design very feminine clothes. She has set up shop with her husband, Bruce, in new premises at Saint-Cloud and has designed her most beautiful shop like a second home. There are personal items, curtains and plush sofas in a setting designed by Jean-Louis Riccardi. You simply have to see it for its charm alone, and then take in the underwear, the necklaces and the soft, fetching dresses.
♡ **CHANTAL THOMASS** 1, RUE VIVIENNE I – 47 03 38 34

ISSEY MIYAKÉ Thanks to Issey Miyaké, the greatest of Japanese creators, a small drawing school has been transformed into a haven of serenity, elegance and Buddhist-influenced simplicity. This is characterized by spotless white, and flower-decked windows which look out on to a garden courtyard. Set up by Tomio Mori, who regularly stages the master's exhibitions and fashion parades, the shop is dedicated to the great collection, with its flagstone floor, its shelving and its cut-out iron mannequins. You will find the whole ethereal range here, the origami-style pleats made in cotton or synthetic materials, the flowing raincoats and the overall-style trousers in avant-garde materials.

ISSEY MIYAKÉ   3, PLACE DES VOSGES IV – 48 87 01 86

JEAN-CHARLES DE CASTELBAJAC puts his world on show at the Palais-Royal. It's a sophisticated space, aglow with light and freshly painted whitewashed walls reminiscent of a monk's cell – but which Patrick de Maupeou, the designer, has maintained in the most charming way. This is the kind of décor which is perfect for showing off men's or women's clothing, sofas, household linen or, indeed, crockery. His ponchos have become classic everyday wear and the whole shop has the prettiest view of the Palais-Royal gardens.

JEAN-CHARLES DE CASTELBAJAC   5, RUE DES PETITS-CHAMPS I – 42 60 37 33

MICHEL KLEIN showed his very first textile designs to Saint Laurent, who accepted them. Next Jacqueline Jacobson took him on as an assistant for the Dorothée Bis knitwear collection. Now he can be counted as one of the most talented creators in Paris: he knows how to work with wool mixes, how to cut his mandarin-style silk or unbleached cotton jackets and how to design little knitted tops, pullovers and cardigans for evening wear. Ideal for the daily needs of busy women.

⚘   MICHEL KLEIN   6, RUE DU PRÉ-AUX-CLERCS VII – 42 60 37 11

ANGELO TARLAZZI The designer Pier Luigi Pizzi has transplanted a Roman-style décor on to this charming Italian's salon with its enormous Corinthian cornice in sun-drenched Mediterranean colours. The man who knows better than anyone how to show off a woman's beauty now has a space in which models and customers double up in mirrors. You will find jersey sheaths, wrap-around skirts and knitwear. The Tarlazzi II range is a lot more affordable.

ANGELO TARLAZZI   3, RUE DU BOCCADOR VIII – 40 69 69 77

KENZO All Parisians are aware of the amazing shop on the Place des Victoires, but you should also investigate the one on the Left Bank. You would think that you are on the veranda of a country house, all done up in glass above a patio with pale rose-coloured walls and a wooden floor enhanced by mosaic tiling. By the entrance you will find the most wonderful wool, cotton and silk scarves in myriad sizes printed with images of Paris. You just have to start forming a collection. They still have the delightful shoes and the Kenzo designs, including the very straight jacket, the skin-tight trousers and the colourful coats that never go out of fashion.

♡ ♣ **KENZO 16, BOULEVARD RASPAIL VII – 42 22 09 38; 3, PLACE DES VICTOIRES I – 40 39 72 01**

FRÉDÉRIC CASTET is a Master of Fur who, for years and years, was in charge at Dior, where he transformed mink and sable into works of art. Naturally, his shops sell fur, but they also sell clothes in a new fabric called 'Castiss', which is a fluffy material woven from cotton and looks like the shorn fleece of a sheep.

FRÉDÉRIC CASTET 52, RUE PIERRE-CHARRON VIII – 49 52 02 45; 45, RUE FRANÇOIS-Iᵉʳ VIII – 42 25 71 09

ALAÏA has opened a shop in a former industrial works which is now the setting in which he both shows his collections and has his shop. You won't find any windows here, in the realm of the king of the sexy undergarment. But you will find brick walls, girders, polished wooden floors and a 30-foot mirror. The whole place looks like an enormous dance studio and the most upmarket customers, models and actresses all come here and gaze at each other scantily clad without the least trace of embarrassment. The only snobbery in evidence is that of quality.

ALAÏA 7, RUE DE MOUSSY IV – 40 27 85 58

ROMEO GIGLI has transformed a former printworks into a Venetian extravaganza. There is a slightly set-back entrance, edged with small shrubs, and, under an enormous glass roof, rugs are strewn across the floor. The court coats are exhibited like the works of art that, indeed, they are. The cashmere jumpers blend in subtle harmonies of colour. The shirts have over-long sleeves, just as the master commands, and are cut in velvet, silk and cotton jersey. The mezzanine level is devoted entirely to men's fashion.

ROMEO GIGLI 46, RUE DE SÉVIGNÉ IV – 48 04 57 08

SONIA RYKIEL The only woman in the world to have constructed an entire empire from a single jumper has now invested in a five-storey building a few yards from her shops in the Rue de Grenelle. In celebration of more than 20 successful years in the trade, she chose the architect Roland de Leu to renovate a private town house, constructed in 1544. It is carpeted in black with white flecks and panelled with light-coloured wood, and creates the private fiefdom from which Sonia can watch over her offices and her studios. On the ground floor there is an amazing glass-covered shop setting the scene for her creations, including the fabled sweaters, the wool and lurex jackets, the T-shirts, the bags that fit into each other, the household linen, the make-up, and even jams.

SONIA RYKIEL   175, BOULEVARD SAINT-GERMAIN VI – 49 54 60 60

ANNE-MARIE BERETTA wears her long plait of hair like a jewel and constructs her designs like an architect. Nowadays, the queen of the overcoat and the raincoat has mellowed a little, and this is reflected in her collection. But her overcoats and her trenchcoats, made up in natural fabrics, are still the best-looking coats in town.

ANNE-MARIE BERETTA   24, RUE SAINT-SULPICE VI – 43 26 99 30

THIERRY MUGLER is located in the Place des Victoires and on the Avenue Montaigne in an area reserved exclusively for top designers. You go in via a long corridor lit up by science-fiction-style space rockets, at the end of which you arrive at an astral space. Come here for suits that create fine silhouettes and for heavily draped dresses.

THIERRY MUGLER   49, AVENUE MONTAIGNE VIII – 47 23 37 62; 10, PLACE DES VICTOIRES II – 42 60 06 37

JEAN-PAUL GAULTIER Worth visiting for the shop itself, which is truly extraordinary. Tourists come simply to gawp. Under a glass roof you will find a two-storey shop which draws its influences from Captain Nemo's craft, from Pompeii and from the Eiffel Tower all at the same time. On the floor are traces of a mosaic and on the wall there are portholes through which the video of the collection is projected. But don't let all this bold design interfere with your actual appreciation of the beautiful, classic clothes. There are waisted jackets, perfectly cut trousers and unimpeachable knitwear.

JEAN-PAUL GAULTIER   6, GALERIE VIVIENNE II – 42 86 05 05

BERNARD PERRIS The Princess of Bourbon-Parma and Eléonore de La Rochefoucauld are both customers of this creator who was trained in the art of haute couture by Guy Laroche, Jacques Heim and Christian Dior. The place for superb cocktail dresses and golden, brocaded ball gowns. Don't look at the price tags unless you want to feel dizzy. They are real couture prices.

BERNARD PERRIS   48 BIS, RUE FRANÇOIS-Iᵉʳ VIII – 47 20 55 62

KARL LAGERFELD has gathered all his deluxe clothes together in one shop. There are the suits with their maxi-skirts as well as the handbags, the blouses, the shoes and the jewels. Karl, who constantly loves to renovate, frequently changes the décor in his shop in time for the new season. You simply have to visit it and discover the very latest thing in interior design.

**KARL LAGERFELD 19, RUE DU FAUBOURG SAINT-HONORÉ VIII –
42 66 64 64**

POPY MORENI is the queen of ruffs and carnival outfits, but
she also knows how to design perfectly cut clothes made of jersey
wool and how to harmonize in black, white and red.
POPY MORENI 13, PLACE DES VOSGES IV – 42 77 09 96

HELMUT LANG He has the nonchalance of the Italian and the
genes of the Viennese. He invented 'city chic' with his little-
boy-blue trouser-suits that also look good on little girls, and his
body-dresses that you wear underneath trenchcoats and with
stretch T-shirts.
HELMUT LANG at MARIA LUISA 2, RUE CAMBON I – 47 03 96 15

COMME DES GARÇONS Rei Kawakubo, the High Priestess
of Japanese haute couture, gives her creations room to breathe on
the scattered uprights in this enormous space that has been
restored by the architect Takao Kawasaki. Scattered all around
you will see books, items of furniture, pieces of artwork,
exhibitions of paintings. Each of the creator's shows delivers a
new sociological message, and this is then reflected in her
boutique.
COMME DES GARÇONS 42, RUE ÉTIENNE-MARCEL I – 42 33 05 21

CLAUDE MONTANA comes top in the creators' Top 50. He
was the golden boy at Lanvin, which he left to spread his own
wings, and now designs the most ethereal organza smocks with
wing-collars, faultless shaped jackets and fitted trousers. All of
which are fine examples of modern haute couture.
♡ **CLAUDE MONTANA 31, RUE DE GRENELLE VII – 42 22 69 56**

DOROTHÉE BIS Elie and Jacqueline Jacobson were the
pioneers of knitted fashion, which they still create with the same
skill. There are long sweater-dresses and flowing jackets over
romper jumpers, and everything is easy-to-wear, modern and
with-it.
⚘ **DOROTHÉE BIS 46, RUE ÉTIENNE-MARCEL II – 42 21 04 00;
33, RUE DE SÈVRES VI – 42 22 00 45**

YOHJI YAMAMOTO is the philosopher of the fashion world.
He expresses it like a Zen incantation in white, black and red
with coils, drapes, knots and slits. His serene tabards slide like
petticoats under tunics. A little less demanding to wear are the
perfectly tailored long overcoats for men.
YOHJI YAMAMOTO 25, RUE DU LOUVRE I – 42 21 42 93

YVES SAINT LAURENT RIVE GAUCHE Of course, Saint
Laurent is a couturier but, for more than a quarter of a century

(since September 1966), he has also been one of the leading creators of ready-to-wear fashion. His marvellous suits, his dinner jackets, his blazers and all his variations on the gender-bender theme are unfailingly fashionable. As, no doubt, Catherine Deneuve would agree.

YVES SAINT LAURENT RIVE GAUCHE   6, PLACE SAINT-SULPICE VI – 43 29 43 00; 38, RUE DU FAUBOURG SAINT-HONORÉ VIII – 42 65 74 59

SMALL COLLECTIONS

The advent of the 'small collection' or 'diffusion range', a by-product of the big names in haute couture, has given Parisian women a rich new seam to mine. The 'junior' lines of senior designers all have their own code-names: 'Variations' (Saint Laurent), 'Solo Donna' (Ungaro) and 'Part II' (Junko Shimada), for example. These are the alternative collections that the top designers are now creating for wider distribution and, most importantly therefore, to sell at more affordable prices. These aren't simply copies of top-of-the-range models, but genuine new creations with the same spirit but cut in less luxurious fabric and made up on a production line.

YVES SAINT LAURENT VARIATIONS The diffusion line of Yves Saint Laurent, 'Variations' was widely distributed at one time through numerous outlets, but had no direct point of sale to the public in Paris. The whole collection has now been gathered together under one roof. White marble, poplar panelling and lilac-coloured wall-to-wall carpeting create the perfect setting for top-notch clothes designed in the studios of the great couture house. Tailored classics like trenchcoats, duffle coats, three-quarter-length jackets, jackets in tweed, wool and velvet, flannel trousers, tops and that perfect little suit for around 4,000 francs – you'll find everything you've ever loved about Saint Laurent here, and, what's more, at a price you can afford.

YVES SAINT LAURENT VARIATIONS 21, RUE DE TOURNON VI – 43 29 38 14

JUNKO SHIMADA PART II is aimed at young women. Junko Shimada dresses them in college-girl suits, waxed-canvas lumber jackets, city shorts, pretty smock-tops. The collection coordinates clothes and accessories with military caps, berets, scarves and belts. You will find all this in a charming little 17th-century house decorated by the Argentinian architect Julio Bernardou in white-leaded oak and slabs of glass. The floor is made of white cement and you can just dimly make out where the old cellars were situated. You enter via a door sporting an enormous porthole.

JUNKO SHIMADA PART II   34, RUE DES SAINTS-PÈRES VII – 42 22 58 55

INSCRIPTION RYKIEL It was Nathalie, Sonia Rykiel's daughter, who started the 'Inscription' label. Her mother made her take her apprenticeship in fashion very gradually, after starting off in the fashion business as a model, more than ten years ago. Nathalie dreamt about creating Rykiel-type clothes, only different, which is an aim that she has realized. Large black woollen sweaters embroidered with pretty names, sweatshirts with matching, loose-fitting jogging pants. 'Freedom within a universe', she says. At more affordable prices, there are fanciful little items and accessories.

INSCRIPTION RYKIEL   4, RUE DE GRENELLE VI – 49 54 61 10

JUNIOR GAULTIER 'It's got nothing to do with age, but everything to do with your wallet', says Jean-Paul Gaultier. And yet it is preeminently the young who take over his shop by Les Halles. His 50s street-style décor gives them a laugh. They like wandering around over his asphalt floor, rummaging through the clothes rails and the shelves that are fitted into scooped-out advertising pillars. And there are changing-rooms that look like public lavatories. The jeans are affordable, the tops irresistible, the pullovers are top-notch. It's all there, avant-garde and witty.

JUNIOR GAULTIER   7, RUE DU JOUR I – 40 28 01 91

PLANTATION Those women who can afford to do so, and can carry it off, should go to the Place des Vosges and treat themselves to the marvellous pleated clothes and the fitted body-suits in Issey Miyaké lycra. But for day-in, day-out wear, the creator designed 'Plantation', consisting of basic items often made of cotton and suited to the personality of the women who choose to wear them. Cognoscenti come to buy the large, windcheater-style trenchcoats and the pure-silk T-shirts.

PLANTATION   17, BOULEVARD RASPAIL VII – 45 48 12 32

KENZO STUDIO   Two boutiques house the cheaper diffusion collections of 'Kenzo Jungle' and 'Kenzo Jeans'. This most Parisian of all Japanese designers has created an enchanting décor in which to show off his clothes: straw-coloured walls, pale woodwork and flooring, and fitting-rooms decorated with poppies. The collections, which are on two floors, comprise pretty, flowery cardigans, matching mini-skirts, well-tailored 'Kenzo Jungle' jackets and tops by 'Kenzo Jeans'.

KENZO STUDIO   60–62, RUE DE RENNES VI – 45 44 27 88; 99, RUE DE PASSY XVI – 42 24 92 92

LOLITA BIS   Lolita Lempicka created her 'Bis' (alternative) range 'for sensible but cheeky young women', she says. It has been an enormous success with almost 100 outlets opening up all over France. There are waisted jackets, sexy little dresses, stretch-cotton T-shirts: the total armoury of the young temptress.

LOLITA BIS   3 BIS, RUE DES ROSIERS IV – 42 74 42 94

ISTANTE   Versace is as well known for his beaded dresses as for his spectacular printed shirts. He created 'Istante', a diffusion label, for simpler, less expensive clothes but still in his own distinctive style. Women Who Lunch will find the collection in a pretty shop with a brightly coloured mosaic floor and walls of circular glass framed in wood. His best-seller is the printed silk shirt at around 4,000 francs.

ISTANTE   11, RUE DU FAUBOURG SAINT-HONORÉ VIII – 49 24 04 74

OLIVER   was named after Valentino's favourite pug-dog. Oliver opened in the spring of 1989 and is very modern and simple. The line consists of superb suits, beautiful raincoats and above all impeccably cut silk tops.

OLIVER at VALENTINO   17–19 AVENUE MONTAIGNE VIII – 47 23 64 61

EMPORIO ARMANI   All the women who gasp with envy at the elegant window displays in Giorgio Armani's shop now rush to the Emporio Armani, the shop that sells the cheaper, younger, more relaxed range of the Italian couturier. On the corner of the Rue des Capucines, on the former site of Wilmart fabrics, you will find two storeys of light-oak, waxed parquet flooring and white granite décor. On the ground floor are the pretty, feminine dresses, the straight, narrow trousers (at around 500 francs) and the narrow-shouldered jackets. A massive wooden staircase leads up to the first floor, where you will only find men's clothes.

EMPORIO ARMANI   25, PLACE VENDÔME I – 42 61 02 34

KLEIN D'OEIL Michel Klein's particular talent is the art of allying creativity with a low price-tag. Out of this talent emerges the Klein d'Oeil range (a pun in French meaning 'a wink'). This includes twisted sweaters, jersey ballerina dresses, much cheaper Chinese jackets, and a quirky young range of evening dresses. Flashily in-Kleined!

KLEIN D'OEIL   6, RUE DU PRÉ-AUX-CLERCS VII – 47 03 93 76

YOUNG DESIGNERS

They don't yet hold their shows at the Louvre with the great masters of fashion. But they are already fashion stars, with well-defined personalities and clothes that are made up in relatively limited editions – which is not unappealing to their acolytes.

JEAN-LUC AMSLER Graduate of the Esmod fashion school who, after a spell with Courrèges, has just set up his sign in a pocket-handkerchief-sized shop. This handsome young Swiss loves body-hugging lines, trouser-suits and clashing colours.

JEAN-LUC AMSLER   9, RUE RAMEAU II – 42 60 29 51

CHRISTOPHE LEMAIRE trained with Yves Saint Laurent, Michel Klein, Thierry Mugler, Dorothée Bis and Christian Lacroix. His shop is peaceful with a pastel-blue ceiling. His jackets have rounded shoulders and an emphatic cut.

CHRISTOPHE LEMAIRE   4, RUE CHÉRUBINI II – 47 03 39 00

CHRISTOPHE LEBOURG knows how to design fine basics, limp jackets which rumple stylishly and long flowing dresses. Always provocative, he also offers in his tiny premises T-shirts signed Lenin or Ho Chi Minh. An avant-garde creator with a revolution in a time warp.

CHRISTOPHE LEBOURG   75, RUE VIEILLE-DU-TEMPLE III – 42 77 10 82

CORINNE COBSON eliminated half her Oedipus complex in one fell swoop by cutting her father's name in two. Mlle Jacobson, known as Cobson, the daughter of one of the creators of Dorothée Bis, made an enormous impact on the fashion scene when she started up in business. Each season's collection takes as its inspiration the spirit of the moment from the summer of 1940 to the 1950s, but in no way does she let this retro-influenced style detract from the modernism of her delicate little knitwear designs, her stretch-lycra dresses that hug the figure, or her broderie anglaise *à la* Brigitte Bardot.

CORINNE COBSON 28, PLACE DU MARCHÉ SAINT-HONORÉ I – 42 60 01 00

ÉTIENNE BRUNEL The super-gifted pupil of the Employers' Federation School of Fashion, Mireille Etienne set up in partnership with Jean-Luc Brunel. Their label, Etienne Brunel, gained recognition for its avant-garde style, which is classic and extravagant and includes items like the very plain black suit totally covered in brightly coloured embroidery.

ÉTIENNE BRUNEL   68, RUE DES SAINTS-PÈRES VII – 45 44 41 14

FRANK JOSEPH BASTILLE, while studying at the Esmod fashion school, won the young talent competition sponsored by Printemps. Since then he has gone his own imaginative way.

FRANK JOSEPH BASTILLE   21, RUE DAVAL XI – 48 07 20 10

PLEIN SUD sells Fayçal Amor's creations in a very austerely decorated setting. This is highly creative fashion with waisted rayon jackets and smock-tops with ornamental front pockets, and the stock changes totally every season.

PLEIN SUD   14, PLACE DES VICTOIRES II – 42 36 75 02

MARTIN MARGIELA is the most Parisian of the stylists of the Anvers group. After years of anonymity, he has now established his rightful place as one of the leading figures in avant-garde fashion. This former Gaultier assistant has his own studio in the Sentier district where he dreams up his idiosyncratic clothes which you can find at:

KASHIYAMA   147, BOULEVARD SAINT-GERMAIN VI – 46 34 11 50

OLIVIER GUILLEMIN was an assistant to both Thierry Mugler and Azzedine Alaïa, while also designing patterns for Claude Montana and Woolmark, the waiters' uniforms for the Palace Hotel, and Miss Gervais outfits for the film festival. Under his own label he likes futurist clothes in unusual materials. He is the most avant-garde of the young lions of fashion.

OLIVIER GUILLEMIN at ABSINTHE 74–76, RUE JEAN-JACQUES-ROUSSEAU I – 42 33 54 44

ATSURO TAYAMA exhibits his creations like paintings. There are huge sweaters, crocheted jackets, and femininely styled men's jackets, his particular speciality.

ATSURO TAYAMA   40, RUE DE SÉVIGNÉ III − 42 78 40 99

And also:

LILI CUBE   60, RUE DE LA ROQUETTE XI − 47 00 37 16

♣ **OXYMUSE   11, RUE DU PRÉ-AUX-CLERCS VII − 45 44 43 35**

WOMEN DESIGNING FOR WOMEN

'Women designers have a more carefully thought-out approach, based as it is on personal experience', remarks Sonia Rykiel. The purists, the front-line fashion gurus, sniff at these creative geniuses for not being daring enough. But women designers know better − after all, they wear the clothes themselves. So throw-on clothes, at once feminine and pretty, are again front-line news. Make way for the women who design for women.

AGNÈS B Her brushed-cotton cardigans, stripy T-shirts and little grey twinsets have become classics, as famous as Hermès scarves and Chanel suits. With her four boutiques and her gallery, this attractive, eternally youthful blonde designer was the pioneer of the Rue du Jour. She is the star of a street that was always destined to be hers, since, in the Middle Ages, a wealthy member of the bourgeoisie had a chapel built here dedicated to Saint Agnes. At No.3 she caters for flirtatious Lolitas with a selection of leggings, pleated skirts, baggy jumpers and crisp, white shirts. Next door is the men's shop, which specializes in sombre-coloured shirts and big raincoats. Further down the street is the babies' shop, where her jersey romper suits make the cutest of presents for a new-born arrival. No.6 is the women's domain offering an impressive rainbow of colours in the classic cardigan with mother-of-pearl fasteners, plain white shirts, tennis outfits and snappy little preppy suits.

AGNÈS B   1,2,3 and 6, RUE DU JOUR I – 40 26 36 87

MYRÈNE DE PRÉMONVILLE   Parisian women are aware of her 'femme femme' (or 'woman's woman') suits. Cognoscenti are also aware that she designs the Hermès collection and dresses Kathleen Turner and Jane Fonda. After unveiling her first collection in a little corner on the second floor of the Galeries Lafayette, Myrène opened her second Parisian boutique in the 'Golden Triangle' of fashion, decorated by Jacques Grange in a mixture of the ultra-modern and the traditional, with harlequin-style marquetry. Reflected in a great mirror are the suit collection and the rails designed by Hervé Van der Straten. Pretty accessories include brooches, gloves and hats.

MYRÈNE DE PRÉMONVILLE 38, RUE DU BAC VII – 45 49 46 96; 32, AVENUE GEORGE-V VIII – 47 20 02 35

INÈS DE LA FRESSANGE   The supermodel who fascinated the couturiers and their women clients has become a stylist. At her deluxe emporium you will find everything she likes and which makes up her own distinctive style: clothes, furniture, sheets, hard-gem necklaces and pumps. In her brightly coloured boutique, amongst deep sofas designed by Alexis de la Falaise, you can choose basic items of clothing: handsome double-breasted jackets, well-cut straight skirts, very narrow velvet trousers or sumptuous dressing-gowns.

INÈS DE LA FRESSANGE   14, AVENUE MONTAIGNE VIII – 47 23 08 94

CORINNE SARRUT   For a long time she was the star stylist at Cacharel. She knows how to dress the young working woman. In the shop that bears her name, slate-grey outside and white inside, working girls come for trouser-suits, pretty raincoats and little knits. The prices are reasonable.

CORINNE SARRUT   4, RUE DU PRÉ-AUX-CLERCS VII – 42 61 71 60

MARIE SARA is the only woman bullfighter to fill the arena since Conchita Cintron. In her tiled shop are outfits influenced by the Spanish carnival and the bullring: torero shirts in violet, pink and turquoise poplin; cropped bolero jackets; embroidered waistcoats; flamenco shoes.

MARIE SARA   9, RUE DES FRANCS-BOURGEOIS IV – 48 87 47 27

CLAUDIE PIERLOT knows how to design a practical wardrobe with really up-to-the-minute detailing. Set up in one of the wings of the old Royaumont building, she designs her pretty

tops, blazers and irresistible little skirts with humour and wit.
CLAUDIE PIERLOT 4, RUE DU JOUR I – 42 21 38 38; 23, RUE DU VIEUX-COLOMBIER VI – 45 48 11 96

POPY MORENI set up business in the Place des Vosges in 1983. The queen of the collarette and the Commedia dell'Arte diamond-patterned style is also an impressive colourist, though purple remains her mascot colour.
POPY MORENI 13, PLACE DES VOSGES IV – 42 77 09 96

POUR SURAH Maud Perl learnt the art of vegetable and chemical dyeing in India. Her gold, silver and sulphur shades of silk are always rare and precious. Her top-quality heavy silks allow for surreal compositions and superimpositions, even in wintertime. Indigo reigns supreme in her kingdom, but she also displays all the myriad colours of the planet.
POUR SURAH 7, RUE DU TRÉSOR IV – 42 77 11 21

RENATA Her little tops embroidered by hand in Madeira are small miracles of sophistication, even to the buttons which she purchases from antique dealers and the buckles from markets. Nathalie Baye, Nicole Garcia and Marie Laforêt are regulars at her little boutique, where the saleswomen are highly skilled dispensers of good advice.
RENATA 17, RUE SAINT-FLORENTIN VIII – 42 60 11 69

LAURENCE TAVERNIER has lived in the intimate aura of lingerie since the age of 18. After 15 years at Printemps and Dior she launched her own collection, which she called 'Cocooning'. There are perfect jackets for indoors and big, quilted dressing-gowns for which you can buy matching, comfortable pyjamas.
LAURENCE TAVERNIER 7, RUE DU PRÉ-AUX-CLERCS VII – 49 27 03 95

CAPUCINE PUERARI As a young assistant having just graduated from the Studio Berçot school, she spent her free time making up little panties for her friends . . . . This jokey hobby turned into a full-time job. 'Frivolous lingerie just didn't exist, you simply had to choose between the sophisticated or the sensible.' Young women adore the scoop-neck basques and the multi-purpose bodies-cum-swimming costumes. Her dresses, which follow the curves of the body and mould the bust, are feminine without being vampish and dressy without costing the earth.
CAPUCINE PUERARI 63, RUE DES SAINTS-PÈRES VI – 45 49 26 90

BARBARA BUI This talented young stylist began her career in a small studio she christened Kabuki, where she only designed clothes made of leather and sheepskin. Now these make up merely a small part of her collection. But she still has a special liking for the softness and pliability of these materials. There are superb, well-cut clothes in pastel shades of velvet, and they are very often embroidered.

BARBARA BUI   23, RUE ÉTIENNE-MARCEL I – 40 26 43 65

EMMANUELLE KHANH An ex-Balenciaga model, she was one of the pioneers of the ready-to-wear collection. And she was the first person to make the classic woman's suit a little more feminine by introducing petal-shaped collars and rounded lines. Regulars roll up to purchase her very well-cut jackets or 50s-influenced chenille knitwear.

EMMANUELLE KHANH   45, AVENUE VICTOR-HUGO XVI – 45 01 73 00

FANNY LIAUTARD promotes the lifestyle of quite another age, an age in which softness and beauty combined. She built her reputation on the lingerie of dreamtime and is still making it in incredibly intricately worked natural fabrics. This ex-Givenchy assistant also designs evening dresses and luxury négligés. You'll find all these items at her boutique, which is painted in glossy rose colours and finished in bronze, with white curvilinear furniture.

FANNY LIAUTARD   2, PLACE DES VOSGES IV – 42 77 73 44

CRISCA is the first shop bearing the Nathalie Acatrini label, the young protégée of Margaretha Ley, the famous creator of the Escada label. She's already designing her own collection, which is more expensive and more sophisticated than that of her mentor. Crisca is targeted at a younger sportier clientèle with its décor of frosted steel, glossy glass, wood and marble setting the scene for leggings, 70s-style T-shirts and psychedelic prints which hang from railings alongside little smock-tops with cotton stitching. The multicoloured, frilly Brazilian-style skirts are irresistible.

CRISCA   78, RUE DES SAINTS-PÈRES VII – 45 49 31 08

SÉVERINE PERRAUDIN has at last set up shop (on the ground floor of the 'Soie de Paris' building, to which she would go as a young woman starting out in business to buy her jersey by the metre just like all the other young stylists). Géraldine Pailhas, the leading actress in the latest Jean-Jacques Beineix film, and a variety of other actresses are already going crazy over her strapless tops and her white satin dresses.

SÉVERINE PERRAUDIN   14, RUE D'UZÈS II – 45 08 12 21

And also:

LOLITA LEMPICKA   13 BIS, RUE PAVÉE IV/3 BIS, RUE DES ROSIERS – 42 74 42 94

SONIA RYKIEL   175, BOULEVARD SAINT-GERMAIN VI – 49 54 60 00

JANO   29, RUE SAINT-SULPICE VI – 43 26 82 30

THE PARISIAN WOMAN'S WARDROBE

KNITWEAR

The elegant little jumper is indispensable for completing the look of a classic suit or of that straight skirt which all Parisian women keep hanging in their wardrobe. Don't forget the baggy sweater with large stitching that everyone in town wears over leggings or tights and everyone in the country wears with jeans. And a special mention for cashmere.

RODIER In 1916 a manufacturer showed Gabrielle Chanel a material that she had never seen before: it was machine-knitted and it was called 'jersey'. Mademoiselle was seized with fervour for the product and launched her famous suits, cut in the new Rodier fabric. Today famous stylists, who remain anonymously hidden behind the brand label, design knitted socks, Mondrian graphic prints and 'outsize' pullovers. Their star material is called 'Kasha', but they are also thought of in connection with lycra and mohair.
RODIER   15, AVENUE VICTOR-HUGO XVI – 45 01 79 88

TEHEN The whole collection is made up of small items which go together like a jigsaw puzzle and are designed by a style bureau, which is set in a framework of bleached wood and natural flecked stone. Their hot-point is sexy little dresses and bodies.
TEHEN   5 BIS, RUE DES ROSIERS IV – 40 27 97 37; 28, RUE DE GRENELLE VII – 45 44 80 42; 30, RUE MONTMARTRE I – 40 26 86 23

MARION ROTH An opulent shop made up of large slabs of stone and 30s-style treated wood, contains Marion Roth's knitwear which, with its distinctive diminutive golfer emblem, is characterized by the use of colour. 36 shades from the most acid to the most neutral.
MARION ROTH   1, RUE DE LA BANQUE II – 40 15 04 38

FAC BAZAAR Sophie Serret, with her sure good taste, has been designing cardigans for almost 20 years now. She has knitwear machined by craftswomen, who then reembroider it by hand (for about 1,000 francs). She matches these up with pretty gathered skirts, retro scarves and romantic blouses.

♡ **FAC BAZAAR   38, RUE DES SAINTS-PÈRES VII – 45 48 46 15**

BLANC-BLEU Enamoured of all things nautical, Patrick Khayat made this space the 'figurehead' of his label. In premises lit by a glass roof, there are gorgeous weekend pullovers and knitwear with matching leggings.

BLANC-BLEU   14, PLACE DES VICTOIRES I – 42 96 05 40

CHANDAIL Pascal Ricaux adores jumpers. This young advertising executive opened a shop to fulfil his own fantasies. He imports Scottish cardigans, John Smedley polo-necks in fine-quality wool, and lambswool sweaters all year round.

CHANDAIL   68, RUE SAINT-HONORÉ I – 40 41 02 72

CHRISTA FIEDLER is a former top model at Eileen Ford, the biggest agency in America. She launched her first sweater collection in 1981. 12 years later her patterns, knitted in natural fabrics with woollen basics in winter and cotton or linen basics in summer, are generally worn by working women.

CHRISTA FIEDLER   28, RUE DU CHERCHE-MIDI VI – 45 48 51 58; 87, AVENUE PAUL-DOUMER XVI – 40 50 84 08

CAROLL in 1963 Joseph Bigio and his friend, Raphaël Levy, arrived in France and launched a little sweater business. Every season they show a stylish collection designed by freelance stylists and always in up-to-the-minute designs.

CAROLL   8, RUE HALEVY IX – 42 65 20 58

JOSEPH is French but he's a star in London, his spiritual home. He makes the most beautiful sweaters in the softest wool, which are enormous and feature high collars and hand-embroidery. They are also expensive (average price 3,000 francs) and he has four shops in Paris including:

♡ **JOSEPH   27, RUE DE PASSY XVI – 45 24 24 32; 44, RUE ETIENNE-MARCEL II – 42 36 87 83**

ABERCOMBIE The pullovers, which are knitted in Scotland but styled in-house, are not at all expensive. Cardigans in cotton jersey, pullovers embroidered with little flowers, crew-neck sweaters in unusual colours – you'll find them all here.

♧ **ABERCOMBIE   38, RUE DU BAC VII – 45 48 48 85**

ALAIN MANOUKIAN They have a very pretty jumper made of high-quality cotton, beautifully finished and with three-quarter-length sleeves, for around 300 francs. The strength of this diffusion range is that it blends fashion with low prices, and this has made the company that Dany and Alain Manoukian started in 1973 very successful indeed. There are shops all over Paris, but one of the most attractive is:

♣ **ALAIN MANOUKIAN   83, RUE DE PASSY XVI – 45 27 38 75**

KERSTIN ADOLPHSON The most beautiful examples of Icelandic, Norwegian and Swedish Jacquard hand-knitting are all gathered together here in a tiny boutique.

KERSTIN ADOLPHSON   157, BOULEVARD SAINT-GERMAIN VI – 45 48 00 14

BENETTON No introduction needed for the 'United Colours of Benetton'. It's the incredible range of colours that lies behind the success of the three brothers and one sister from the Venice area. There are around 20 shops in the Paris area, but one of the best-stocked is:

♣ **BENETTON   59, RUE DE RENNES VI – 45 48 32 29**

PÔLES There's furniture moulded from thick solid pieces of wood and a door leading on to a courtyard, made of glass and verdigrised wrought-iron sculpted by Marco de Gueltz. It's the perfect setting that Maïté Michel created for his Pôles label. His faithful followers come to buy artistically styled knitwear and velvet stitching.

PÔLES   17, RUE DU JOUR IV – 45 08 93 67

FABRICE KAREL Under his real name, Gérard Karel, a croupier by trade, married a decorative arts student whose parents ran a small knitwear shop. And Bob's your Uncle, he's launched his own label, distributed through hundreds of outlets. The secret is that his wife Babette's patterns are charming. They capture the spirit of the season and there are six boutiques in Paris, including:

♣ **FABRICE KAREL   39, AVENUE VICTOR-HUGO XVI – 45 00 59 22**

CASSAGNE Cashmere and alpaca in an incredible rainbow of colours. No shade is too difficult for them. You will find almost the exact colour you've been looking for, and all the clothes match.

CASSAGNE   42, RUE DE L'UNIVERSITÉ VII – 42 61 09 50

MARGO Didier Romi and his wife Laurence launched a knit-wear collection: Margo. It includes pullovers but also cotton-lycra clothes in sophisticated styles, both loose and fitted. These are simple, eminently wearable clothes for around 500 francs.

MARGO   84, AVENUE DES CHAMPS-ÉLYSÉES VIII – 43 59 24 27

BREIZ-NORWAY A right hotch-potch, a bit of a shambles, but very charming. An Aladdin's cave of a collection from Francis and Marie Vatinel, in which all the pullovers come in from the cold at acceptable prices.

BREIZ-NORWAY 33, RUE GAY-LUSSAC V – 43 29 47 82

ANVERS Two Belgian designers, Ann Kegels and Martine Hillen, set up shop in an old 18th-century stone setting, with untreated, unpolished parquet flooring. This makes a pretty setting for the simple, almost austere clothes, cut in jersey wool at reasonable prices.

♡ ANVERS 7, RUE DU PRÉ-AUX-CLERCS VII – 42 86 84 40

PLÜCK Having arrived in Paris in 1970 to learn French, Louise Becker simply never went home again. Her Plück label specializes in coordinated items of knitwear and all in 100% wool. These are fashionable outfits that will never cease to be so.

PLÜCK 18, RUE PIERRE LESCOT I – 45 08 10 40

GILLIER Arnaud created the European Business Institute. Thierry has a BA Hons from New York University. Born into a dynamic textile dynasty, the two Gilliers salvaged an old factory whose workforce specialized in camelhair, which remains their forte. But there are also collections of small, coordinated knits which are perfect for the office or just for going shopping.

GILLIER 8, RUE DE L'AMIRAL COLIGNY I – 42 60 82 42 (showroom); 27, RUE SAINT-SULPICE (boutique)

KOOKAÏ No need to introduce Kookaï and his funny kook-aïettes, unbearable and chic at very low cost. The boutiques just keep on opening up, but we have a particular soft spot for a little one with a waxed oak floor.

♧ KOOKAÏ 3, RUE DES CANETTES VI – 40 46 04 58

CHAUMETTE ET POIRIER Pretty Jacquard pullovers from Chaumette and Poirier are bought up rapidly by total fashion victims. This is because Marie Chaumette and Patrick Poirier, interior designers who both graduated from the Camondo School, have a very individual style, classic but contemporary, which eludes pretentiousness. They make up the clothes in their own manufacturing studio, and the knitting is done by craftspeople and finished by hand. The styles are exclusive.

CHAUMETTE ET POIRIER 68, RUE VIEILLE-DU-TEMPLE IV – 43 29 71 96

And also:

GÉRARD MABÉ 37, RUE DE PASSY XVI – 42 88 82 71

BRITISH STOCK 10, RUE GUICHARD XVI – 45 25 25 52

Cashmere

Cashmere yarn, plucked from the fleece of Himalayan goats, is a luxury product. Various astute business people import it from China. Besides the perfect, well-known labels like 'Old England', 'Ralph Lauren', 'Hermès', 'Aux laines écossaises' and 'Kenzo', there are also other lesser-known names:

ERIC BOMPARD After several visits to China, Eric Bompard, a specialist in mail order, got the go-ahead to import cashmere pullovers directly from Mongolia. His extensive control is the secret behind his low prices (at around 1,000 francs for a double-knit cardigan) and there is a vast range of colours.

♧ ERIC BOMPARD 28, RUE MONTROSIER 92200 NEUILLY – 47 47 76 56; 4, RUE DE VARENNE VII – 42 84 04 36; and by mail order from BP 221 SOPHIA ANTIPOLIS 06561 VALBONNE CEDEX

CENTRE DE LA MODE A source of supply to which retailers themselves come when they want to stock up. But, although you won't find anything to indicate the fact, it's also open to the general public. A whole host of regulars turn up at the door to purchase goods at a 50% discount, including quality cashmere made at Hawick in Scotland. There are genuine bargains to be found if you can be bothered to hunt around for them among the piles of heaped-up packages all over the floor.

♧ CENTRE DE LA MODE 101, RUE RÉAUMUR II – 42 36 68 53

RICHARD GRAND is a manufacturer who opens his shop to private individuals. At his Scottish factory they manufacture 30 different styles of jumper, not including his classic items in all 42 of their regular colours.

RICHARD GRAND 229, RUE SAINT-HONORÉ I – 42 60 18 75

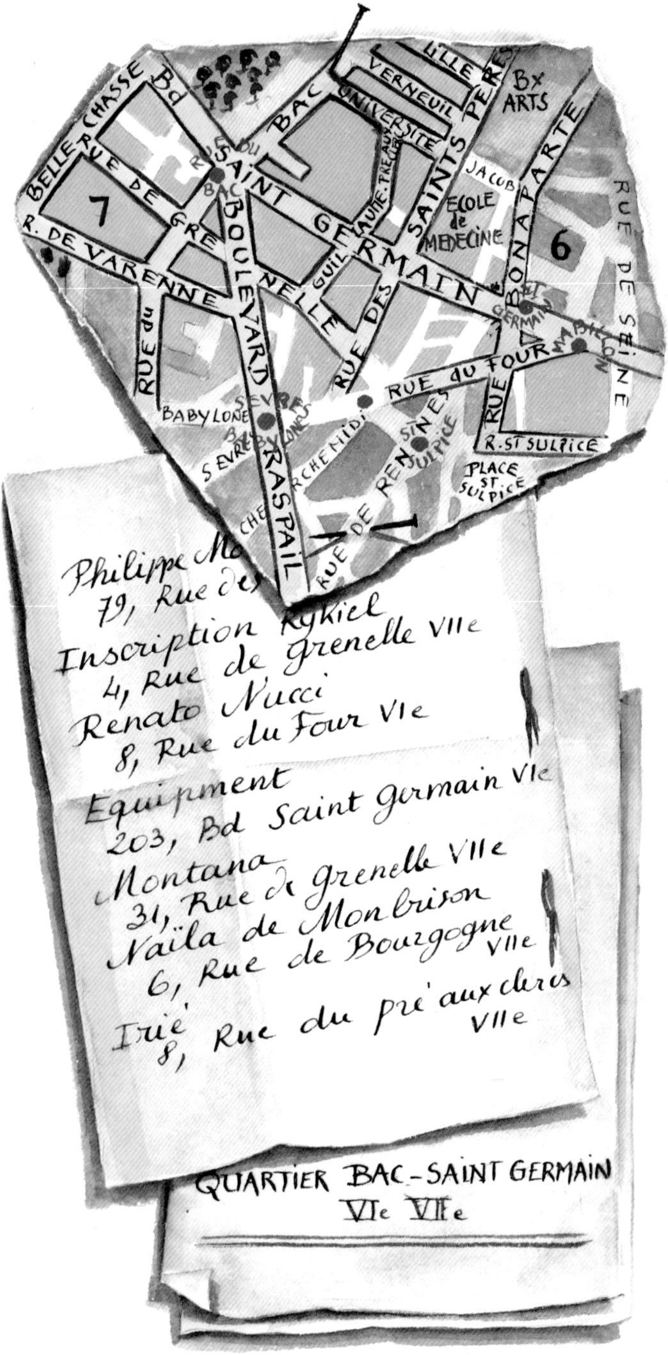

LILLE
VERNEUIL
UNIVERSITE
SAINTS PERES
Bx ARTS
BELLECHASSE
Bd SAINT GERMAIN
BAC
RUE DE GRENELLE
7
6
JACOB
ECOLE de MEDECINE
RUE BONAPARTE
RUE DE SEINE
R. DE VARENNE
BOULEVARD RASPAIL
RUE DES SAINTS PERES
RUE du BAC
RUE du FOUR
MABILLON
RUE DE RENNES
BABYLONE
SEVRES BABYLONE
CHERCHE MIDI
R. ST SULPICE
PLACE ST SULPICE
Philippe Mo
79, Rue des
Inscription Rykiel
4, Rue de Grenelle VIIe
Renato Nucci
8, Rue du Four VIe
Equipment
203, Bd Saint Germain VIIe
Montana
31, Rue de Grenelle VIIe
Naïla de Monbrison
6, Rue de Bourgogne VIIe
Irié
8, Rue du pré aux clercs VIIe
QUARTIER BAC-SAINT GERMAIN
VIe VIIe

SHIRTS

The shirt is the 'top' that allows the 'bottom' not to sink hopelessly out of fashion. It adds that certain something to a plain suit or, dresses up a skirt whether that skirt is made of leather, wool or silk.

EQUIPMENT All the trendy girls have two or three of these famous washed-silk shirts in their 24 glorious colours. Having started in premises in the Place des Victoires, Equipment invested, as convention demanded, in the more traditional site of the Boulevard Saint-Germain, in an austere environment enhanced by natural stone flooring and spacious fitting-rooms, complete with immense frosted-glass mirrors. The décor was designed by an English architect called David Chipperfield.

EQUIPMENT 203, BOULEVARD SAINT-GERMAIN VII – 45 48 86 82;
♡ **46, RUE ÉTIENNE-MARCEL II – 40 26 17 84**

CORINA This is a tiny shop that only sells shirts made of a kind of polyester crêpe de chine, which is a super fabric, similar to a heavy silk, machine-washable and which you can drip-dry. There are over 100 different styles in the collection.

♣ **CORINA   10, RUE ROYALE VIII – 42 60 57 62**

RENATO NUCCI For over ten years now, he has been designing romantically tailored shirts in natural materials including cotton, linen, poplin, cambric or voile. All the styles are gathered together in a pretty boutique on old-fashioned dummies.

RENATO NUCCI 8, RUE DU FOUR VI – 46 33 29 08

MOHOLY NAGY The grandson of one of the Bauhaus School artists, André Moholy-Nagy has given over almost his entire shop to the plain white shirt – from the highly feminine, ruffed-collar, puffed-sleeve blouse to the men's shirt.

♡ **MOHOLY NAGY** 2, GALERIE VIVIENNE/5, RUE DE LA BANQUE II – 40 15 05 33

LE GARAGE A ceiling painted with bucolic garlands of flowers and external hoardings fixed permanently under glass. The young come to this former bakery to buy inventive, original samples of embroidered, braided shirts, decorated with lace and even semi-precious beading.

LE GARAGE 21, RUE SÉVIGNÉ IV – 48 04 73 72

POUR SURAH In a beautiful, pure, illuminated space Maud Perl exhibits her range of colours as a painter does his palette. Her speciality is fine, heavy silk which means she can effect surreal compositions and superimpositions even in mid-winter. Indigo reigns supreme, but the whole extensive range of earth tones, from the desert to the volcanic, are there. Isabelle Adjani, Nicole Garcia and Claire Brétécher are some of her biggest fans.

♡ POUR SURAH 7, RUE DU TRÉSOR IV – 42 77 11 21

BERESFORD In 1912 Antoinette and William Beresford opened a blouse shop not two yards from Coco Chanel's. Today there are more than 300 styles in the range, made of lawn, Swiss voile, linen, muslin, silk, taffeta and even, since women of today demand it, machine-washable polyester. The saleswomen, who are former designers themselves, can alter any style to fit the particular individual and can take down sleeves or take up plunging neck-lines according to taste.

BERESFORD 384–386, RUE SAINT-HONORÉ I – 42 60 03 15

RENATA Old-fashioned embroidery is Renata's selling-point. She sells crêpe-de-chine tops, which are hand-embroidered in Madeira on silk satin worked with the smooth side facing inwards. This makes it softer on the skin. She also works in cotton and linen, and everything is beautiful.

♡ RENATA 17, RUE SAINT-FLORENTIN VIII – 42 60 11 69

BRITISH HOUSE is one of the great specialists in cotton poplin or Oxford flannel shirts. They come plain or striped, with Mandarin collars, or school-girl collars or necklines with bows. There are around 10 shops including:

BRITISH HOUSE 7, AVENUE DES TERNES XVII – 47 66 96 89

CHRISTIANE KOVITZ is a specialist in the very pretty, sophisticated shirt, which Christiane designs and manufactures in her own studio. All the styles, even the most elaborate ones with pleats, tucks and frills, can be easily machine-washed and ironed. One of her particularly enchanting designs is a T-shirt made of polyester seersucker and embroidered with a croquet-mallet motif. She has this made up every year.

FASCINO 130, RUE DU FAUBOURG SAINT-HONORÉ VIII – 42 25 05 31;
♡ 10 RUE GUSTAVE-COURBET XVI – 45 53 06 41

CHEMISERIE CACHAREL In 1987 Cacharel decided to return to their first love – the shirt. It comes in cotton and silk, in 19 colours and 300 different materials and is sold in franchised shops all designed by Jean-Michel Wilmotte. The biggest selling-points are the Liberty prints and the low prices.
♣ **CHEMISERIE CACHAREL** 34, RUE TRONCHET VIII – 47 42 12 61

And also:
ARMANI 6, PLACE VENDÔME VIII – 42 61 55 09
MARKS AND SPENCER 68, RUE DES MATHURINS IX – 47 42 42 91
NINA RICCI 39, AVENUE MONTAIGNE VIII – 47 42 18 12
GUY LAROCHE 29, AVENUE MONTAIGNE VIII – 40 69 68 00
CHANEL 31, RUE CAMBON I – 42 86 28 00

SUITS

The lady's suit was conceived at the end of the 19th century and christened 'the tailored suit'. It was thought up by the House of Redfern in the 1880s but really took off in the 1920s when Coco Chanel launched her famous jacket-and-skirt ensemble cut in soft flowing materials like jersey. Today it's the 9-to-5 girl's standard uniform, from Claire Chazal, who chose to wear the Dior version, to Catherine Deneuve, the mascot of Yves Saint Laurent. A change of blouse is enough to pep up a whole outfit – making the suit the Secret of Success from dawn to dusk.

IRÈNE VAN RYB Having started with almost nothing in the 80s, she has made a startling breakthrough with her pure, modern, straight-up style. Her speciality is crêpe wool suits, or, indeed, linen or stretch-cotton ones in classic navy or ivory, although she also makes up clothes in acid orange or fuchsia pink. The new, hip thing is the trouser-suit with its short jacket with Beatle collar and drainpipe trousers.

♣ IRÈNE VAN RYB at GALERIES LAFAYETTE   40, BOULEVARD HAUSSMANN IX

RÉGINA RUBENS Her career really took off thanks to her bouclé wool and pepper-and-salt suits, which are perfectly cut and not too expensive. Find out for yourself in the intimate ambience of her showroom-shop in which the best samples are exhibited on a screen.

♣ RÉGINA RUBENS LES TROIS QUARTIERS 23, BOULEVARD DE LA MADELEINE I – 42 96 24 81

ESCADA It was love at first sight for Margaretha, a Swedish model, and Wolfgang Ley, a self-taught German. They got married and out of their fiery passion was born a new label, Escada. Trendy shops turned up their noses but the upper-middle-class, city-style talent of Margaretha and her feel for top-quality materials launched the label successfully into the Parisian Top 50 list. Their best-seller is an impeccable suit with a straight skirt and in bright colours.

ESCADA 57, AVENUE MONTAIGNE VIII – 42 89 83 45

LAUREL Escada's baby brother is sportier and less expensive. Make way for the two-coloured suit in wool gabardine forming part of a knitted ensemble.

LAUREL 402, RUE SAINT-HONORÉ I – 42 60 13 89

GEORGES RECH Visiting the Rechs has always been a well-tailored experience. Following in his father's footsteps, the young Georges, ambitious and talented, dreamt of launching his own collection. This former fine arts student now creates in pure, architectural lines, out of which he has carved the success of his perfect suits. These are all made in the finest-quality wool, cotton or linen and are not too expensive.

GEORGES RECH   273, RUE SAINT-HONORÉ I – 42 61 41 14; 23, AVENUE VICTOR-HUGO XVI – 45 00 83 19

DANIEL HECHTER hung up his modern pieces of artwork in his shop in order to create a space in which you can stroll around, look at the décor and choose yourself something to wear, all at the same time. The clothes are laid out attractively on travelling-trunks and the fitting-rooms are decorated with poems by Jacques Prévert and Paul Verlaine. The suits have a particular look that makes them easy to wear to the office, although you will think you're in more casual gear, and they come in warm colour schemes.

DANIEL HECHTER   66, RUE FRANÇOIS-Ier VIII – 40 70 94 98; 31, RUE TRONCHET VIII – 49 24 96 15

LOLITA LEMPICKA All the fashion victims want to be seen in her little, waisted suits which make for a shapely figure and a feminine form. In a couture setting, women come to be welcomed without snobbery but with kindness and sympathetic service.
♡ **LOLITA LEMPICKA**   13 BIS, RUE PAVÉE III – 42 74 50 48

EMMANUELLE KHANH The queen of the suit knows exactly how to enhance her favourite piece of clothing with velvet panels or harmonize it with little ice-skater's skirts, or decorate it with braid. The prettiest masculine ensembles are made more feminine.
EMMANUELLE KHANH   45, AVENUE VICTOR-HUGO XVI – 45 01 73 00

CERRUTI He dresses Kathleen Turner, Glenn Close, Annette Bening and Christine Ockrent. Nino Cerruti has a certain natural elegance, nonchalance and ease. His executive women's suits have no rigidity or affectation. These are classics of colour and quality.
CERRUTI 1881   42, RUE DE GRENELLE VII – 42 22 92 28; 17, AVENUE VICTOR-HUGO XVI – 45 01 66 12; 15, PLACE DE LA MADELEINE VIII – 47 42 10 78

DAKS In the only Parisian outlet, you will see women fighting over these famous classic tweed suits with their leather-trimmed buttonholes and their 'DD' initialled buttons. The skirt is perfection itself with its elasticated waist and pleats in the front and back, and it comes in either plain or herringbone material.
DAKS   269, RUE SAINT-HONORÉ VIII – 42 60 22 19

RENOMA had its heyday in the 60s. Today in their six-storey shop the Renoma brothers mostly stock sportswear, but you can still find the odd well-cut suit with delicate detailing on the buttonholes and in good-quality material.
RENOMA   129 BIS, RUE DE LA POMPE XVI – 47 27 13 79

VENTILO invites you to stroll around as well as to shop; lots of light and unvarnished wood floors. There are delicately elegant ensembles of natural linen and ivory cotton, and don't forget to pay a visit to the shirt department.
VENTILO   25, RUE DU LOUVRE II – 42 33 18 67

And also:
ARTHUR ET FOX   40, RUE VIGNON IX – 47 42 00 32
BERTEIL   3, PLACE SAINT-AUGUSTIN VIII – 42 65 28 52
and, of course,
SAINT LAURENT RIVE GAUCHE, VARIATIONS and **CHANEL**

DRESSY DRESSES

The little black dress, the draped stole, the spectacular ballgown: whatever the formal occasion everyone will be wearing them, whether to a private view, a film première, a wedding or a simple dinner party. Don't be left out.

14.18 For some years now all the most chic and well-connected young ladies have been running to visit Christiane Hélouis. This former journalist is never short of an idea, and, in her private house, taffeta skirts, velvet strapless tops and stoles all hang alongside one another. You get a 20% discount for clothes you're prepared to finish off yourself.
14.18 75, RUE DES VIGNES XVI – 42 88 18 14

ESCADA knows how to create a party atmosphere with beaded embroidered dresses, sophisticated wraps and invaluable Spencer jackets.
ESCADA   418, RUE SAINT-HONORÉ VIII – 42 60 14 97

ISABELLE ALLARD The elder daughter of the Marquis de Grailly was brought up in the old château at Charentes and always enjoyed dressing up both herself and her friends in mummy's ballgowns. She now creates sexy wraps and tight-fitting dresses which simply have to be seen.
ISABELLE ALLARD   218, BOULEVARD SAINT-GERMAIN VII – 47 03 49 58

CATHERINE PUGET Her reputation is confirmed. All elegant women like to wrap themselves in her silk, satin and crêpe clothes. Silver lamé decorates her T-shirts and blouses, and the Duchess of Württemberg buys all her clothes here.
CATHERINE PUGET   58, RUE BONAPARTE VI – 46 34 60 04; 416, RUE SAINT-HONORÉ VIII – 42 60 57 80

MAUD DEFOSSEZ Chic ladies meet up at the boutique of Maud Defossez and her daughter, Stéphanie. This is the realm of the velvet suit, brocaded satin and the elegantly finished dress, all at affordable prices. They are specialists in the little basque suit with its sophisticated top half and in the sexy little dress.

MAUD DEFOSSEZ   33, RUE DES SABLONS XVI — 47 27 34 33; 24, AVENUE DE BRETEUIL VII — 45 67 31 69

ZADIG ET VOLTAIRE With its small 50-square-metre space and large glazed façade, this shop stakes its reputation on the austerity of its décor, which is totally white and therefore emphasizes the spangly collection in frothy, colourful yet simple young shapes. This is temptation for any young lady.

♧ **ZADIG ET VOLTAIRE   18, RUE SAINT-GUILLAUME VII — 45 49 04 77**

APOSTROPHE In a sober boutique Patrick Hazan designs dresses for active women. The heavy silk patterns are easy to wear for dining out of an evening.

APOSTROPHE   93, RUE DU FAUBOURG SAINT-HONORÉ VIII — 42 66 30 35

HERVÉ LÉGER makes up one-off designs tailored specially to fit each individual customer. His thing is to use strips of crêpe viscose in matt or lurex which he wraps around a Stockman dummy similar to the particular client involved. Then he corrects the tailoring to the exact centimetre on the client herself. The result is an extraordinary dress which is not easy to wear, since you have to have an incredibly good figure with a super-sexy image. It's an exercise in high style for this former assistant to Tan Giudicelli, Karl Lagerfeld and Merryl Lanvin, but he dresses the whole of Parisian society.

♡ **HERVÉ LÉGER   7, RUE DU LOUVOIS II — 49 27 08 85**

PAULE KA Serge Cajfinger, who has adopted Lille as his home town but was actually brought up in Brazil, knows a thing or two about classic, refined and opulent collections. The prices are affordable and you try on the clothes in an ivory setting, which is austere, although the fitting-rooms are large and supplied with leather sofas and big mirrors.

♧ **PAULE KA   20, RUE MALHER IV — 40 29 96 03; 192, BOULEVARD SAINT-GERMAIN VII — 45 44 92 60**

JEANNETTE was the woman who first brought deluxe fashion to this 'quartier' of Paris and was, also, the first person to distribute the 'Chloé' label when Karl Lagerfeld created it. She remains faithful to her roots as well as to Bernard Perris and Tan Giudicelli. She is the mentor and fashion guru to her customers, whom she supplies with unceasingly good advice. She is also the recourse of all elegant women and members of the jet-set brigade.

JEANNETTE   2 BIS and 3, RUE DE GRIBEAUVAL VII — 45 44 21 90

MICHEL LÉGER This stylist is skilled in the art of making women of larger, more rounded physiques look slim. But he also knows how to carve tight little dresses in stretchy fabrics.

MICHEL LÉGER   22, PLACE DU MARCHÉ SAINT-HONORÉ I – 42 60 47 90

VICKY TIEL At the back of a pretty paved courtyard in the heart of Saint-Germain you will locate the shrine of the dressy dress. It is always very sexy.

VICKY TIEL   21, RUE BONAPARTE VI – 46 33 53 58

CANDICE FRAIBERGER This beautiful lady creates impossibly sexy dresses and outfits, laying emphasis on the cleavage and the attractive legs of her customers, whom she receives not a stone's throw from the Elysée Palace.

CANDICE FRAIBERGER 7, RUE D'AGUESSEAU VIII (1st floor) – 42 66 23 74

And also:

UNGARO   2, AVENUE MONTAIGNE VIII – 47 23 61 94

MOSAÏQUE   17, RUE DE SÈVRES VI – 45 48 53 06

LIGNE PARIS BY NIGHT by MICHEL KLEIN   6, RUE DU PRÉ-AUX-CLERCS VII – 42 60 37 11

VICTOIRE   1, RUE MADAME VI – 45 44 28 14

MARGO   84, AVENUE DES CHAMPS-ÉLYSÉES VIII – 47 73 09 99

ANGELO TARLAZZI   67, RUE DU FAUBOURG SAINT-HONORÉ VIII – 42 66 67 73

LINGERIE

Now an essential element of any woman's wardrobe. Particularly since, diverted from their purely functional uses, the body and the crop-top have replaced the blouse and the skirt as outerwear.

ANN STEEGER A former model and already the owner of a range of products for the bathroom, she has now added a lingerie collection to the contents of her shop, and thus mixes the two great loves of her life. On her second-hand, painted pine furniture, you can choose between fern-scented cologne or perfumes inspired by country smells, thick soft sponges and pretty underwear. Her hot point is that you can make up your own gift-box by matching up one of her heart-shaped gift-boxes with the objects of your choice, including little slippers with matching pochettes, bodies and vanity cases.

ANN STEEGER   130, RUE DE GRENELLE VII – 45 55 81 82

NATORI Josée Cruz Natori's sumptuous black marble shop was decorated by Jacques Grange. The satin inlay panels on the household linen are embroidered in the Philippines. Naturally, before she set up her business, Josée, who was born over there, studied economics in New York and became, at the age of 28, the first female vice-president of the merchant bankers Merrill Lynch. She then decided to start her own company and to make full use of her native country's greatest traditional skill – embroidery – which still comes with a finesse that we no longer encounter under our own northern skies. For the extreme fastidiousness of the East, mixed with the design traditions of the West, this is the place to go. She also has a range of accessories, including a delightful selection of mule slippers.

NATORI   7, PLACE VENDÔME I – 42 96 22 94

MARKS AND SPENCER The prices and the quality are unbeatable. They sell little cotton knickers, hemmed with perfect lace trimmings. And, as long as you keep the receipt, you can exchange anything or get your money back. They've got the biggest choice and the greatest variety.

♧ **MARKS AND SPENCER   35, BOULEVARD HAUSSMANN IX – 47 42 42 91**

FANNY LIAUTARD used to have a boutique in the heart of the Marais. An ex-seamstress at Givenchy, she is now the queen of the lavish négligé in all its Art Deco glory, made up in sheerest chiffon and diaphanous lacework. She also makes dressing-gowns in Pyrenean wool but, naturally, lined in silk.

FANNY LIAUTARD – 42 72 92 99

UNE FEMME EN PLUS In a vast shop, in the pastel shades of a Victorian boudoir, a former department store buyer has devoted her entire store to lingerie and household linen. You will always find simple masculine-style pyjamas on sale, but cut in silk satin. You will also find sophisticated underwear.

UNE FEMME EN PLUS   142, RUE DE COURCELLES XVII – 40 53 06 06

CAPUCINE PUERARI A pretty brunette designs the most charming, most youthful collections of lingerie. For nymphets there are Turkish-style peasant tops, strapless cotton bodies and even flirtatious little basques.

♡   **CAPUCINE PUERARI   63, RUE DES SAINTS-PÈRES VI – 45 49 26 90**

CHANTAL THOMASS remains the queen of the sexy under-garment. She was the first designer to make underwear a fashion item and still sells the most gorgeous net and lace body-stockings, dainty little knickers, bras and suspender belts, which are all deeply arousing but never vulgar.

♡   **CHANTAL THOMASS   11, RUE MADAME VI – 45 44 57 13**

LAURENCE TAVERNIER A pretty, blonde lady who specializes in casual 'Homewear', she knows how to match pyjamas and dressing-gowns, and then harmonize them with Chinese cotton, tartan, particoloured cashmeres and plain fabrics. This is quality with perfect finishing. People love the coordinated ballet dresses, and above all the two candles scented with genista and magnolia.

♡   **LAURENCE   TAVERNIER   7,   RUE   DU   PRÉ-AUX-CLERCS   VII – 49 27 03 95**

PRINCESSE TAM-TAM Two Madagascans, the daughters of the owner of the local cotton plantations, came to Paris to study and never went home. Imagination running wild and general all-round daring rule the roost here and create the wittiest, most original prints made into sexy bras and frilly French knickers.

PRINCESSE TAM-TAM   9, RUE BRÉA VI – 43 54 03 58; 23, RUE DE GRENELLE VII – 45 49 28 73

SEDUCTION Charm as well. In a cosy setting given over to 35 square metres of intimacy, this is a brand-new shop dedicated to underwear. The aim is in the name: seduction. And everything seduces: lace-trimmed uplift bras, suspender-belts, bodies . . . and the latest Wolford tights in the softest of micro-fibres.

SEDUCTION   12, RUE DU CHAMPS-DE-MARS VIII – 45 56 08 31

SABBIA ROSA Monette Moati was one of the pioneers of 'seductive' lingerie. Actresses and singers all go mad over her velvet and satin dressing-gowns. She also sells Sarah Bernhardt-style négligés.

SABBIA ROSA   71–73, RUE DES SAINTS-PÈRES VI – 45 48 88 37

LA BOÎTE À BAS They don't sell anything except tights and stockings in this shop, but they do stock all the top names in all the desirable materials including net, lace, opaque and satin. And they have all the colours.

LA BOÎTE À BAS   77, RUE DE LONGCHAMP XVI – 47 55 11 55; 27, RUE BOISSY D'ANGLAS – 42 66 26 83; 16, AVENUE MOZART XVI – 42 24 89 98

LES FOLIES D'ÉLODIE maintain their pole position in the world of lingerie. For millionaires, stars of stage and screen and other 'Pretty Women', this is *the* place to shop. But you will, consequently, only find silk, satin, lace and macramé.

LES FOLIES D'ÉLODIE   56, AVENUE PAUL-DOUMER XVI – 45 06 93 57; 1 BIS, AVENUE MAC-MAHON XVII – 42 67 68 95

SOPHIE D'ANNUNZIA She's a former journalist but she's redeployed herself very effectively in the world of lace. Her strong point is her tights, which she sells from the ultra-classic to the ultra-trendy, including names like Wolford, Chantal Thomass and Pierre Mantou. Her other speciality is bodies.

SOPHIE D'ANNUNZIA   17, RUE DU CHERCHE-MIDI VI – 45 44 46 54

LES DIVINES Monique Vissot made a wise business decision opening her boutique next to Chanel's. The customers from the couture house and the guests at the nearby Ritz Hotel can't avoid going past her shop and, once inside, they will never see a more sophisticated selection of wares than her lingerie for refined people.

LES DIVINES   23, RUE CAMBON I – 42 61 75 54

SWIMWEAR

The prelude to throwing yourself into the water is looking for a swimming costume, and this can be a painful exercise for any Parisian woman. There is nothing more humbling than exposing pale, winter flesh to the glare of a fitting-room mirror. To make it easier, however, we provide a selection of the top specialists.

ÉRÈS is the chic and expensive temple of the swimming costume. In the middle of winter, travellers to foreign shores find their dream design. The staff are all corset-makers by trade and the costumes are checked by hand. There are no androgynous models here. This is the home of the precise, fitted shape for either the slim or the more amply proportioned and you will also find matching, sexy little dresses, shorts and T-shirts to complete your holiday wardrobe.

♡ ÉRÈS 2, RUE TRONCHET VIII – 47 42 24 55; 4 BIS, RUE DU CHERCHE-MIDI VI – 45 44 95 54

CAPUCINE PUERARI This delightful young lady designs the prettiest collections of junior lingerie and bodies without gussets that you can wear as outerwear also. Her speciality is the uplifting, deep-plunge model and styling for the young.

CAPUCINE PUERARI 63, RUE DES SAINTS-PÈRES VII – 45 49 26 90

À LA PLAGE On speed-boat flooring and with white-varnished fitting-rooms complete with widely striped deckchairs, the two A La Plage boutiques bring to mind the landscape of Normandy at the turn of the century with its picturesque little ports. In winter as in summer, Isabelle de Maistre, the owner, stocks an impressive range of top labels and designer costumes. They have all the colours and all the prints for even the most unaccommodating of figures.

À LA PLAGE 6, RUE DE SOLFÉRINO VII – 47 05 18 51; 17, RUE DE LA POMPE XVI – 45 03 08 51

DIVA Three sisters, Murielle, Maud and Violette, try on 800 prototypes themselves, every season, in order to weed out the ones that are so fashion-orientated or so over-the-top that no real woman could actually wear them. Their favourite labels are La Perla and Pascal and they sell sizes up to 44 (16). They even have some models in 46 (18). The saleswomen here are friendly, competent and unusually patient with all their customers.

DIVA 54, AVENUE CHARLES DE GAULLE 92200 NEUILLY-SUR-SEINE – 47 47 90 99

MANUEL CANOVAS Everyone knows about the delightful prints that this textile designer produces. But not everyone knows that you can find these same prints made up into beach bags, sarongs, bath sheets and softly moulded swimming costumes with narrow straps, which are rather athletic-looking.

MANUEL CANOVAS 7, PLACE DE FURSTENBERG VI – 43 26 89 31

AU REFUGE The pilot shop of this sportswear firm is the meeting-place for breast-stroke and front-crawl champions. The whole year round they stock an impressive department full of indoor and competitive poolwear. The sporty swimmer takes precedence here.

♧ **AU REFUGE   46, RUE SAINT-PLACIDE VI – 42 22 27 33**

DAC In this shop they specialize in clothes for tropical climes. Since the 50s all their customers have been aware that they sell swimming costumes even in the middle of winter. They have a very wide selection of Jannie Rolin outfits and sizes right up to 52 (22).

DAC   18, BOULEVARD SAINT-MARTIN X – 42 06 44 59

V DE V In winter the shop is more or less taken over by skiwear but there is a permanent swimwear department. In the summer, sailing, surfing and water-ski enthusiasts, who also want to feel the benefits of an all-over tan, come to purchase one-piece costumes that roll down to become bikini bottoms, and also adjustable wraps.

V DE V   4, RUE DE SÈVRES VI – 42 22 39 15

SPORT ET CLIMAT In this very old shop, safari-lovers, cruise-fanatics and journalists all gather to get their tropical gear and their safari hats. There's a permanent swimwear department and it's all very classical.

SPORT ET CLIMAT   223, BOULEVARD SAINT-GERMAIN VI – 45 48 80 99

PIERRE KLIMO and his daughter Nathalie design and manu-facture dance and gym leotards and they have tailored their style to suit swimwear. It's made of lycra and elasticated cotton so that it dries quickly, and there are 30 styles at comfortingly low prices. The rounder amongst us can choose from swimwear made to measure.

PIERRE KLIMO   72, RUE D'ALÉSIA XIV – 45 42 40 49

DOROTENNIS STOCK Sporty types like Dorotennis's cos-tumes because of their simple, comfortable shapes. Slyer creatures looking for a bargain know that they can buy last year's collection from the 'still in fashion' stock.

DOROTENNIS STOCK   74, RUE D'ALÉSIA XIV – 45 42 40 68

RALPH LAUREN In a Newport kind of style, this is elegant, sporty swimwear in the consistently classic designs of Ralph Lauren, one of the most famous of the American designers, and it is sold on the first floor of his shop in the 'Country and Western' department.

RALPH LAUREN   2, PLACE DE LA MADELEINE VIII – 44 77 53 00

LA PETITE PLAGE In a quiet, almost provincial district of Paris, in the shadow of the bells of Saint-Cloud, a kindly saleswoman will help you try on the most up-to-the-minute designs by A La Plage and Nautic, in winter just as in summer, in her spacious fitting-rooms.

LA PETITE PLAGE   27, RUE CASIMIR-PERRIER VII – 47 05 33 57

And also:

AU VIEUX CAMPEUR   6, RUE DE LATRAN V – 43 29 12 32

The department stores and the CRUISE sections in designer stores.

COUNTRY WEEKEND

As soon as the leaves turn brown, the hunting and shooting season begins. Clothes worn for the chase are then worn in the city and, fashion being what it is, everyone buys the gear even if they don't know the first thing about holding a gun or the meaning of the huntsman's calls. Even the environmentally sound are into it all. The women go shopping in their Barbours, leave for the office wearing loden coats and go out to dinner in Spencer jackets with gold buttons. For weekend presents they will offer you a wide variety of objects all to do with field sports. So join the pack!

KETTNER An arms merchant and a specialist in hunting clothes, he first came to public attention with a mail-order catalogue which still exists. He then opened a vast shop in Paris with 1,000 square metres on two levels. The armoury collection is displayed in the basement. This Man from Lorraine knows all about choosing equipment that will shelter you from the cold as well as the damp, and his traditional Barbour jacket is one of the cheapest on the market. He also sells it in waxed poplin with a gamebag, and even in Goretex.

KETTNER   23–27, BOULEVARD GOUVION-SAINT-CYR XVII – 45 74 10 77

MARIE-CLAUDE ET ALAIN SIRAS were the pioneers of Sologne style and they have adapted it to city lifestyles. Now they have two shops under the name 'Interchasse' and a mail-order business. There are featherweight and ultra-warm jackets made of 'polarplus' (a synthetic material like shaven teddy-bear fluff but which is not in the least restrictive). There is also a handsome selection of Austrian sweaters and, by way of accessory, bootjacks made of solid wood.

♡   INTERCHASSE   12, RUE DE PRESBOURG XVI − 45 00 04 34; 104, BOULEVARD HAUSSMANN VIII − 43 87 90 87; CATALOGUE BP 30616, 75767 PARIS CEDEX 16

HENRY COTTON'S kits out all the sporty types with parkas made of canvas material and this year's in-thing, which happens to be quilted wool. You will find this near the Place des Victoires and, once you've got past the locked entrance guarded by a stern-faced porter, in a superbly decorated shop of solid oak and exposed stonework.

HENRY COTTON'S   52, RUE ÉTIENNE MARCEL II − 42 36 01 22

GASTINNE-RENETTE held the title 'King's Arquebusier' and has had a shop in the Avenue Franklin-D.-Roosevelt since 1936. The armourer now busies himself with the rest of his clients' requirements, which include black quilted hunting jackets and shooting bags. If you feel a sudden urge to practise your shooting skills, you can go down to the basement where you will find a superbly equipped firing range − which is apparently the same one used by the Swiss Army − and which has a complete set of hunting videos. Perchance to dream and let yourself drift into your emotional fantasies.

GASTINNE-RENETTE   39, AVENUE FRANKLIN-D.-ROOSEVELT VIII − 43 59 77 74; PRINTEMPS DE LA MODE, BOULEVARD HAUSSMANN

AIGLE Since 1853 they have been making rubber boots for hunters. And they now sell them as part of a wide range of clothes adapted to open-air activities on land or sea. They also sell perfect, inexpensive sweatshirts, made of a soft, light and warm fabric called 'polarfleece', which is just wonderful for both town and country; they come complete with truck-drivers' collars and velvet yokes. They also have trappers' jackets, and genuine parkas made of Scotchguard (a waterproof anti-stain material) which are both sporty and very fashionable.

♡ ♣ ESPACE   AIGLE 141,   BOULEVARD   SAINT-GERMAIN   VI − 46 33 26 23

OK'DUCK opened a shop in Paris in 1990, after Constance de La Rochefoucauld had been distributing her goods for several years by a pretty mail-order catalogue, which she sent to her customers from her home in the Loiret area (south of Paris). Her choices are always sophisticated and include flowing woollen riding-skirts with horn buttons. There are also Tintin-style wool trousers and crockery with hunting motifs.

OK'DUCK   6, RUE DU LAOS XV — 45 67 98 93

And also:

HERMÈS   24, RUE DU FAUBOURG SAINT-HONORÉ VIII — 40 17 47 17

BURBERRYS   8, BOULEVARD MALESHERBES VIII — 42 66 13 01; 55, RUE DE RENNES VI — 45 48 52 71

OLD ENGLAND   12, BOULEVARD DES CAPUCINES IX — 47 42 81 99

LOEWE   57, AVENUE MONTAIGNE VIII — 42 89 06 61

METTEZ   12, BOULEVARD MALESHERBES VIII — 42 65 33 76

TUNMER   5, PLACE SAINT-AUGUSTIN VIII — 45 22 75 80

FAURÉ LEPAGE SAILLARD   8, RUE DE RICHELIEU I — 42 96 07 78

DUPREY   5, RUE TROYON XVII — 43 80 29 37

EQUISTABLE   177, BOULEVARD HAUSSMANN VIII — 45 61 02 57

PADD   20, RUE DU LAOS XV — 43 06 56 50

KINETON   40, RUE VITAL XVI — 45 04 67 21

FASHION ACCESSORIES

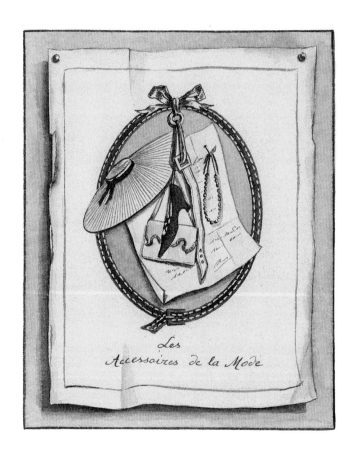

Les
Accessoires de la Mode

FOOTWEAR

Footwear designers dress supermodels and elegant women everywhere. Between the moment of inspiration and that of manufacture, they have also learnt the secret of the perfect fit. And it's thanks to them that the shoe has become an essential fashion item in its own right.

CHRISTIAN LOUBOUTIN The happening thing in style for feet. The most astonishing of the designs at his Véro-Dodat gallery is the 'lovebird' or 'inseparable' shoe, with motifs like the word 'Love', knots and comets extending across both feet. Christian learnt his trade with Roger Vivier, so it's no wonder, then, that his models, fanciful and extravagant though they are, also combine sophistication and tradition. His beechwood heels are gilded with gold leaf and his satin slippers are set with precious stones and crystals. All of which you will find displayed in the surrealist décor of his 'home'.

CHRISTIAN LOUBOUTIN 19, RUE J.-J.-ROUSSEAU / 2, PASSAGE VÉRO-DODAT I – 42 36 05 31

FAUSTO SANTINI From Milan to Rome everyone knows his name. Here he is for the first time in 'Parigi' in the middle of its 'artiest' district. With a deep-purple frontage and a vast slab of white stone for a display unit, the architecture of the shop is due to Antonio Citterio. In its sober way, it highlights every shoe. The originality lies in the heels; whether horseshoes, half-cylinders or pyramids, they are all perfectly stable to walk in. Other accessories are also irresistible, with simple shopping bags, holdalls or mini-handbags. The American actress, Lauren Hutton, is a big fan.

FAUSTO SANTINI 4 TER, RUE DU CHERCHE-MIDI VI – 45 44 39 40

HAREL From Catherine Deneuve to Hélène Rochas, from Nadine de Rothschild to Paloma Picasso, the most elegant of Parisian women treat themselves to Harel pumps and the other women just dream of doing so. They come in lizard and are cut, made up and finished by hand. There are 26 different colours and the styles vary from the classic to the eccentric (fuchsia-pink, ivy-green). There are also 16 half-sizes, 2 widths and 5 heel heights. You will find all this in the sumptuously appointed two-storey shop behind a stone façade with a little garden, and all fitted out like an English library.

HAREL 8, AVENUE MONTAIGNE VIII — 47 20 75 00

K JACQUES It all began in Saint-Tropez. A customer rolled up at the workshop in the summer of 1933 and ordered Roman centurion sandals, made to measure. The Tropezian sandal was born and, with it, Jacques Keklikian's reputation. His company, K Jacques, set up in Paris in a shop decorated in the colours of the sun, the sand, the sea and the forest. Mediterranean décor, then, for the famous sandal (at around 500 francs) and made up in every possible shade of leather.

K JACQUES SAINT-TROPEZ 16, RUE PAVÉE IV — 40 27 03 57

CHARLES JOURDAN Started in 1921, the Charles Jourdan label is distributed in over 100 shops world-wide. In Paris, the pilot store in the Champs-Elysées gathers together the whole collection under one roof. This is a vast space filled with his very high-heeled walking shoes, his moccasins and his clumpy-heeled platforms, all laid out on very low display tables.

CHARLES JOURDAN 86, AVENUE DES CHAMPS-ÉLYSÉES VIII — 45 62 29 28; 12, RUE DU FAUBOURG SAINT-HONORÉ VIII — 42 65 35 22

PARABOOT This is the shop for hikers, bikers and hard kids. Founded in 1919, Paraboot offers 83 models including hand-sewn shoes from 'Goodyear', Norwegian designs like the classic 'Saint-Michael' range and more sophisticated styles in ankle boots, brogues and fabulous hunting boots.

PARABOOT 9, RUE DE GRENELLE VII — 45 49 24 26

WALTER STEIGER At 16 years of age, Walter was a young Swiss shoemaker. After the early days as a crafstman, he started working for Bally, where for four years he designed the collections while also learning manufacturing techniques. He launched his own name by creating accessories for Karl Lagerfeld, Montana and Gérard Pipart at Ricci. His designs for low-heeled shoes are among the most perfect in the whole world.

WALTER STEIGER 83, RUE DU FAUBOURG SAINT-HONORÉ VIII — 42 66 65 08; 5, RUE DE TOURNON VI — 46 33 01 45

STÉPHANE KÉLIAN He made his name into a designer label thanks to a master's skill: the art of braiding by hand. An office integrated with stylists thinks up a new avant-garde collection every season.

STÉPHANE KÉLIAN   13 BIS, RUE DE GRENELLE VII – 42 22 93 03; 6, PLACE DES VICTOIRES II – 42 61 60 74

MOI MES SOULIERS is the label of Miss Gratounette. Marthe Lagache sells her detailed shoes here, in flirtatious and even classic styles. A fresco sets the tone on the ceiling and portrays Adam and Eve fighting over a red slipper. You can have the colour of the fabric changed for a small supplement.

MOI MES SOULIERS   14, RUE DU ROI-DE-SICILE IV – 42 78 84 04

SALVATORE FERRAGAMO He supplies shoes to everyone in Hollywood, from Hayworth to Bacall, and dreams up cork platforms with transparent soles. Now he's arrived in Paris.

SALVATORE FERRAGAMO 68–70, RUE DES SAINTS-PÈRES VII – 45 44 01 24

TIMBERLAND The models are stuck together thermally and soldered before being hand-sewn and coated with silicone to make them totally rainproof. This is the major asset of the American brand founded in 1918 through the imagination of Nathan Swart, a lumberjack by trade.

TIMBERLAND   52, RUE CROIX-DES-PETITS-CHAMPS I – 45 08 41 40

CAREL After studying style in Italy, Tony Carel, the boss's son, took over the family business, founded in 1952, keeping creativity to the fore. There are charming ballet shoes and white satin pumps, dyed to any colour you want in 48 hours.

CAREL   22, RUE ROYALE VIII – 42 60 23 06

JOAN AND DAVID White marble façade, black lacquered columns, a maplewood counter and black granite floor all characterize this pure, austere space, the shop of the famous American shoe manufacturer. At its head sits Joan, a graduate in Social Science from Columbia University, and her husband and business partner, David Helpern. She designs shoes for women who, like her, are constantly plane-hopping, and thus gives priority to flat heels.

JOAN AND DAVID   6, RUE DU FAUBOURG SAINT-HONORÉ VIII – 42 65 65 37

RENÉ MANCINI produced the first pair of black-tipped shoes for Chanel so that 'the eye doesn't notice the dark part' (and the foot appears more petite). Claire, his daughter, took over the shop with a best-seller: the 8-centimetre-heeled pump.

RENÉ MANCINI   20, RUE DU BOCCADOR VIII – 47 23 01 03

DELAGE The famous decorator Barbara Wirth is responsible for the design. Primrose Bordier is in charge of the colour scheme. They have sea-green shark, yellow crocodile and purple lizard moccasins and pumps, all of which make this shoemaker irresistible.

DELAGE   6, RUE DE MÉZIÈRES VI – 42 84 15 24

STUDIO LARIZZI Sidonie Larizzi designed extraordinary boots in suede flecked with braid for Lacroix. She now supplies the other couturiers with shoes but, for those of us on a smaller budget, she has designed a collection that you can discover for yourself in a small shop with beige suede-like wallcovering, a counter made of light-coloured oak and astonishing baroque chairs. They also have pretty pumps with cork heels.

STUDIO LARIZZI   28, RUE DE LA TRÉMOILLE VIII – 47 23 35 08; you will find the large couture collection at **8, RUE MARIGNAN VIII – 43 59 38 87**

LAURENT MERCADAL Mercadal's perfect pumps and ballet shoes are made in his own workshops and they cost around 900 francs a pair. The pumps have low heels, the moccasins are made of granulated leather and they also sell satin sandals. You can also have your purchases mended.

LAURENT MERCADAL   3, PLACE DES VICTOIRES I – 45 08 84 44

GELATI Elegant, fashionable and inexpensive, Gelati shoes are designed by Elie Jacob. They have very fitted ballet shoes with rounded, pointed or square toes for around 600 francs.

GELATI   20, RUE DU CHERCHE-MIDI VI – 45 48 41 01

ROBERT CLERGERIE His shoes have their feet firmly on the ground. Simple, classic and comfortable, they are fashionable but not overly so. There are pumps with soft curves and little heels and ballet shoes with platform soles.

ROBERT CLERGERIE   5, RUE DU CHERCHE-MIDI VI – 45 48 75 47

BALLY The Swiss shoe shop set up in a grand style in the building which was once the studio of Renoir, the painter. This is the biggest shoe shop in Europe and was designed by Yves Taralon. 'Active' women (cyclists or dancers) will find what they want on the ground floor. On the first floor they have a VIP suite for made-to-measure shoes.

BALLY   BOULEVARD DE LA MADELEINE I – 42 61 11 60

FREE LANCE The shop is totally fitted out in iron, copper and Mad Max-style recycled lead. It is part of the hardline ecological movement, continued in the young, avant-garde collection. There are Indian moccasins and 50s-style ballet shoes.

FREE LANCE   30, RUE DU FOUR VI – 45 48 14 78

And also:
lizard shoes at **SARTORE 14, RUE CAMBON I – 40 15 02 44**
avant-garde shoes at **ACCESSOIRE-DIFFUSION 8, RUE DU JOUR I –
40 26 19 84**

BAGS AND BELTS

*There are the almost legendary bags like the Hermès Kelly bag
and the quilted Chanel number and then there are the practical,
useful bags like the pouch and the classic shopper. There are
evening bags, embroidered like ball-gowns and beaded bags like
pieces of jewelry and then there are the fashion items, which are
small, angular and rigid. Parisians carry them in their hands or
hanging off their forearms like Jackie Kennedy. And then there
are the belts which might match, but, equally well, might not. All
in all, there's something for everyone and every occasion.*

RENAUD PELLEGRINO comes from a family of potters from
Vallauris (on the Côte d'Azur) and, more specifically, from the
town of Cannes. He moved up to Paris and owes his success to
Maria Carita who entrusted him with the design of her accessories. You will find his shop on the Right Bank, with its wrought-
iron gate, designed by André Dubreuil, and conceived in white
marble and exotic wood. It serves as a showcase for an
astonishing collection of jewelry-bags: satin pouches and heart-
shaped bags made of ottoman and moire and manufactured to
order from samples.
**RENAUD PELLEGRINO 348, RUE SAINT-HONORÉ I – 42 60 69 36; 15,
RUE DU CHERCHE-MIDI VI – 45 44 56 37**

AÏCHA In her small, white shop with its beige floor, Aïcha
Nadau, a young Algerian designer, exhibits her highly con-

temporary creations, in clashing colours. These are genuinely original.

AÏCHA   19, RUE PAVÉE IV – 42 77 62 65

DELVAUX This master leather craftsman from Brussels can number King Baudouin amongst his clients. This house, created in 1829, on the Rue de l'Empereur in Brussels, specializes in travelling-trunks. Here the décor is stone, marble and glass, which creates a sumptuous atmosphere in which to show off the magnificent bags. These will always be classics.

DELVAUX   18, RUE ROYALE VIII – 42 60 85 95

DIDIER LAMARTHE The floor of this magnificent shop resembles a French garden with its stencilled decoration of paths and shrubbery, setting off to perfection Didier Lamarthe's leather goods. It was in 1970 that he took over the small failing family business. Today he has a factory in Brittany and a workshop in Paris. Hence the very reasonable prices for his handbags in washable leather and his multipocketed wallets. Creativity combined with durability.

DIDIER LAMARTHE   219, RUE SAINT-HONORÉ I – 42 96 09 90; 19, RUE DAUNOU II – 42 61 02 66

LESAGE There are silk bags embroidered in a variety of colours and enriched with semi-precious stones and braided with trimmings. The prettiest creations for evening use are the wonderful baroque items made by hand in the workshops of the embroiderer François Lesage, and you can admire all of these designs in a shop you will find located on the site of the former couture house of Schiaparelli.

LESAGE   21, PLACE VENDÔME I – 40 20 95 79

EMILIA Cognoscenti are only too well aware of Emilia Weinberg's bag shop which is located in a former historic palace. The rigid styles are inspired by the 50s, and they also sell bucket-bags. Their strong point is the fine quality of the smooth leather and the pure forms.

EMILIA   9, RUE DE GRENELLE VII – 42 22 37 67

SOCO was a clog manufacturer in Bort-les-Orgues in the Corrèze area of France. In order to use up the hides from the local tannery, he used grainy calfskin leather to make Wild West bags, often in two-tone colours.

SOCO   50, RUE CROIX-DES-PETITS-CHAMPS I – 42 60 12 80

JEAN-LOUIS IMBERT Models designed by Jocelyne Imbert and manufactured in the family factory in Marseilles tend to be in touch with the times and reasonably priced.

JEAN-LOUIS IMBERT   44, RUE ÉTIENNE-MARCEL II – 42 33 36 04

PALOMA PICASSO Picasso's dove has landed in the Rue de la Paix, in a setting designed by Jacques Grange, comprised of purple carpet, red benches and parchment walls. Paloma has created bags which are easily identifiable as hers by the gold cross which is executed with audacious skill. Equally, guests at the Ritz Hotel, and anyone else who happens to wander in for that matter, will find a delightful boutique in the shopping gallery inside the hotel. It looks on to a garden and has a sharp collection of designs.

PALOMA PICASSO   5, RUE DE LA PAIX II – 42 86 02 21; HÔTEL RITZ 17, PLACE VENDÔME II – 42 60 00 48

LA BAGAGERIE was the shop that pioneered leather goods as fashion items. As early as 1954, Jean Marlaix was designing avant-garde bags which exploded on to the traditional leather-goods market. They still supply the accessories for the haute couture fashion shows, but they also now sell a basic line of goods, from pouches to shopping bags, at reasonable prices.

LA BAGAGERIE   12, RUE TRONCHET VIII – 47 42 79 13; 41, RUE DU FOUR VI – 42 22 66 84

MULBERRY In 1969 Roger Saul began designing leather bags and belts in the kitchen of his London flat. Then, with help from his parents, he started his own label in the former smithy of his family estate in Bath. Today the crocodile-print bags, the personal organizers and the belts are classic items for all Parisian women.

MULBERRY   45, RUE CROIX-DES-PETITS-CHAMPS I – 40 41 07 69; 14, RUE DU CHERCHE-MIDI VI – 42 22 95 05

HERVÉ CHAPELIER has no reason to be modest about his achievements. His two-tone nylon shopping bags with their internal pockets have become the featherweight, indispensable accessory of the 'Executive Woman'. Model number 913 is the best-seller and can hold shopping, your handbag, the file you're working on and 15 kilos of bumph without giving way. Number 901 is very small and can be used as an evening bag or a vanity case.

HERVÉ   CHAPELIER   55,   BOULEVARD   DE   COURCELLES   VIII – 47 54 91 27

GUNILLA LINBLAD is one of the most famous supermodels (you will undoubtedly have seen her face on the cover of one of the glossies), and she has now opened a shop devoted to the real McCoy. She vanished to the States for ten years with her husband and, whilst there, the beautiful Gunilla Linblad had time to think over just which seductive items she wanted to sell herself. There is, in fact, a mixture of the American and the classic with shades of her first Upla shop, which they created. Cévennes shepherds' pouches made of sheep's leather and Spanish bags made up by craftsmen from the world of bullfighting are all to be found in this collection.

GUNILLA LINBLAD   1, PLACE ALPHONSE-DEVILLE VI – 42 84 05 83

SAC ET SAC Before launching his first collection, Maurice Doulka used to direct 'Le Tanneur'. His individual desire was to break the mould of classic leather manufacture and, in order to do so, he asked all the young avant-garde designers to come up with new designs and then hallmark them. Go and stroke them, try them out in your own time in this beautiful, grey space decorated by Bernard Eric.

SAC ET SAC   5, RUE DU SABOT VI – 42 22 90 84

LANCEL In 1876 the Lancels opened a shop for smokers. Gradually they extended their activities to include leather and opened a shop in the middle of the Paris of the Belle Epoque. Now that this has been taken over by Edouard and Jean Zorbibe, the firm has its own creative bureau, which works hand-in-glove with the studio, fine-tuning avant-garde work at reasonable prices.

LANCEL   8, PLACE DE L'OPÉRA IX – 47 42 37 29

GROOM They sell the prettiest purses in Paris, designed by Corinne Greffay. This young designer won the prize at the annual leatherworkers' show for her very first bag design and now shows her entire collection in her all-black shop. At the entrance door is a bell-boy with painted face, dressed in red from head to toe. There is also a very pretty selection of belts.

GROOM   13, RUE DU CHERCHE-MIDI VI – 45 48 49 36

CHABRAND Set up in Marseilles 50 years ago, this family leather business brings a modern touch to a classic label. There are bucket-bags and duffle bags in bright colours. The firm, all of whose staff are meticulously well-informed about matters leathery, also sells wooden bags made in a traditional saddler's way.

CHABRAND   18, RUE MARBEUF VIII – 47 20 02 13

BRISKA made its Paris début after New York and Tokyo. The Rioland clan, saddlers from father to son for three generations, carry on the tradition of manufacturing bags that are moulded round wood. It is through this process that the rigid shapes are achieved, carved, as they are, with straight edges, dyed and waxed by hand, and requiring eight manhours for each bag. You can also have them made-to-measure either less rigidly, or in ostrich or crocodile in a colour chosen from a swatch.

BRISKA   38, RUE DE GRENELLE VII – 45 48 41 90

And of course:

CHANEL 31, RUE CAMBON I – 42 86 28 00

HERMÈS 24, RUE DU FAUBOURG SAINT-HONORÉ VIII – 40 17 47 17

VUITTON 54, AVENUE MONTAIGNE VIII – 45 62 47 00

FRANÇOIS MAROT 95, RUE DU FAUBOURG SAINT-HONORÉ VIII – 47 42 15 00

SYLVAIN LEFEBVRE 97, RUE RAMBUTEAU I – 42 36 08 65

ROCHAS 33, RUE FRANÇOIS-Iᵉʳ VIII – 47 23 54 56

ADELINE ALBINET 24, RUE DU ROI-DE-SICILE IV – 42 78 92 78

MILLINERY

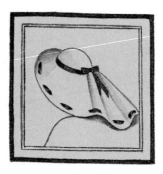

You will never see an entire catwalk show without noticing the skills of a master milliner. The hat, after all, heads the fashion scene.

JEAN BARTHET has supplied hats to Romy Schneider and Sophia Loren, Brigitte Bardot and Jackie Kennedy. He made the wide-brims in the film *Les Demoiselles de Rochefort* and the turned-up look which Catherine Deneuve modelled in *Fort Saganne*. In his workshop you might bump into Stéphanie of Monaco or even Michael Jackson. He also supplies the hats for numerous couture houses who love his beautiful wide-brimmed hats and his upmarket design skills.

JEAN BARTHET 13, RUE TRONCHET VIII – 42 65 35 87

MARIE MERCIÉ 'Tradition doesn't interest me', says this milliner, 'I just do my own thing.' And so she does, with her own particular brand of humour. She's an art history graduate but she's also a painter, and a visit to her jumble of a shop will turn into a beauty session. Her designs are funny, poetic, crazy but never ridiculous. She dares to suggest a top hat planted with roses, or a wide-brimmed hat that looks like a famous pirate's.

MARIE MERCIÉ   56, RUE TIQUETONNE II – 40 26 60 68

In her Left Bank shop, which features varnished planks and tall mirrors, windows open on to a romantic courtyard and peach-coloured décor sets off a simpler, more affordable collection.

MARIE MERCIÉ   23, RUE SAINT-SULPICE VI – 43 26 45 83

PHILIPPE MODEL, one of the most talented young milliners in Paris, has a workshop on the banks of the Yonne. For the 'Prix de Diane-Hermès', an annual horserace, his sister Laurence, the director of the elegant little shop, hires out 200 to 300 extravagant new hats every year. She also sells gloves, bags and shoes.

PHILIPPE MODEL 33, PLACE DU MARCHÉ SAINT-HONORÉ I – 42 96 89 02

Philippe Model also has a Left Bank shop. There are felt hats with double crowns and hats that are easier to wear for everyday. Do take note of the famous elastic, coarse-grained shoes, with or without their little heels.

PHILIPPE MODEL   79, RUE DES SAINTS-PÈRES VI – 45 44 76 79

JEAN-CHARLES BROSSEAU Untreated walls, pale-green parquet flooring and a boudoir atmosphere serve as the setting for Jean-Charles Brosseau's collection. He was a pioneer who has designed for Jacques Fath and was the first to create hats in soft fabrics made in the off-cuts of designer studios. In 1960, he opened a shop in the Rue Vaneau and then he set up at the Place des Victoires. He maintains his reputation for simple, strong, sophisticated designs.

JEAN-CHARLES BROSSEAU   26, RUE DE L'UNIVERSITÉ VII – 40 15 98 72

GABRIELLE CADET knows how to make a fetching, unex-pected hat out of the tiniest piece of fabric. She drapes ribbons and intertwines pieces of silk, so don't hesitate to climb the three dusty staircases which lead up to her studio near the Place de la République. It takes her a day to create a new design and her speciality is hats covered with dress material, which start at around 1,500 francs.

GABRIELLE CADET   7, RUE BÉRANGER III – 42 74 53 07 (found on the third floor, the staircase on the left in the courtyard, and by appointment only)

OLIVIER CHANAN was trained in the school of entertain-ment and advertising. He took history of art and window-dressing classes before he started doing fashion styling and making the hats for the actors at the Théâtre de la Colline and the models at Jean-Paul Gaultier. He is a specialist in draping fabric and the most creative milliner in town.

OLIVIER CHANAN   6, RUE DES ROSIERS IV – 42 77 15 87

LUGGAGE

'An Invitation to Travel' was the title of an exhibition donated by Louis Vuitton to the Museum of Decorative Arts 5 years ago. This is because the concept of travel goes hand-in-glove with the purchase of luggage. Whether a heavy trunk or a light knapsack, this is an accessory which makes you dream of becoming an eternal bird of passage.

Louis **VUITTON** was the trunk and box maker of the Empress Eugénie. He opened a factory in 1854 at Asnières and the mahogany wood he used then is still rigorously selected today, along with leather and coarse-grained monogrammed canvas, to make the most famous luggage collection in the world, on the exact same premises. For sailors there's a sailor's bag as a tribute to the Louis Vuitton Cup, one of the events in the America's Cup. Go and admire the superb window displays in the shop on the Avenue Marceau and the large stone portico of the Avenue Montaigne shop. In the former family residence at Asnières, his descendants have opened a museum, which is definitely a must.

VUITTON 78 BIS, AVENUE MARCEAU VIII – 47 20 47 00; 54, AVENUE MONTAIGNE VIII – 45 62 47 00

LANCEL Has been manufacturing leather for more than 100 years, and has represented comfort for travellers during the whole of that time. He puts little rollers on his cases, intelligently thinks up ways to transport clothing, makes up travel bags in all shapes and colours, works with leather, uses both leather and canvas as all-purpose materials, supplies his solid wares with handles and long shoulder straps and, to add to all this, has recently had the Opéra store redecorated so that it now has a granite floor of lightly flecked maple wood.

♡   LANCEL   8, PLACE DE L'OPÉRA IX – 47 42 37 29; 127, AVENUE DES CHAMPS-ÉLYSÉES VIII – 47 23 66 03; 4, ROND-POINT DES CHAMPS-ÉLYSÉES VIII – 42 25 18 35

DIDIER LAMARTHE uses a gilded double unicorn as his logo as well as the colour yellow. He takes light materials like PVC and coated canvas and embellishes these with corner pieces, piping and leather handles.
DIDIER LAMARTHE   219, RUE SAINT-HONORÉ I – 42 96 09 90

AUX ÉTATS-UNIS is 100 years old and at the time it was founded the leather manufacturer didn't have to worry about baggage handling. As he has now adapted to the times, François Dereisme uses a reinforced nylon which is both supple and tear-resistant, and the scales that are a permanent fixture of the shop will let you weigh your purchases very accurately.
AUX ÉTATS-UNIS   229, RUE SAINT-HONORÉ I – 42 60 73 95

GOYARD have been trunkmakers since 1853 and can now count Jeanne Moreau, the actress, amongst their many customers. They hang red and white ribbons from their luggage, which is a handy idea and helps you spot it instantly as it goes round the conveyor belt.
GOYARD   233, RUE SAINT-HONORÉ I – 42 60 57 04

LONGCHAMP has invented the nylon X-Tra Bag, which will convert in seconds from a small, pocket-sized object into a holdall the size of a duffle-bag. This is an indispensable item for those amongst us who can't even imagine going for a quick breath of air without returning laden with purchases. The other speciality of Philippe Cassegrain is the very fine-quality leather he uses.
LONGCHAMP   390, RUE SAINT-HONORÉ I – 42 60 00 00

LE TANNEUR   has been a master of leather manufacture since 1898. In this two-storey shop decorated in pink cabinet-wood and black and pink granite panelling, you can just stand there, for ages, gazing at the beauty of the merchandise.
LE TANNEUR 72, RUE DU FAUBOURG SAINT-HONORÉ VIII – 40 17 06 91; 102, AVENUE VICTOR-HUGO XVI – 47 55 48 06

LE MONDE DU BAGAGE was thought up by a former dentist, Gisèle Pomeranc, who wanted it to be 'practical and cheapish'. Brightly coloured nylon and black rubber are partly responsible for their best-selling items.
LE MONDE DU BAGAGE   4, RUE DES PETITS-CHAMPS II – 42 86 90 45

HERVÉ CHAPELIER was initially a tremendous hit with college students and sixth-formers. But then their mothers caught on. Your first purchase is bound to be a rucksack and your second will be one of the shoppers which come in all shapes and sizes. People collect them because of the beautifully harmonizing colour-schemes like emerald and red, purple and pink, and so on.

HERVÉ CHAPELIER   55, BOULEVARD DE COURCELLES VIII – 47 54 91 27; 13, RUE GUSTAVE-COURBET XVI – 47 27 83 66

MANDARINA DUCK comes from Italy; to be more precise, it comes from Bologna. The stylists who work there prefer avant-garde materials, which they weld, thermally, with steel or nickel springs and anodized handles. This is solid, futuristic gear.

MANDARINA DUCK   7, BOULEVARD DE LA MADELEINE I – 42 86 08 00; 6, RUE SAINT-SULPICE VI – 46 33 40 08

MULBERRY COMPANY comes from Somerset (in England), the home county of Roger Saul, the founder. He likes crocodile-style leather, from which he makes his suitcases.

MULBERRRY COMPANY 45, RUE CROIX-DES-PETITS-CHAMPS I – 40 41 07 69; 14, RUE DU CHERCHE-MIDI VI – 42 22 95 05

MANUEL CANOVAS travels all over the world to promote his fabrics. He makes up enormous, impressive bags out of some of the coarser fabrics. The most recent creations have contrasting lining material and, in order to spot his own suitcases straight away, as they go spinning round the conveyor belt in airport lounges, Manuel paints his motif colours, yellow and blue, discreetly on to his luggage. This is really the height of sophistication.

MANUEL CANOVAS   30, AVENUE GEORGE-V VIII – 49 52 00 36; 5, PLACE DE FURSTENBERG VI – 43 26 89 31

PATRICK FREY is just as much a textile manufacturer but has now launched a line of cases and bags, made up in some of his own fabric designs, which he has waterproofed.

PATRICK FREY   47, RUE DES PETITS-CHAMPS I – 44 77 36 00; 5, RUE JACOB VI – 46 33 73 00

And also:

LA BAGAGERIE   74, RUE DE PASSY XVI – 45 27 14 49

ARCO   5, RUE CAMBON I – 42 96 45 34

MCM   243, RUE SAINT-HONORÉ I – 42 60 08 74

LA DILIGENCE   102, BOULEVARD DES BATIGNOLLES XVII – 43 87 28 04

INTERCHASSE   12, RUE DE PRESBOURG XVI – 45 00 04 34

PRADA   5, RUE DE GRENELLE VI – 45 48 53 14

COMPTOIR SUD-PACIFIQUE   17, RUE DE LA PAIX II – 42 61 74 44

CHAPITRE 3   86, AVENUE PAUL-DOUMER XVI – 45 24 59 32

HIDEO WAKAMATSU   77, BOULEVARD SAINT-MICHEL V – 43 54 71 63

NOBILIS   29, RUE BONAPARTE VI – 43 29 21 50
ETRO   66, RUE DU FAUBOURG SAINT-HONORÉ VIII – 40 07 09 40

COSTUME JEWELRY

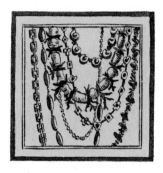

Chic and cheap costume jewelry has to be reckoned with for its sheer effrontery in colour, creativity and force – just as long as it makes no attempt to look 'real'. Coco Chanel brought it into fashion at a time when real jewels, which were very ostentatiously designed, seemed extravagantly inappropriate. Mademoiselle was the first person to mix real and false gemstones, which takes skill combining wit, irony and elegance. Following in her footsteps, women today succumb to the real, deluxe charms of fake jewels. But, naturally, only the right ones.

YVES SAINT LAURENT You might well imagine that you've entered an 18th-century House of Sin. There's an emerald velvet screen and parchment lit by four crystal chandeliers in a setting specially designed by Jacques Grange for this shop which is entirely devoted to the haute couture accessories of the famous designer. You will see necklaces made up of cascades of crystal, earrings tumbling down to the shoulders, bracelets made of precious woods and inlaid with 'fools' gold'. He also sells studded handkerchiefs, silk handkerchiefs and reversible silk scarves. These are accessories that you will also find in a special boutique nestling in the ground floor of the couture house.
YVES SAINT LAURENT   32, RUE DU FAUBOURG SAINT-HONORÉ VIII – 42 65 01 15

KATINKA DE MONTAL She's a multi-talented artist (who started in the world of murals) and knows just how to show off her jewelry collection to best advantage in the showroom which also contains her other designs.

KATINKA DE MONTAL　9, RUE VANEAU VII – 40 20 03 94

AGATHA Michel Quiniou is the son of a costume jewelry manufacturer and, after a spell with the perfumer 'Bourgeois', he created his own label, 'Agatha'. Nowadays he sells an incredible selection of some 2,000 designs, which are all fashion-conscious and include necklaces and charm bracelets with diminutive representations of the famous Paris monuments hanging off the links. There are also cameos and 50s-style brooches and the customer services department allows you to go back to the shop when you've lost an earring and buy a single one to replace it, or, when the metal on your bracelet loses its shine, you can go back and have it polished up.

AGATHA　97, RUE DE RENNES VI – 45 48 81 30; GALERIE DU ROND-POINT 12-14 ROND-POINT DES CHAMPS-ÉLYSÉES VIII – 43 59 68 68

DOMINIQUE AURIENTIS Having been a serious-minded student of literature at the Sorbonne and then done her apprenticeship at Dior and four years' training with Isabel Canovas, Dominique was highly qualified to launch her own label. Her style consists of neo-classic jewelry: charm bracelets (domes and cupolas), crystal necklaces and studs of amber-coloured glass or rubies mixed with white mother-of-pearl. She even sells reversible earrings, with one side in gold and the other in paste. You'll find the largest selection at:

DOMINIQUE AURIENTIS at ZENTA　6, RUE MARIGNAN VIII – 42 25 72 47

FABRICE Jackie Riss studied fine art and, once she'd finished, she sold her little old Citroën to finance her first collection and launch her own label, which she christened 'Fabrice'. In 1970 she set up in the Rue Bonaparte where Fabrice remains the market-leader in avant-garde jewelry. You will find absolutely super necklaces made of solid silver or mother-of-pearl and 30s-style bracelets.

FABRICE　33, RUE BONAPARTE VI – 43 26 57 95

NAÏLA DE MONBRISON This is a gallery consecrated to jewelry-makers of all ethnic origins and even of all periods in history. They throw the most elegant private view soirées in Paris and you might well rub shoulders with Loulou de la Falaise or Paloma Picasso if you're lucky enough to be invited. Marcial Berro, Tina Chow and Mattia Bonetti have all exhibited there.

GALERIE NAÏLA DE MONBRISON 6, RUE DE BOURGOGNE VII – 47 05 11 15

LOLA PRUSAC was one of the first designers to specialize in

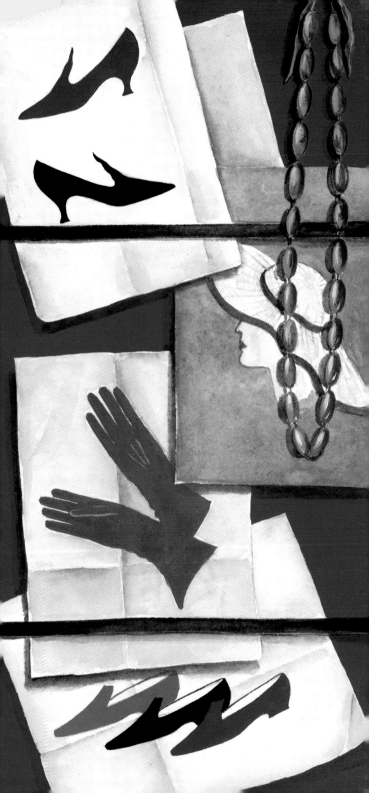

accessories. After studying fine art, this young Pole became a stylist at Hermès. Her brooches and necklaces became indispensable items in any elegant woman's wardrobe and nowadays her nephew has taken over the reins of control. As the inheritor of the family archives, he has had all the old jewelry reproduced in braidwork, from the amber bracelets to the distinctive Prusac-style metal chokers.

LOLA PRUSAC 179, RUE SAINT-HONORÉ I – 42 60 63 66

YAMADA This is the label that makes the jewelry for Kenzo, Moschino and Sonia Rykiel. They have a reputation for the beauty of their coral and other gemstones, and Yamada, a substantial Japanese company, distribute their designs direct to the public. They specialize in ruby jewelry which comes in heart-shapes and pendant crucifix forms.

YAMADA 30, RUE DANIELLE-CASANOVA II – 42 86 94 81

ROCHAS The Rochas boutique, which has been redesigned by Yves Taralon, is truly scrumptious! It features soft yielding carpet, warm panelling and gentle lights. Discover it at the same time as the superbly designed jewelry, in its strange and baroque forms, thought up by the artistic director, Christian Astuguevieille.

ROCHAS 33, RUE FRANÇOIS-Ier VIII – 47 23 54 56

PAUL CAILLOL designed Saint Laurent's jewelry for 11 years, until he began his own collection. And he's only ever used one medium – a matt black material that he inlays with jet and transparent or coloured crystal. In his treasure trove of a shop with its garnet-marble floor, lovers of romantic jewelry will find their heart's desire. Nowadays, Marilyn Sfadj sells his designs.

PAUL CAILLOL at SHADÉ 63, RUE DES SAINTS-PÈRES VI – 45 49 30 37

MADEMOISELLE ZAZA trained as a pattern cutter and, at the age of 20, opened a shop selling second-hand clothes and 50s' memorabilia. At the same time she began buying old jewelry, which she revamped and then sold. Gradually she began designing her own jewelry in an up-to-the-minute fashion-conscious way. Pop or 70s, whatever the season demands.

MADEMOISELLE ZAZA 29, BOULEVARD RASPAIL VII – 45 48 24 37

SOPHIE LEVY In a little rococo shop with candy-pink décor, Sophie Levy displays her funny, naive jewelry designs, which will delight adults as much as little girls.

SOPHIE LEVY 8, RUE DES ÉCOUFFES II – 48 85 17 83

MERCEDES ROBIROSA She arrived from Buenos Aires in 1975 and Mercedes first experienced the world of Parisian fashion in her role as a model. Then she followed Karl Lagerfeld to Chanel where she worked on the accessories. In 1987 she launched her own label and now dreams up fairy-tale jewelry. She works in metal, which is plunged into baths of gold, crushed, embossed and made baroque, with a new theme each season. This might be gifts from the sea, the Incas or pirate treasure, and you will find the biggest selection at:

MERCEDES ROBIROSA at VICTOIRE 10, PLACE DES VICTOIRES II – 42 60 96 21

ANDRÉ GAS This is an Aladdin's cave of a shop and was wonderfully well designed by Marc Berthier. André Gas will coat you with pearls, sequins, pendant bracelets made of dark ribbon and rings that open wide, metamorphose or can be added to.

ANDRÉ GAS 44, RUE ÉTIENNE-MARCEL II – 45 08 49 46

MICHAELA FREY Stylists graduating from the Viennese School of Fine Art create a collection of enamelled jewelry for this shop. It is always in a naive, folksy sort of style but has Art Deco leanings.

MICHAELA FREY 42, RUE DU DRAGON VI – 45 44 12 20

MIGEON ET MIGEON Christian and Marie-Thérèse Migeon unite in both their private and personal spheres to work solely for themselves. Their speciality is resin work, which they carry out in colour. They polish it, gloss it or decorate it with gold and silver leaf. It's incredible!

♡ **MIGEON ET MIGEON at EN ATTENDANT LES BARBARES** 50, RUE ÉTIENNE-MARCEL II – 42 33 37 87

SWAROVSKI The king of cut-glass. Born in Bohemia, Daniel Swarovski, the founder of the firm, set up in the Tyrol in 1895 where he perfected a technique for cutting gems by machine, a technique which is still in use today. For four generations now, his descendants have been building up the business by working with the haute couture designers to create costume jewelry which is not the slightest bit tacky and draws its inspiration from the world of high design.

SWAROVSKI 7, RUE ROYALE VIII – 40 17 07 40

BURMA Picture a façade of black glass, small and precious window displays, benches and a counter made of cabinet wood, on which the sales assistant will show you the jewelry laid out on a velvet tray, just like a 'real' jeweller's. Their new thing is the stick-pin which comes shaped like a tortoise or a teddy. It all comes presented in a gift-box and is guaranteed for 10 years.

BURMA 16, RUE DE LA PAIX II – 42 61 60 64

JACQUES GAUTIER He is a silversmith, master glassmaker and painter and he sells his jewelry from a narrow gallery of a shop. Max Ernst, Simone de Beauvoir and Sonia Delaunay have all bought goods here and he works using a medieval technique which involves laying crystal on to silver and then adding coloured enamel.

JACQUES GAUTIER 36, RUE JACOB VI – 42 60 84 33

CHRISTIAN LACROIX really loves genuine fake jewelry. He hangs crucifixes from necks, heart-shaped earrings from lobes and includes all his regular obsessions. The sun, Provence and the Baroque all light up the blackest of little black dresses.

CHRISTIAN LACROIX 73, RUE DU FAUBOURG SAINT-HONORÉ VIII – 42 65 79 08; 26, AVENUE MONTAIGNE – 47 20 68 95; ground floor at GALERIES LAFAYETTE and PRINTEMPS DE LA MODE

ANTIQUE JEWELRY

You might well prefer antique jewelry but never have the good fortune to inherit your grandmother's delightful ruby-studded ring or, indeed, her extraordinary diamond brooch. Still, some women hang around the sales at Drouot (the famous auction room), which are always interesting, or rummage around in specialist shops just hoping to pick up that special item (and occasionally selling jewelry of their own). It's a love thing.

MILLER is run by a young graduate from the Gemological Institute of America called Carine Miller. She's the daughter of a diamond merchant and began by setting up a stall at the flea market in the north of Paris. Her proximity to the Place Vendôme allows her to check the authenticity of any of her finds, whether they are hallmarked Cartier, Boucheron, Van Cleef or any of the other famous names of the area. 'Second-hand', she tells us, 'simply means half the price of brand-new'.

♡ **MILLER 233, RUE SAINT-HONORÉ I – 42 61 63 13**

PERRONO has been in the Rue de la Chaussée-d'Antin since the middle of the last century. At the time it was open until 2 o'clock in the morning so that the customers at the Café des Italiens could buy their evening companions a special little thank-you gift, if they so desired. Now the wares are displayed on little tables, from which you can sell, exchange or buy. The choice is very important and Christian Lacroix is a regular.

PERRONO 4, RUE DE LA CHAUSSÉE-D'ANTIN IX – 47 70 83 61; 37, AVENUE VICTOR-HUGO XVI – 45 01 67 88

BARBOZA is run by Annette Gribe, who inherited it from her parents. Seated on squat armchairs, embroidered in petit point, the customers sometimes ask to swap their purchases. There is a large selection of crucifixes to be worn, as Christian Lacroix's wife Françoise wears hers, hanging from a velvet ribbon.

BARBOZA 356, RUE SAINT-HONORÉ I – 42 60 67 08

BIJOUX À TROQUER You should go fairly regularly since the turnover of goods is high. Eve Cazes has designed the surroundings to look like a treasure trove with shades of gold and black that set off her beautiful merchandise.

BIJOUX À TROQUER 20, RUE DE MIROMESNIL VIII – 42 65 95 44

BRUNELINE offers a substantial choice of tie pin, worn less and less often by men, but with increasing frequency by women as brooches. The top designers are getting into them as hat pins, just like in the old days.

BRUNELINE 26, RUE DANIELLE-CASANOVA II – 42 86 96 30

LE VIEUX SAINT-HONORÉ opened in 1893 and the jewels sold there include examples of Second Empire (1852–1870) right through to the 1930s. These always come with a Certificate of Authenticity and you can also find old designs from the big names in the Place Vendôme.

LE VIEUX SAINT-HONORÉ 334, RUE SAINT-HONORÉ I – 42 60 44 75

MARTINE FAIVRE-REUILLE has a penchant for Second Empire design and takes it as the source for the décor in her shop. There are exquisite gold bracelets and plaited tresses. You can even have jewelry mended.

MARTINE FAIVRE-REUILLE 231, RUE SAINT-HONORÉ I – 42 60 61 29

SYLVIE NISSEN likes the original, the astonishing and the unusual. You will find her during the afternoon at the Hôtel Westminster (the boutique is on the left as you enter the foyer) and she will, no doubt, recount at great length but with panache the story behind any of the goods she shows you.

SYLVIE NISSEN at the HÔTEL WESTMINSTER 13, RUE DE LA PAIX II – 42 61 61 70

GARLAND was on the Left Bank in the 60s and 70s but came to the Rue de la Paix in 1978. They have a very substantial stock indeed of old jewelry and customers include Barbra Streisand, Caroline de Monaco and Anne-Aymone Giscard d'Estaing. In the workshop in the basement you can have any items that are damaged beyond repair, or are too difficult to wear, altered to taste.

♡ **GARLAND   13, RUE DE LA PAIX II – 42 61 17 95**

And also:

LEÏ   15, RUE DES PETITS-CHAMPS I – 42 86 00 16

TROC DE BIJOUX   3, RUE COETLOGON VI – 45 48 93 54

TIANY CHAMBARD   32, RUE JACOB VI – 43 29 73 15

MINERVE   89, RUE DE PASSY XVI – 45 20 44 15

At the **LOUVRE DES ANTIQUAIRES, PLACE DU PALAIS-ROYAL; BRUNO PÉPIN (ALLÉE ODIOT), BALIAN (ALLÉE ODIOT), CASTIGLIONE (ALLÉE BELLANGER), MARTIN DU DAFFOY (PLACE DU PALAIS-ROYAL).**

DESIGNER JEWELRY

As Marilyn Monroe sang so prettily, 'Diamonds are a girl's best friend.' When we go past the Place Vendôme or the Rue de la Paix, the windows make us dream just like Audrey Hepburn in Breakfast at Tiffany's. *In these beautiful shops you will always receive a warm welcome and all the jewellers now have reasonably priced collections. The simplest way to go about it is just to say how much you want to spend and take it from there. No one will think the less of you and you can still stand and admire the more sumptuous creations.*

FRANÇOIS HÉRAIL Many years ago he created the Poiray range of jewelry which he subsequently had to leave. At last he has opened his own shop in a pretty courtyard off the Place Vendôme. It has charming Italian décor shown to great effect under the subdued lighting of chandeliers covered with silk taffeta, and he sells jewelry which bears no relation to that of his famous neighbours. There are pieces of yellow gold wrapped inside grey gold, damascening, gems studded with gold or mounted like mosaics.

♡   **FRANÇOIS HÉRAIL   16, PLACE VENDÔME (in the courtyard on the left)**
I – 42 60 70 10

JEAN DINH VAN was the first person to pare down jewelry to its essential forms. His square wedding ring, his bracelets which are worked like bangles, his rectangular linkchains, his handcuff-style clasps and his little chain bracelets with round plaques are the best-selling lines and, in fact, sell better than the classics. They come in jade or 24-carat gold, hammered, or in simple disc-shaped pendants pierced simply, with a single, pure hole.

♡   **JEAN DINH VAN   7, RUE DE LA PAIX II – 42 61 74 49**

CARTIER has existed for more than one and a half centuries but only opened in the Rue de la Paix in 1898. Their current lines demonstrate a return to the engraved gem and are sublime. It was in 1973 that they launched the 'Must de Cartier' range, and the best-selling item is the ring with its three intertwined colours of gold thread that was a particular favourite of Jean Cocteau. The panther has been the house mascot since the 20s, and has also launched a range of perfumes.

CARTIER   13, RUE DE LA PAIX II – 42 61 58 56; 51, RUE FRANÇOIS-Iᵉʳ VIII – 40 74 60 60

MAUBOUSSIN is run by two brothers, Alain and Patrick Mauboussin. They had the bright idea of working on mother-of-pearl by hollowing it out, shaping it, damascening it or encrusting it with diamonds, precious and semi-precious stones. They make the perfect engagement ring but also feature low prices, charming enamel and gold models on the theme of the harlequin and diamond-shaped patterns.

MAUBOUSSIN   20, PLACE VENDÔME I – 42 60 32 54

BOUCHERON This now occupies the building in the Place Vendôme that was once the town house of the Contessa di Castiglione, Napoleon III's mistress. The great-grandson of Frédéric, the founder, Alain Boucheron, currently uses acacia wood or rock crystal for his jewelry and has just created a divine collection in enamel. Even stick-pins in animal shapes form part of the collection in the same material. The gold brooches and precious stones are cleverly designed to slide into rings, bracelets and necklaces and change the whole look. For a long time now, the best-seller has been the first-name tags which are presented to mothers at the birth of each child and which they hang from charm bracelets or on a chain around baby's neck. A new addition to the range, and very fragrant it is too, is the men's perfume, but there is also women's perfume and household scent. This all comes in a stunning ring-shaped flask.

BOUCHERON   26, PLACE VENDÔME I – 42 61 58 16

MELLERIO is the oldest jeweller in Paris and opened its doors to the French market more than 375 years ago. At the helm stand François and Olivier Mellerio, direct descendants of the young Italian emigré who started the whole thing. The house speciality is the presentation cup they design for great sporting moments including the French Tennis Open at the Rolland-Garros stadium. There is a delightful jewelry collection in which one gem is set into another, a blue sapphire, for example, into a yellow one.

MELLERIO   9, RUE DE LA PAIX II – 42 61 57 53

CHAUMET gladly reminds us of the two great events that happened on the first floor of this very shop: Chopin died here and the future Empress Eugénie admired a show here just a few days before she got engaged to Napoleon III. The Jonc collection is reasonably priced and includes gold rings, rings adorned with stones, bracelets and a particularly attractive watch. You should make sure you pay a visit to the museum where you will find models of crowns, diadems and tiaras all on display. These are the house specialities and the curator is bound to regale you with their individual histories with incredible enthusiasm.

CHAUMET   12, PLACE VENDÔME I – 42 60 32 82

VAN CLEEF ET ARPELS was founded in 1906 and is famous for its 'minaudières' or precious little evening bags. In 1954, they were the first people to create low-price jewelry in the form of animal-shaped brooches and pendants that are still very recherchés. There are two house perfumes: 'First' and 'Arpels'.

VAN CLEEF ET ARPELS   22, PLACE VENDÔME I – 42 61 02 36

RENÉ BOIVIN is 100 years old and its jewelry is top-of-the-range stuff. The mixed-media work is very daring and includes combinations like pebbles with lemon-coloured stones.

RENÉ BOIVIN   12, RUE DE LA PAIX II – 42 61 06 23

POIRAY was founded by the talented François Hérail and is now run by Nathalie Hocq. Their best-seller is the large ring plaited in three kinds of gold. They also sell a rather witty ring with interchangeable studs.

POIRAY   1, RUE DE LA PAIX II – 42 61 70 58

O.J. PERRIN is Nicolas Perrin's tradename and he has totally grasped the strength of the 'small range'. His best-selling item is a watch with gold gadrooning on the frame. Next to his shop in the Avenue Montaigne, he has now opened a modern art gallery.

O.J. PERRIN   8, RUE ROYALE VIII – 42 61 88 88; 36, AVENUE MON-TAIGNE VIII – 47 23 88 88; 33, AVENUE VICTOR-HUGO XVI – 45 01 88 88

TECLA was the first jeweller to have the sheer audacity to work with cultured pearls, a Japanese turn-of-the-century invention. The façade is decorated in sculpted red Chinese lacquerwork and sumptuous Japanese screens decorate the interior. There are necklaces, chokers and strings of pearls as far as the eye can see, and you can even buy pearls blended with gold, coral and lapiz. These are fastened with a clasp worked like a jewel in its own right. The webs of Tahitian pearls are particularly wonderful, but they also sell freshwater pearls which are very small and irregularly oblong in shape. The prices are eminently affordable and you could go there to buy a teenage girl's first bracelet or the classic 18th-birthday present – a pearl necklace.

TECLA   2, RUE DE LA PAIX II – 42 61 03 29

CIPANGO is designed by Micheline Washberg, who mixes semi-precious stones that she occasionally finds on exploratory missions. The results are magnificent necklaces made of agate, malachite and quartz or peridot, quartz and aquamarine, or even crystal and granite. You can also bring her your own pearls or pieces of amber which she will string together for you into something quite original and marvellous.

♡   **CIPANGO   14, RUE DE L'ÉCHAUDÉ VI – 43 26 08 92**

And also:

BUCCELLATI   4, PLACE VENDÔME I – 42 60 12 12

HARRY WINSTON   29, AVENUE MONTAIGNE VIII – 47 20 03 09

POMELLATO   66, RUE DU FAUBOURG SAINT-HONORÉ VIII – 42 65 62 07

BULGARI   27, AVENUE MONTAIGNE VIII – 47 23 89 89

MARINA B   18, AVENUE MONTAIGNE VIII – 40 70 16 17

ILIAS LALAOUNIS   364, RUE SAINT-HONORÉ I – 42 61 55 65

ZOLOTAS   318, RUE SAINT-HONORÉ I – 42 60 98 63

FRED   6, RUE ROYALE VIII – 42 60 30 65

MIKIMOTO   8, PLACE VENDÔME I – 42 60 33 55

ALEXANDRE REZA   23, PLACE VENDÔME I – 42 96 64 00

ANSHINDO   8, RUE DE LA PAIX II – 40 20 07 65

A. ET A. TURNER   16, AVENUE GEORGE-V VIII – 47 23 88 28

HUGUES DE PAILLETTE   16, BOULEVARD RASPAIL VII – 45 48 51 56

CHRISTINE ESCHER CARRÉ D'OR   46, AVENUE GEORGE-V VIII – 47 23 07 38

FRANÇOIS PAULTRE   13, RUE SAINT-SULPICE VI – 43 25 63 90

ARNOULD 7, RUE RACINE V – 43 54 77 98

DOMINIQUE ARPELS at **TROIS QUARTIERS**, 23, BOULEVARD DE LA MADELEINE I – 42 96 22 33

ALDEBERT 1, BOULEVARD DE LA MADELEINE I – 42 61 58 27

AUROR 20, BOULEVARD DU MONTPARNASSE XV – 47 34 16 58

ARFAN 35, BOULEVARD DES CAPUCINES II – 42 61 66 74

CHARLEY CARRÉ D'OR 46, AVENUE GEORGE-V VIII – 40 70 11 00

CHRISTIAN BERNARD 21, RUE DE LA PAIX II – 40 07 10 64

Three great couturiers have launched themselves on to the jewelry market. **CHANEL** was first with the extravagantly designed watch they call 'Mademoiselle', which you can buy in gold, lacquer, pearl and now diamond (at 7, **PLACE VENDÔME** I – 42 86 29 87). In a rather more affordable price range you can go to **YVES SAINT LAURENT** who has designed Jonc gold rings for which he uses 'close-set' gemstones (telephone 49 26 16 46 for information), and **NINA RICCI** who has commissioned the Italian jeweller **BUCCELLATI** to design gold lacework and diamond pieces (telephone 47 23 78 88 for information).

THE ART OF BEAUTY

THE PERFUMERS

To step inside the premises of Guerlain or Caron is to discover the very essence of the great perfume-makers. But there are also small-scale perfumeries in Paris, where sensitive 'noses' compose new and original scents.

GUERLAIN was born in 1828, when Pierre-François-Pascal Guerlain opened a little business as a perfumer-cum-vinegar maker on the Rue de Rivoli. There he created 'Senteurs des Champs' and 'Esprit de Fleur', but the big time came when he moved to the Rue de la Paix, becoming perfumer by appointment to the Empress Eugénie, wife of Napoleon III. For her he created his 'Eau Impériale' cologne, which you can still buy in the shop to this day. The best-selling 'Shalimar' was created in 1925. Today, along with 'Jardin de Bagatelle', 'Chamade' and other famous perfumes, Guerlain sells a voluptuous range of products for the bath, including soap, talc, deodorant and body lotion, as well as the 'Issima' beauty products and a range of make-up in sumptuous gilded compacts. There are five shops in all, including:

GUERLAIN 68, AVENUE DES CHAMPS-ÉLYSÉES VIII – 43 59 96 30

CARON With its grey marble altars and its dramatic drapes, the Caron boutique is a veritable temple of perfume. The illustrious house was created in 1903 and later bought out by a dandy and keen traveller called Ernest Daltroff. On a grey and golden background you can still become intoxicated by the ritual scents of the past, contained in Baccarat crystal bowls or bottles designed by famous artists. There are perfumes called 'Nuit de Noël', 'En avion', 'Tabac blond', 'Narcisse noir' and now a new scent contained in a golden bottle called 'Parfum sacré'.

PARFUMS CARON 34, AVENUE MONTAIGNE VIII – 47 23 40 82

GRAIN DE BEAUTÉ Odile Malardier fills houses with her fragrant perfumes. As well as the English eaux-de-toilette 'Penhaligon' and 'Floris', she also sells pomanders, floral pot-pourris and thyme- or lavender-scented balls.

GRAIN DE BEAUTÉ   9, RUE DU CHERCHE-MIDI VI – 45 48 07 55

LES PARFUMS DE ROSINE Marie-Hélène Rogeon is a direct descendant of the perfumer, Panafieu. Her small 15-square-metre boutique in the gardens of the Palais-Royal pays tribute to the Rosine perfumes created by Paul Poiret, a famous couturier at the turn of the century who named the perfumes after his daughter. But retrospection stops at the name of the business, for the new 'nose' creates absolutely new perfumes, like 'Rose de Rosine' with an iris and violet base, contained in an Art Deco flask. In this little salon, dominated by wrought iron, moiré and taffeta, they sell exclusively this perfume and the range of bath products.

LES PARFUMS DE ROSINE   43, GALERIE DE MONTPENSIER I – 42 60 47 58

PERLIER After Milan but before Tokyo and New York, Parisians discovered the delights of soap, face packs and shampoos made of honey. A marvellous range of products gathered together in a sunflower-coloured boutique.

PERLIER   8, RUE DE SÈVRES VII – 45 48 48 05

DETAILLE The Comtesse de Presles bought herself a convertible car at the end of the last century. She just loved driving around at 15 miles an hour but she was frightened of ruining her complexion. In 1895, therefore, her friend Marcellin Berthelot created a liquid cream for her from a base of egg-white and plant extracts. You will still find her today in this delightful shop, with its intact wood-panelling and its mosaic floor, since all packets and bottles are printed with the portrait of the sporting flirt. Nowadays the products are made in a tiny laboratory and there are even powders made of rice, peach, tea or Rachel rose blossom.

DETAILLE   10, RUE SAINT-LAZARE IX – 48 78 68 50

BOUCHERON PARFUMS In order to sell his perfume in its superb ring-shaped bottles, Alain Boucheron the jeweller opened a treasure trove of a shop with a large stone façade. There are blue-lacquered columns topped with cornices, crystal show-cases behind which to display the perfumes, eaux-de-toilette and a line of bathroom products wrapped in sapphire and gold packaging and decorated like jewels.

BOUCHERON PARFUMS   134, AVENUE VICTOR-HUGO XVI – 47 55 81 87

SHU UEMURA A wonderful Japanese-style shop with a real make-up counter: more than 150 eye-shadows, almost 100 lipsticks and foundation powders all displayed on a black marble table. A beauty therapist will advise you and make up half your face. After that it's up to you. Shu Uemura also sells a whole range of beauty products from face cream to a fabulous make-up removing oil (which you can also buy at the chemist). Other indispensable accessories include 60 different types of brushes in all shapes and sizes, made of sable, goat or pony hair, magnifying glasses, toilet bags and wonderful professional-style overnight bags with drawers and compartments.

SHU UEMURA   176, BOULEVARD SAINT-GERMAIN VI – 45 48 02 55

CARLA Three sisters, Violette, Muriel and Maud, and their mother opened up a pilot shop in Neuilly almost 30 years ago. It was a fabulous success due in no small part to the warm welcome and solid advice of the saleswomen. You will find the best selection of well-known products in this shop.

CARLA   7, RUE DE LONGCHAMP 92200 NEUILLY-SUR-SEINE – 46 37 01 83

ANNICK GOUTAL Presented like great fat sweeties in an abundance of transparent wrapping paper, the Annick bottles and perfumes hold all the scent and charm of turn-of-the-century herbalists. She was a concert pianist but she became a composer of perfumes: 'Passion' and 'L'Eau d'Adrien' to name but two. There are two perfumes especially for little girls called 'Les Eaux de Charlotte' and 'Camille'. There are three shops including:

ANNICK GOUTAL   3, RUE GUSTAVE-COURBET XVI – 45 53 61 62

MAÎTRE PARFUMEUR ET GANTIER Jean Laporte is a passionately committed botanist. A chemist by training and a world-traveller, he became a perfumer thanks to his technical know-how and his taste for the natural. His originality lies in the way he takes the concepts of flowers, spices, fruit and wild gardens and recomposes them in perfumes, pot-pourris and household scents. There are two shops in Paris including:

MAÎTRE PARFUMEUR ET GANTIER   84 BIS, RUE DE GRENELLE VII – 45 44 61 57

DIPTYQUE In 1961, Desmond Knox-Leet, a painter and furnishing-fabric designer, opened a shop. In 1968 he invented an eau-de-toilette and a perfumed candle. Regular customers at the old-fashioned shop include Isabelle Adjani, Lauren Bacall, Sophie Marceau, Catherine Deneuve, Givenchy and Karl Lagerfeld. Today you can buy the candle in 31 scents (best-seller cinnamon) and there are 7 eaux-de-toilette.

DIPTYQUE   34, BOULEVARD SAINT-GERMAIN V – 43 26 45 27

BAIN PLUS With blue-grey tiling on the floor and a view of the beautiful trees of the Blancs-Manteaux church from the back of the shop, Claude Mingeon has given over his entire boutique to the pleasure of the bathroom. There are brushes, combs and essence of lime, the fragrant perfumes of Creed or the scrubland of Provence, and perfumed candles.

BAIN PLUS   51, RUE DES FRANCS-BOURGEOIS IV – 48 87 83 07

CRABTREE AND EVELYN An English brand that combines perfumes with sweet things. And which packages them both in an absolutely charming way. There are pot-pourris, lining-papers and household perfumes and it's all terribly refined!

CRABTREE AND EVELYN 177, BOULEVARD SAINT-GERMAIN VI – 45 44 68 76

COMPTOIR SUD PACIFIQUE A harmony of ochre and lagoon blue in the shop of Josée and Pierre Fournier. They import monoi, a coconut oil perfumed with flower scents, from Tahiti. They bring back vetiver, sandalwood and vanilla from Morocco, Turkey and the Caribbean. You are guaranteed to experience exoticism and sophistication in their pretty shop.

COMPTOIR SUD PACIFIQUE   17, RUE DE LA PAIX II – 42 61 74 44

SUR LA PLACE A blue façade decorated with a stylized tree is the shop's emblem. The perfume bottles designed by Jean-Jacques Granval are used as packaging for the house perfumes in amber, Persian fruit and vanilla.

SUR LA PLACE   12, PLACE SAINT-SULPICE VI – 43 54 93 06

PATRICIA DE NICOLAÏ has one of the most creative noses of her generation. The grand-daughter of Pierre Guerlain she was the first woman to receive the perfumer's award. With her sense of smell she created 'Number one' out of white blossom, 'Jardin secret' and 'Odalisque'. All of which are sold exclusively in her own shops in bottles designed by Serge Mansau. Two shops including:

PATRICIA DE NICOLAÏ   69, AVENUE RAYMOND-POINCARÉ XVI – 47 55 90 92

ANN STEEGER Thick cotton drapes and wine-coloured carpet, pine furniture bargained over at second-hand shops, hundreds of fragments of splintered light, all of which Ann Steeger wanted in order to create a comforting setting for her perfume shop. She creates custom-made perfumes and specially requested cosmetics.

ANN STEEGER   130, RUE DE GRENELLE VII – 45 55 81 82

BEAUTY SALONS

Parisians who visit beauty salons are not pampered odalisques who spend their days at home, supported by men. Quite the contrary, in fact, according to a recent survey which stated that these are busy women (40% held managerial positions), young and well-off. From reshaping to depilation, from make-up to manicure, each salon has its own particular speciality.

LANCÔME hasn't changed location since 1935 but its technology is light years removed from that date. The efficiency, the iron hand and the warm welcome of Béatrice Braun, its director, make themselves felt in the tiniest details. Allow two hours for your first appointment. The first step will be to have your skin-type analysed by a computer. The beauty programme in the computer will microscopically measure the contours, the elasticity, the moisture level and the sebum factor. Then the printer will produce a prescription. The star treatment is a four-handed body massage, which is exclusive to the salon and lasts for an hour, an hour in which two beauticians will relax, soften and massage the muscles in your legs, arms and back!
INSTITUT LANCÔME 29, RUE DU FAUBOURG SAINT-HONORÉ VIII – 42 65 30 74

MATIS 320 square metres and three floors devoted to beauty on a site between the Madeleine and the Opéra. They've done away with the cramped cubicle and have instead installed spacious treatment rooms in which you'll have no trouble relaxing. This part of town, however, is full of customers who have very little time to spare for beauty treatments and so they have developed the 'express treatment' in which you'll get the comprehensive service in just an hour and a half: facial; therapeutic pedicure;

Map labels:

PLACE VICTOR HUGO

VICTOR HUGO R. COPERNIC

AVENUE VICTOR HUGO

RUE BOISSIERE

BOISSIERE

AV. R. POINCARÉ

RUE DE POMPE

LYCÉE JANSON DE SAILLY

PLACE DES SABLONS DE MEXICO

LONGCHAMP

AV. R. KLÉBER

H. MARTIN

AV. G. MANDEL

16

RUE DE LA TOUR

RUE DES

RUE CORTAMBERT

TROCADÉRO

PLACE DU TROCADÉRO

CIMETIÈRE DE PASSY

AV. du PRT

PALAIS DE CHAILLOT

RUE DE LA

RUE DE LA TOUR

PAUL DOUMER

MUETTE

AVENUE

R. VITAL

R. NICOLO

GUICHARD

R. FRANKLIN

RUE DE PASSY

BOIS le VENT

QUARTIER PASSY-VICTOR HUGO

La Chatelaine
170, Av. Victor Hugo XVIe

British Stock
10, Rue Guichard XVIe

Nouez-moi
27, Rue des Sablons XVIe

Franck et Fils
80, Rue de Passy XVIe

Patrick Divert
7, Place de Mexico XVIe

Joseph
27, Rue de Passy XVIe

hand treatment; make-up and a quick hairdo. Another strong point is the do-it-yourself make-up classes which are held in these warmly decorated premises with stencilled walls and trellised floors.

INSTITUT MATIS PRESTIGE 22, RUE DES CAPUCINES II – 42 86 07 24

REVLON The new salon has taken over from the one in the Champs-Elysées. And faithful customers immediately made for the new establishment because of the selective 'club' atmosphere. Real cognoscenti ask for Ginette, whose hands are skilled in pummelling, softening and oiling skin.

REVLON 19, RUE DE BASSANO XVI – 47 20 05 42

SOTHYS Refined down to the smallest detail with its luxurious décor, its green plants, its soft music and its scent of seaweed, you will find bathrobes and towels freshly washed and ironed just as if you were in your own home. A cordless phone connects the treatment rooms to the outside world. You can reserve airline or theatre tickets while you're having yourself pampered. Their particular brand of care is a kind of body-sculpture that gets rid of wrinkles and lightens the skin after a deep and detailed cleansing treatment and three consecutive face packs.

SOTHYS 128, RUE DU FAUBOURG SAINT-HONORÉ VIII – 45 63 98 18

ANNE SEMONIN These ravishing premises, completely tiled in white, have no suggestion whatever of the kitchen or the laboratory. To have a session there is pure pleasure. One of the specialities is freezing, a scaling treatment that is more regenerative and less traumatizing than peeling.

ANNE SEMONIN 2, RUE DES PETITS-CHAMPS II – 42 60 94 66

INSTITUT GEORGE-V Antoinette rules the roost from the top of the building that also accommodates the Crazy Horse nightclub. From her perch she wages a pitiless war against all superfluous hair. Her weapon is warm, pink-coloured wax of the very finest quality. For sensitive skin she applies a product which is mildly anaesthetic and her clients include showbiz stars, members of the jet-set and the social set.

INSTITUT GEORGE-V 12, AVENUE GEORGE-V VIII – 47 23 49 77

CLINIQUE The grand-daughter of herbalists and the daughter of a perfumer, Sylvie Braguier knows how to combine an almost 'clinical' cleanliness, a good diagnosis and general efficiency. In a refined atmosphere you will find an impressive skin-cleansing process, make-up removal, a rubber treatment for the fingers and a special exfoliation product. Blemish removal is far more efficient after brushing with a swivel-headed brush. The electric high-frequency heals the red marks left on the skin. Ten minutes under the ozone lamp and then you'll get the 15-minute facial with the menthol face pack.

CLINIQUE   7, RUE DE PONTHIEU VIII – 42 56 32 30

KANEBO In order to try this famous Japanese brand you will have to go to the Printemps de la Maison store, where you will find a high-tech treatment room which provides an exceptionally good service. They clean your face three times before applying the 'eye contour cream' at the same time as 'Sansai', the face-pack cream used for shiatsu massage. Then they will apply a strengthening cream. Success guaranteed.

KANEBO at PRINTEMPS DE LA MAISON   BOULEVARD HAUSSMANN IX – 42 82 50 00

ORLANE The treatment rooms are laid out around a tiny patio filled with seasonal plants. First the customer is encouraged to take off her make-up on her own and then spray her face with cleansing lotion. The key treatment is the 'Antifatigue Absolu B21' which begins with a thorough pore-cleansing scrub. The massage takes place amid the aroma of essential oils and the relaxing face pack is applied in an ionized environment enriched with oxygen.

ORLANE   163, AVENUE VICTOR-HUGO XVI – 47 04 65 00

PAYOT can be found in the former home of the Contessa di Castiglione. The Grade I listed wrought-iron staircase which leads to the beauticians' training school was lent by Napoleon III at the time of his amorous encounters with the lady of the house! It was Nadia Grégoire Payot, a graduate of the University of Lausanne in 1913, who discovered the first beauty salons when she went to the United States. On her return to Europe in 1919, she opened a laboratory in Paris. Today the house is at the cutting edge of beauty techniques. The beautician will make up an individualized treatment according to your skin-type. The principle behind the treatment is the mixing of two different products in order to create either a relaxing warmth or an astringent chill factor.

PAYOT   10, RUE DE CASTIGLIONE I – 42 60 32 87

INGRID MILLET Here you don't eat caviar by the ladle, you rub it into your skin. This is the speciality of Ingrid Millet's deluxe beauty salon. In this haven of peace and greenery, Elya Boutin, the director, will supply you with a quite exceptional rub down of the face, back and bust. The electro-therapy tones up pressure points and muscles are treated with shiatsu massage. You finish up with a moisturizing face-pack. It's fabulous!

INGRID MILLET   54, FAUBOURG SAINT-HONORÉ VIII – 42 66 66 20

JUVENTHERA Because she loved the area Michèle Chetboune chose the 17th arrondissement in the 80s to launch both her range of products and her beauty salon, with its sober, luxurious décor and its soft background music. Here you will be pampered in a whole variety of ways, inspired by Chinese massage in order to relax and maintain your well-being. They use a new, manual slimming treatment, to do with the lymph glands, called 'Fisio Minci Tonic' which counters weight-gain on the hips and thighs. There are four centres in Paris including:

JUVENTHERA   140, RUE DE COURCELLES XVII − 47 66 14 04

CLARINS Cool cubicles, orchid and sandalwood essential oils but no sign of any electronic gadgetry. Here everything is natural and you will have to rely on the efficient hands of the beauticians alone.

CLARINS   4, RUE BERTEAUX-DUMAS 92200 NEUILLY − 46 24 01 81

DECLEOR specializes in aromatherapy and light therapy. Unique to this salon is a pre-sun treatment for skin which involves a special mud pack, a deep-cleansing scrub and a seaweed treatment.

DECLEOR   97, RUE DU BAC VII − 45 48 30 30

GUERLAIN As soon as you enter the totally white marble establishment the perfumed atmosphere will seduce you completely. In the tastefully furnished large salon, under the light of a crystal chandelier and with its windows draped in red, someone will tend your hands in style. The warm manicure is reserved for ingrowing nails which can be cured in only six sessions. There is a terrific depilation service using pink beeswax, which is translucent like a boiled sweet and is changed completely for every customer.

GUERLAIN   68, AVENUE DES CHAMPS-ÉLYSÉES VIII − 43 59 31 10

SIMONE MAHLER At the back of her newest shop, she has built a skin-diagnosis centre and three treatment rooms. The most frequently requested treatments are the 'pressotherapy' for tired legs and the anti-wrinkle treatment which is carried out with the aid of a special pen. There are four centres in Paris including:

SIMONE MAHLER   57, AVENUE VICTOR-HUGO XVI − 45 00 22 66

SIMONE NAHMIACH Her phenomenal hands remove all traces of fatigue and tone up the muscles. She is a specialist in face care but she also treats the body with rubbing, scrubs and massage. At one of the prime Parisian addresses, an answering-machine will take your calls.

SIMONE NAHMIACH   10, RUE CAMBON I − 42 60 23 53

And also:

CARITA   11, RUE DU FAUBOURG SAINT-HONORÉ VIII – 42 68 05 74
BIOSUN   13, RUE DUPIN VI – 45 44 73 22
CAROLE FRANCK   6, PLACE DU GÉNÉRAL-CATROUX XVII – 46 22 03 33
JEANNE PIAUBERT   129, FAUBOURG SAINT-HONORÉ VIII – 43 59 36 46

HAIRDRESSERS

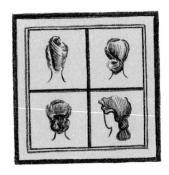

They gave us hair-sculpture, crimping and highlights. Our Figaros are constantly reinventing ways of fashionably styling our hair. But each one has his own up-to-the-minute method of execution.

JACQUES DESSANGE Pure hygiene: each customer has her own cellophane-wrapped brush, is offered a laundered gown, and the combs and scissors are disinfected. The house-stylists are fully trained by Dessange, not only in how to cut and blow-dry but also in how to interrelate with the client, to listen to her and to take her views on board. Which is all why lawyers, business-women, journalists and Parisian office-workers all go to this effective salon, luxurious without being over-the-top, where each hairdo is tailored to the individual's style and face. Their speciality is a new way of pleating hair. They've named it the 'Rollernews' since they've got rid of curlers and now use long pieces of foam rubber (in six lengths) which they curl the hair round without pulling it too tight. The result is a frothy, bouncy hairstyle.

JACQUES DESSANGE INTERNATIONAL   37, AVENUE FRANKLIN-D.-ROOSEVELT VIII – 43 59 31 31

MOD'S HAIR The least conventional and the trendiest of the hair salons. Decorated in a highly baroque way, you can wander around there as if you were in someone's flat. The bar and the little studio of Frédéric and Guillaume, who take portrait photos, have endowed the whole place with a certain flair and a relaxed quality. The whole fashion and promo crowd go there, including David Hallyday and Estelle, Julien Clerc and Christine Ockrent. If you want to look like a model you can have your hair done in a 50s' or 60s' style. Just as in the world of fashion, there's a new selection of extensions and styles every six months.

MOD'S HAIR   5, AVENUE MATIGNON VIII – 45 62 57 32

JEAN-LOUIS DAVID INTERNATIONAL Your gaze will be transfixed by an entire wallful of television screens. You choose your style from a chart with 157 designs and everything comes up on the screen. Colour, daring and the avant-garde define the style and the hairdos are carried out using clippers, which gives them a certain spring and aggressive quality. They've got no time for the cute but spend their time searching for that elusive quality which makes women more seductive.

JEAN-LOUIS DAVID INTERNATIONAL   47, RUE PIERRE-CHARRON VIII – 43 59 82 08; 4th floor at PRINTEMPS DE LA MODE – 42 83 41 41; JEAN-LOUIS DAVID QUICK-SERVICE 5, RUE CAMBON I – 42 97 47 26 – no messing, not expensive, not bad, no appointments.

LLUIS LLONGUERAS He calls himself Lluis with two 'l's, he's Catalonian and he's got 50 salons in Spain. His is the only salon from which you might emerge with a lion's mane of hair, curled to the point of backcombing, just like the Duchess of Alba in Goya's painting. The ringleted 'Ricci' look, the blue-black tinting and hairdos that are fixed with just a hint of wax.

LLUIS LLONGUERAS   229, RUE SAINT-HONORÉ I – 42 60 64 48

SABERNY set up in the Golden Triangle and also on the Right Bank in a salon managed by Pascal, his star stylist. He lavishes attention on one's hair and cares for it with a treatment he has brought over from California.

SABERNY   17, RUE DE TOURNON VI – 43 29 39 89

HERVÉ BOUDON In Italy he has been hailed as one of the most creative hairdressers in the country and works with the top fashion photographers like Gilles Bensimon and on shows and presentations of people like Diane Dufresne and Patricia Kaas. People in the forefront of fashion roll up at his salon to have their hair done in the trendiest possible way.

HERVÉ BOUDON   150, RUE MONTMARTRE II – 42 33 54 20

ALAIN DIVERT His salon is imbued with a sense of charm,

femininity and discretion. Great mahogany panels and baroque ceilings with stucco garlands of flowers decorate the salon in which Alain Divert does the hair of Michèle Morgan, the Princesses of Norway and Per Spook models. He knows better than anyone how to set his clients' minds at ease, how to get rid of grey hair and how to give each one of his clients a certain elegance.

ALAIN DIVERT   35, AVENUE GEORGE-V VIII – 47 23 36 41

JEAN-CLAUDE GALLON Wearing John Lennon glasses, Jean-Claude Gallon does the hair of the Miyaké, Castelbajac and Maud Perl models. He's not only adept at avant-garde hairstyles but is also very good at Grace Kelly chignons.

JEAN-CLAUDE GALLON   20, RUE VIGNON VIII – 42 66 21 09

ALEXANDRE ZOUARI Members of the jet-set meet up at her salon in the Alma district. On ball nights they might do as many as 100 women in one day. These women exchange news over mosaic sinks. Alexandre Zouari did Brigitte Bardot's and Nathalie Wood's hair when he was just 16 years old. Still young, still handsome, he loves sophisticated glamorous women, and despises the badly dressed. Don't go there if you have a taste for the natural look, which he will wipe out totally.

ALEXANDRE ZOUARI   1, AVENUE DU PRÉSIDENT-WILSON XVI – 47 23 43 35

Jean-Marc **MANIATIS** is constantly updating his cutting techniques. He photographs customers who want to change their hairstyle. This man of the moment has grasped the concept that women no longer want restrictive hairstyles. He's a purist who cuts hair perfectly but he has rejected the idea of grooming hair and teaches women to use his hair-care products for themselves. There are no dictates about length, and so on; everyone does their own thing in a sober, bright salon on two floors.

MANIATIS   18, RUE MARBEUF VIII – 45 44 16 39

CARITA Catherine Deneuve, Paloma Picasso and Inès de la Fressange all bump into each other at Carita's. The colourists here know the secret of the perfect 'natural' platinum-blonde look which they achieve by a careful assessment of waiting times and bleaching products that work only on roots. Ash, golden or silver, these luminous, transparent 'blond' colours are the house speciality.

CARITA   11, RUE DU FAUBOURG SAINT-HONORÉ VIII – 42 65 79 00

LOUIS G. He is a herbalist-hairdresser and each hair-type receives individual, natural attention ranging from eggs which are cracked and beaten in front of the customer to colours made from a henna and nut-leaf base and warm olive oil used to massage the scalp. All the same treatments that women did for themselves in the old days. They particularly enjoy dressing long hair here.

LOUIS G. 4, RUE DE BOURGOGNE VII – 45 51 30 39

LYNE BERTIN The tall, narrow mirrors alternate with the soft beige-coloured marble. Bach sonatas play in the background. You're not in a hairdressing salon, you're in a sanctuary with no visible philistine benches, sinks or hairdryers. Not a comb or a razor to be seen. Lyne Bertin sculpts with her scissors. The girlfriend of the fashion designer Dominique Morlotti does the hair of Brigitte Fossey, Dorothée Lalanne and Sabine Azéma. She studies the shape of the skull and the movement of the hair. Precision and beauty.

LYNE BERTIN 78, RUE JEAN-JACQUES-ROUSSEAU I – 42 36 04 59

MICHEL BROSSEAU Having learnt his trade in London, he came back to buy up Jacques France's famous salon. He can carry out great hairdos following the flow of the hair with the sure hand of a master and has two strong points: dry cutting and colour, which is subtle, transparent and undetectable.

MICHEL BROSSEAU 122, RUE DU FAUBOURG SAINT-HONORÉ VIII – 45 62 75 06 and 43 59 66 54

ALEXANDRE They call him the hairdresser of royalty since he did the Begum Aga Khan's hair for her wedding, Princess Grace of Monaco, the Duchess of Kent and all the most famous stars from Elizabeth Taylor to Liza Minelli, as well as most of the top designers' models from Yves Saint Laurent to Christian Lacroix. He has now reopened in a salon with a white wooden floor, Provençal mosaics, sofas and coral-coloured armchairs. You can have your hair done in an individual cubicle. A treatment exclusive to Alexandre is a henna wash that will give your hair new tone and colour in between bleaches. And, of course, they create the most spectacular of hair-knots. Cocteau called him 'the sphinx of hairdressing' and he now has another very boudoir-like salon in the old 'Trois Quartiers' building.

ALEXANDRE 3, AVENUE MATIGNON VIII – 42 25 57 90

LUCIE SAINT CLAIR has a faithful, chic clientèle. Charlotte Rampling has been going there for ages. They repair split ends, dye hair very gently and work away the rust-colour that sets into hair after you've used henna too often.

LUCIE SAINT CLAIR 4, AVENUE PIERRE-Ier-DE-SERBIE XVI – 47 20 53 54

PATRICK ALÈS A keen user of plant extracts and the star-stylist at Carita, he used to make his own colour-dyes himself.

Now he is known as one of the pioneers of phytotherapy. Women come to his salon for the quality of his haircare, in which he gives priority to health and shine. He also gets top prize for his hair colourings which contain Alès oil, specially designed not to harm your hair.

PATRICK ALÈS   37, AVENUE FRANKLIN-D.-ROOSEVELT VIII – 43 59 33 96

ROCK HAIR Jean-Paul Gaultier might meet a Harley Davidson groupie or a rock star here. 'We don't have any prejudices', the receptionist will tell you. You can have anything you like from yellow to pink, short-back-and-sides to dreadlocks.

ROCK HAIR   7, BOULEVARD BEAUMARCHAIS IV – 42 77 01 97

JEAN-PIERRE EUDES is the person who specializes in long hair and sophisticated hairdressing. You will find his discreet, padded salon after a long climb up a narrow staircase where regulars know they'll get a fashionable but not overly outrageous haircut.

JEAN-PIERRE EUDES   40, AVENUE PIERRE-Iᵉʳ-DE-SERBIE XVI – 47 20 38 11

SOPHIE GATTO Having started her career at Claude Maxime's and cutting her teeth at Dessange, she then opened a charming salon of her own, lined with mirrors. The staff are trained on site and Sophie herself specializes in cutting.

SOPHIE GATTO   15, AVENUE KLÉBER XVI – 45 00 91 00

JEAN-CLAUDE BIGUINE He made a name for himself by introducing a new concept in hairdressing – the democratization of hair! A concept that made him one of the cheapest, most popular Parisian hairdressers. There are no appointments and no standard styles, which doesn't mean that the salon lacks imagination. His latest invention is the 'Suave' perm, which doesn't use ammonia and lives up to its name.

JEAN-CLAUDE BIGUINE   15, RUE DES HALLES I – 42 21 39 49

CLAUDE MAXIME invented Brigitte Bardot's sauerkraut bun, as it was called. Women come to the shop to have their hair highlighted with a toothless comb and three different kinds of tinting colour, a process that creates a natural, shiny look.

CLAUDE MAXIME   27, AVENUE GEORGE-V VIII – 47 20 78 08

LÉONOR GREYL cares for dry, flyaway hair with wheatgerm poultices. He is one of the best haircare specialists.

LÉONOR GREYL   15, RUE TRONCHET VIII – 42 65 32 26

JEAN-FRANÇOIS LAZARTIGUE treats heavy heads of hair with massages, grain poultices and vegetable dyes.

JEAN-FRANÇOIS LAZARTIGUE   5, RUE DU FAUBOURG SAINT-HONORÉ VIII – 42 65 29 24

And also :

BRUNO   15, RUE DES SAINTS-PÈRES VI – 42 61 45 15

For haircare:

CAMILLE DARMONT   61, RUE DE LA TOUR XVI – 45 03 10 99

JEAN-YVES LE GOFF   63, RUE DE PONTHIEU VIII – 45 62 51 55

CENTRE HÉLÈNE CLAUDERER   346, RUE SAINT-HONORÉ I – 42 61 28 01

LARGE AND SPACIOUS
STORES

DEPARTMENT STORES

Created in the 19th century by true visionaries, Paris's great department stores have been substantially revamped over recent years. There are five of them on the Right Bank – three on the Boulevard Haussmann and two on the Rue de Rivoli. But on the Left Bank one store reigns supreme.

PRINTEMPS Jules Jaluzot's store opened its doors in 1865. His second building, devoted to fashion, dates from 1910 and was still called the 'new shop' 60 years later. The first Printemps shop continued to cater for household needs (the fifth floor being devoted exclusively to upmarket contemporary furniture). In 1912 the management set up a workshop called Primavera, where furniture and household items were designed under the aegis of a well-known art critic of the time, René Guillère, some pieces even finding their way into art exhibitions. They are occasionally reissued. Nowadays the place to draw up a wedding list is the second floor, while, for the perfect honeymoon, romantic nightwear is to be found in the fabulous lingerie department in the basement. A third store, Brummell, caters exclusively for men. Printemps offers a number of additional services and facilities: racket-stringing, a book and record exchange, a cloakroom and hairdressing salon (Jean-Louis David), a travel agency and a mother-and-baby room. If you find yourself flagging, there is a choice of restaurants – the Brasserie Flo, the Café Flo and the deli – where you can relax and regain your strength under the magnificent listed glass roof. You can even hire the place out for the evening.

PRINTEMPS 64, BOULEVARD HAUSSMANN IX – 42 82 50 00

GALERIES LAFAYETTE In 1895 this was a long, narrow

shop at the Ecrasés crossroads, on the corner of the Chaussée d'Antin and Rue Lafayette. Eleven years after the opening, the founders, Théophile Bader and Alphonse Khanh, extended it on to the Boulevard Haussmann, adding (like Printemps) a superb dome. Almost a century later, the store's strong point is its fashion departments, which include 'cutting edge' fashion. Gentlemen are catered for by the 'Galfa-Club' department. Lifestyle is spread out in the basement, where you will find 'Table Arts' sumptuously displayed with the wedding-list department just next-door. Contemporary furniture is on the fourth floor and you have to go back down to the basement for books and records. A security room for furs, photo-developing, clothes alterations, a travel agency and even the Micro school, where you can learn how to use your computer, complete the list of services on offer. Two years ago, they opened a wonderful self-service grocery department called 'Lafayette Gourmet'. It is vast (2,300 square metres) and luxuriously decorated (the shopping baskets and trolleys are gilded and messengers will make home deliveries if you live in town; just call them on 48 74 37 13 or 48 74 46 06), the goods are attractively displayed and, here and there, a little snack-bar will enable you to sit down for a moment and have a slice of salmon, a steak tartare, hot snacks or a quick glass of champagne. There is a car park.

GALERIES LAFAYETTE   40, BOULEVARD HAUSSMANN IX − 42 82 34 56

MARKS AND SPENCER crossed the Channel in 1975. The founder Michael Marks was a Lithuanian refugee who arrived in Great Britain in 1882. His first shop was called the 'Penny Bazaar'. The Paris store has just had a two-storey extension built, and everyone has gone mad over the food department where you will find muffins, smoked salmon, legs of lamb from Ireland, traditional English apple pies, marmalade and Christmas puddings. They sell incredibly fresh sandwiches with a wide variety of fillings, the best-selling line being salmon and cucumber. The underwear and the jumpers (including cashmere) are excellent quality and very affordable. Their particular selling-point is that you can return the goods whenever you like and get all your money back, as long as you keep the receipt.

MARKS AND SPENCER   35, BOULEVARD HAUSSMANN IX − 47 42 42 91

LE BON MARCHÉ opened in 1852. The founders were called Aristide and Marguerite Boucicaut and their ideas were revolutionary for the time. They believed in set prices, goods exchange facilities, getting your money back and delivery by horse within the Paris area. They also invented the sale of household linen and the idea of the sale, which happened in order to shift goods whenever the customers were a bit strapped for cash. A few years ago Bon Marché was revamped and Andrée Putman redecorated the restaurants. A superb central double escalator was constructed and they had sculptures commissioned from Lalanne, Georges Ferrato, César and Etienne. The basement, which is known as 'Entretemps'(or 'Meanwhile'), is given over to 'the world of words, images and music', and the bookshop and record shop are self-service. The stationery department has a workshop area. A few steps further on you will come across 'Trois Hiboux', the children's department, where books, games, art supplies and toys are all on display; it is an exceptional selection for a Parisian store. The grocery department is also vast and opens earlier and closes later than the rest of the store. There's a great wine selection and an excellent delicatessen counter. There is also a car park.

LE BON MARCHÉ   RUE DE SÈVRES-RUE DU BAC VII – 45 49 21 22

BHV was initially called the 'Bazar Napoléon' and only became the 'Bazar de l'Hôtel de Ville' in 1870. It was then that Xavier Ruel, the founder, invented the fixed-price counters, opened a restaurant for members of the public and set up a staff clinic and a rest-room. Six years ago the store was renovated and, having developed a specialist line in decoration and gardening, became the Mecca of DIY enthusiasts with a large selection of cut-glass and wood, tool-hire facilities and a panelling and parquet department. However, it still maintains its position as a general department store with a perfume department and a fashion section. There is a Métro entrance actually in the store and a car park.

BHV   52, RUE DE RIVOLI IV – 42 74 90 00

SAMARITAINE opened in 1870 but the buildings we see today were not commissioned until much later by the founders Ernest Cognacq and his wife Louise Cognacq-Jay. In 1906 Frantz Jourdain built a steel and glass store in the Art Nouveau style of which the great staircase, the polychrome façade and the fifth-floor mural still remain intact. In 1926, the other architect involved, Henri Sauvage, created two Art Deco buildings. On the top floor you can go out on to a terrace from which you will have a view of the roofs of Paris which stretch out in front of you as far as the La Défense Arch. Household goods and sport take centre stage in this store which is affectionately known as 'Samar'. There is a large DIY department, free consultations with pharmacists, lampshades made-to-measure and a service whereby you can take the carpets home and try them out. For enthusiasts of all kinds of sporting activities there are numerous customer service facilities. You can have new wheels put on to your roller-skates; you can have mountain and rock-climbing boots resoled and repaired; you can have your skis totally remodelled and your swimming goggles correctly adjusted to suit your vision. There is a workshop where they repair and service bicycles and a section in which they will lend you a new Mitchell reel while you have the one on your fishing rod repaired. You can also hire a brand-new tennis racquet (but you have to leave a deposit). There is a whole shop devoted to television sets, hi-fi equipment, video machines, audio equipment and a bookshop, and there's a car park.

SAMARITAINE   19, RUE DE LA MONNAIE I – 40 41 20 20

STUDIOS AND MEGASTORES

These aren't department stores but their size, between 800 and 1,300 square metres, and sometimes even larger than that, puts them into a category of their own. The choice is vast and there is a free mix of fashion and decorative objects. Occasionally you will come across a sweet counter or a snack-bar. The two great designers Yves Saint Laurent and Gianni Versace stick to fashion in their vast shops on the Faubourg Saint-Honoré. Saint Laurent's was decorated by Didier Gomez and Versace's by the Italian designers Rocco Magnoli ard Lorenzo Carmellini. You should not miss paying a visit to either of these stores at any price!

FRANCK ET FILS   In 1899 this was a haberdasher's in Passy, which at the time was just a village. Emma and Léon Franck didn't have much money and couldn't afford a more central location, which has been a godsend for their descendants! This Mecca of upmarket fashion has retained one of Emma's innovations, the 'fortnights', which are still as successful as they were at the turn of the century.

FRANCK ET FILS   80 RUE DE PASSY XVI – 46 47 86 00

TATI 40 years ago this was a little shop opened by Jules Ouaki at No. 22 Boulevard Rochechouart. Now that it extends from No. 2 to No. 30 it has become a whole universe of a shop at which you can dress your entire family from top to toe, purchase your beauty products and even accessorize your home. The labels with their blue lettering on a Vichy-pink-and-white background were inspired by the work of Schnabel, the painter, and Azzedine Alaïa, the fashion designer. Everyone goes there, including Nadine, Baroness Rothschild, who wrote in one of her books that she even buys her tights there. Take care of the pennies and the pounds will take care of themselves! There are numerous bargains as long as you're prepared to rummage around and not have a panic attack as a result of the good-natured masses milling around you.

♠ TATI   2 to 30 BOULEVARD ROCHECHOUART XVIII – 42 55 13 09

L'ENTREPÔT was the first of the 'loft'-style shops. Jean-Pierre and Nicole Hennequet opened their store up a staircase in the Rue de Passy and the little window displays that look on to the street below must surely tempt passers-by to come on up. Marc Berthier, the designer, recently redid the décor behind those displays. On behalf of the young trendies of the super-plush 16th arrondissement, and their parents come to that, Nicole and Jean-Pierre scour the world and have a nose for the next item that everyone will simply have to possess. All the fashions, all the 'gotta have it' objects, you'll find them all here in the shop, from mini-skirts to cups, sticks of barley sugar to postcards, watches to chaises longues, or whatever. And they sell swimwear all year. At the back of the shop there's a bar called the 'Paris-Plage' which serves both lunch and tea, prepared by lively young Americans who all cook very well indeed.

♡ L'ENTREPÔT   50, RUE DE PASSY XVI – 45 25 64 17

BONPOINT Over the years they've taken over a whole section of the Rue de l'Université. In 1973, two sisters, Marie-France Cohen and Dominique Swildens started up a business, making up refined but unfancy children's clothes. It was a success. Their husbands got involved, one in administration and the other in décor, and now they dress babies as well as young children. And, indeed, they also dress schoolgirls going to their first dance, young people, couples, couples' mothers and couples' fathers. And now they've given over an entire shop to children's bedroom furnishings. What they're good at is mixing street fashion with top-drawer chic, and everything they sell is top quality. The label with its little cherries reminds one that Marie-France and Dominique are still the daughters of a confectioner.

♡ BONPOINT   62, 65 and 86, RUE DE L'UNIVERSITÉ VII – 45 50 32 18

AUTOUR DU MONDE brings together under one painted wooden roof combat shirts, army trousers, jodhpurs and all the other paramilitary gear gathered by Serge Bensimon in a colonial-style shop, decorated in shades of beige, brown, blue and green. They also sell their famous round-ended baskets covered in elastic, which are, quite simply, referred to as 'bensimons'. In the next-door shop the walls are painted in ochre like Mexican houses and they are permeated with the sweet smell of cedar. The polished wooden wardrobes open to reveal patchwork quilts, floral pot-pourris and dishcloths. On the shelves of the dressers you will find heavy earthenware crockery, gardening manuals and cookbooks. In the basement there are armchairs with rests and rocking-chairs which create a Wild West atmosphere. You can just about hear the folk music playing in the background, and the children's boutique completes this particular universe.

AUTOUR DU MONDE   8, 10 and 12, RUE DES FRANCS-BOURGEOIS III — 42 77 06 08, 42 77 96 98 and 42 77 16 18

L'ÉCLAIREUR mixes designer clothes and furniture in a former printworks dominated by a magnificent glass turn-of-the-century roof. Martine and Armand Hadida commissioned the architect Maurice Marti to design the shop which is in daringly good taste.

♡   L'ÉCLAIREUR   3 TER, RUE DES ROSIERS IV — 48 87 10 22

NATURE ET DÉCOUVERTES An interesting concept created by François Lemarchand, the man behind Pier Import in the 70s. Red hexagonal floor tiles and rust-coloured furniture are finished in turquoise. The whole shop is conceived in the colours of the earth and the sea. You can buy a telescope or a T-shirt with a rhino print, a kaleidoscope or an amber necklace, a cycling map of the whole Paris region or a tape of bird songs. Here, at least, ecology and business co-exist harmoniously.

♡   NATURE ET DÉCOUVERTES   10 BIS, RUE DE L'ARC-EN-CIEL, FORUM DES HALLES I — 40 28 42 16; 23, BOULEVARD DE LA MADELEINE I — 49 27 07 58; 24, PLACE D'ITALIE XIII — 45 88 28 28

CHEVIGNON TRADING POST is entirely given over to Wild West culture and sells its customers both household objects and clothes heavily influenced by the genre and its wonderful 'General Stores'. A coffee shop serving Tex-Mex food completes the picture.

CHEVIGNON TRADING POST   4, RUE DES ROSIERS IV — 42 72 42 40; 49, RUE ÉTIENNE MARCEL I — 40 28 05 67

AU VIEUX CONTINENT is the result of a partnership between the Ventilo brothers, Jean-Michel Signoles of 'Chipie' and a businessman from Grenoble. The secret of their success is the American Dream of a 15-year-old schoolboy, which, put into practice, means the 50s alongside New England and a bit of Wild West thrown in for good measure. They sell clothes as well as records and crockery and there's even a second-hand section. There is also a restaurant area where you can have a bottle of Mexican beer. Armand Ventilo has said that he wanted the public to 'find the unexpected when they go shopping'.

AU VIEUX CONTINENT   5, RUE D'ARGOUT II – 40 39 94 94

LANVIN   At the crossing of the Faubourg Saint-Honoré and the Rue Boissy-d'Anglas, the two buildings, superbly renovated by Terence Conran, contain 1,800 square metres dedicated to elegance. The English designer explains that he wanted to rediscover the roots, the symbols and the spirit of the founder. Blue is everywhere, as are also the distinctive design of the Arpège bottle and the wave and frieze that are so dear to Armand-Albert Rateau, Jeanne Lanvin's favourite decorator. No. 22 is reserved for women. As with the men's fashion, the designer is the talented Dominique Morlotti. At No. 15, women go straight to the third floor, called 'Il pour Elle' (He for Her), because it is there that they can finally discover men's suits adapted to the female form. On the fourth floor there are gift items signed by Hilton McConnico and Joy de Rohan-Chabot. A pleasant place to stop is the Café Bleu in the basement, open to all for a refreshing cup of coffee, tea or chocolate.

LANVIN   15 AND 22, RUE DU FAUBOURG SAINT-HONORÉ VIII – 44 71 33 33

And also:

♡   RALPH LAUREN   2, PLACE DE LA MADELEINE VIII – 44 77 53 50

THE CLASSICS

THE CLASSICS

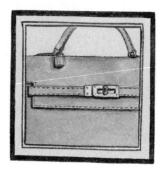

Wallet or scarf, necklace or T-shirt, blankets or glasses, we've listed 41 items that have become, in our humble opinion, eternal, immortal classics. They are bigger than their designers, sociologists and the vagaries of fashion. They are timeless, universal and they will never go out of fashion. In contradistinction to the fast-moving world of high fashion, these items are more fashionable now than when they were created. Lots of people copy them, naturally, but you really have to have the Real Thing because, once you have, or once someone's bought it for you, you will hold it forever dear. They'll never be unfashionable, they're top-quality goods and they are the hallmarks of elegance for yourself or your home. Cult items, each and every one.

THE HERMÈS SCARF Since its creation in 1937 not a single change has been made to the design. It is made of silk, measures 90 centimetres square and weighs 75 grams. 820 designs have been produced since the original 'Omnibus et dames blanches' and now, once again, women are hanging them from the handles of their bags.

THE HERMÈS BAG We've seen them styled from the mini to the maxi. The first one was enormous and was used by riders to carry their saddles and their bridles, which created the need for the anti-theft padlock device. Evolving as a ladies' handbag in 1935, it would still be another 20 years before it attained cult status thanks to Princess Grace of Monaco who was to give it its name, the Kelly bag. The current model is the 'Bugatti' which is rounded in shape.

HERMÈS   24, RUE DU FAUBOURG SAINT-HONORÉ VIII – 40 17 47 17

THE OLD ENGLAND TWINSET 100 years ago Alexandre Henriquet, a hosier from the Ardennes, and his Irish partner began selling tea, whisky, plum puddings and gabardine raincoats made-to-measure for chauffeurs. Nowadays Parisians are perfectly well aware that here the choice of twinset, a cardigan with mother-of-pearl buttons and a crew-neck single-ply sweater, is the most significant in Europe, after Harrods's.

OLD ENGLAND   12, BOULEVARD DES CAPUCINES IX – 47 42 81 99

THE PETIT MATELOT REEFER JACKET Since 1790, the crews of Seine barges have been kitting themselves out at the sign of the Petit Matelot, chez Monsieur Rattier, on the Ile Saint-Louis. The shop very quickly became involved with more modern wares and in 1902 it moved to the Avenue de la Grande-Armée. Lovers of Brittany come to buy navy wool reefers with red woollen linings.

AU PETIT MATELOT   27, AVENUE DE LA GRANDE-ARMÉE XVI – 45 00 15 51

THE RICCI CAPE Created in 1980 by Gérard Pipart, it has become one of the firm's best-selling items. It is made of two-ply cashmere jersey and is a 160-centimetre square shape with an 80-centimetre slit in the middle. It comes in no less than 30 different colours.

NINA RICCI   39, AVENUE MONTAIGNE VIII – 47 23 78 88

CHANEL EARRINGS Even Princess Diana wears them. American and Japanese women fight over them and French women just adore them. They are one of the prime symbols of the Chanel style. She didn't like pierced ears, preferring to design clip-ons inspired by pigeons' nests. The single pearl coiled into golden threads is the result of this ecological inclination way before it became fashionable.

THE 'BAVOLET' BAG Quilted according to the precise specifications of the designer with a gold chain for a shoulder-strap, this design, which is called No. 255 because of the day and year it was created, is the most requested and most frequently imitated of the Chanel handbags.

CHANEL   31, RUE CAMBON I – 42 86 28 00; 42, AVENUE MONTAIGNE VIII – 47 23 74 12

THE LACOSTE SWEATER 'The Crocodile' was the nickname of René Lacoste, the tennis champion, one of the four musketeers who won the Davis Cup for France in 1925. The crocodile symbolized Lacoste's tenacious personality, for he never loosened his grip on his opponent, and it became the logo of the most famous jersey sweater in the world. Until 1951 the Lacoste sweater only came in white. Now it is woven with 20 kilometres of long-fibred cotton and comes with either short or long sleeves and in 30 colours.

LACOSTE   37, BOULEVARD DES CAPUCINES II – 42 61 58 20

HAREL PUMPS From Catherine Deneuve to Paloma Picasso the world's beautiful women wear Harel pumps, made of lizard skin which is cut, sewn and finished by hand. They come in 30 colours and the leather is carefully selected and treated with a special slow tanning process which gives it its suppleness and its rainproof qualities. It takes a worker a whole day just to make two pairs of these shoes.

HAREL   8, AVENUE MONTAIGNE VIII – 37 20 79 01

THE YVES SAINT LAURENT BLAZER It's perfect. The shoulders, the lapel and the dimensions. Since his first collection in 1966 Yves Saint Laurent has carried on selling this design while only imperceptibly changing the cut.

YVES SAINT LAURENT RIVE GAUCHE   6, PLACE SAINT-SULPICE VI – 43 29 43 00; 38, RUE DU FAUBOURG SAINT-HONORÉ VIII – 42 65 74 59

THE PRADA WALLET In the past, women in the know went to look for their little black nylon wallet, printed with the gold triangle, Prada's symbol, in the Via della Spiga in Milan. Today they only have to go as far as the Right Bank. It is lined with morocco leather and sewn in a material made on water looms and according to the standards of strength demanded by the Italian army.

PRADA   5, RUE DE GRENELLE VI – 45 48 53 14

CASSEGRAIN NOTEBOOKS They come in gold, black, blue, red or green leather, with gilt edges and yellow pages striped with blue. Their 15 themes range from croquet to yachting, from hunting to books, and of course addresses. Irresistible.

CASSEGRAIN   422, RUE SAINT-HONORÉ VIII – 42 60 20 08

MADELEINE GELY UMBRELLAS Madeleine Gely's pretty shop, which opened in 1834 on the site of one of the old shops of the Charité hospital, can now be found in the heart of the Saint-Germain district. You should go to discover the charms of her sunshades and the artistry of her hand-made umbrellas which have handles carved from fruitwood.

MADELEINE GELY   218, BOULEVARD SAINT-GERMAIN VI – 42 22 63 25

UNGARO'S SWATHED DRESS Anouk Aimée and Ivana Trump are devotees of Ungaro's little swathed dress. Emanuel showed us the first model as part of his summer '80 collection and since then he has constantly reproduced the same design but always with that special extra something of course. It may seem an old-fashioned idea but it's not, and, boy, is it sexy! The colours and the prints change with the seasons.

UNGARO 2, AVENUE MONTAIGNE VIII – 47 23 61 94

THE ÉRÈS COSTUME is worn the whole year round. In winter it's low-cut, curvaceous and ultra-fine, sticking to the curves of your body like a second skin and worn as a body under a long skirt. In summer you wear it with jeans or even to swim in. It was designed by the daughter of the firm's founder, Irène Leroux, who is constantly striving to improve the line and the cut. For more than 20 years now Parisian women have known where to go to find the ultimate silhouette.

ÉRÈS 2, RUE TRONCHET VIII – 47 42 24 55; 4BIS, RUE DU CHERCHE-MIDI VI – 45 44 95 54; 6, RUE GUICHARD XVI – 46 47 45 21

CHEZ PEINTURE'S WOOL LACE SHAWL is knitted by an English hosier, supplier to the babies of the English royal family. Anita Saada, a Frenchwoman, has them made in several sizes and in the colours of her choice.

CHEZ PEINTURE 18, RUE DU PRÉ-AUX-CLERCS VII – 45 48 18 52

JEAN DINH VAN'S GOLD CHAIN is made up of elongated rectangular links with variable cross-sections. From it you should hang small pieces of gemstone such as coral, malachite and jade.
JEAN DINH VAN'S WALLET is made of Breteuil goatskin. It's tough, flat, round and has a gold clasp.

JEAN DINH VAN 7, RUE DE LA PAIX II – 42 61 74 49

THE CARTIER TANK WATCH is square and mounted on an unfurled buckle. It was designed by Louis Cartier in the 20s as a tribute to the American soldiers and to their revolutionary, freedom-fighting combat vehicles. You can buy it in silver, gold or vermilion.

CARTIER 7, PLACE VENDÔME I – 42 61 55 55

THE TECLA PEARL NECKLACE is worn tight round the neck, like a choker, or much longer, Charleston style. The clasp comes in plain or engraved gold, either more or less covered in diamanté or semi-precious stones, and is a jewel in its own right if you want to wear it that way.

TECLA 2, RUE DE LA PAIX I – 42 61 03 29

CHARVET'S BRAIDED CUFFLINKS were designed in the 60s, an age in which the shirt relaunched musketeer-style cuffs. They come in 60 different shades.

CHARVET 28, PLACE VENDÔME I – 42 60 30 70

THE LHUILLIER FRESH FLOWER BUTTONHOLE DECORATION The pleasures of which are as ephemeral as they are sophisticated. The florist launched it as a fashion item at the turn of the century and you can wear it now and then instead of a brooch.

LHUILLIER   2, PLACE VENDÔME I — 42 60 52 15

TROUSSELIER ARTIFICIAL FLOWERS are made from satin, organdy, silk, cotton, voile and gauze. There are roses, camellias, peonies and mimosas. Pin them to your hats, in your hair or to the lapel of your jacket.

TROUSSELIER   73, BOULEVARD HAUSSMANN VIII — 42 66 97 95

GÉLOT'S FELT HAT (at **LANVIN**) Get it out of your wardrobe when cold weather sets in and acquire an enigmatic allure.

LANVIN   2, RUE CAMBON I — 42 60 38 83

THE HANES COTTON T-SHIRT was invented in 1901 by John Wesley Hanes. His first customers were American farmers but they were followed in quick succession by the US Army and US Navy. Marlon Brando and James Dean brought them into the public eye and, since then, Hanes, who was the first man in the world to make T-shirts, has dyed them in 30 different colours and added long sleeves in a winter version.

HANES at GALERIES LAFAYETTE

THE BURBERRY RAINCOAT was very quickly taken up by the English armed forces during the Boer War and subsequently during the two World Wars. Made of Egyptian cotton, the famous check lining was introduced in 1924.

BURBERRYS   8, BOULEVARD MALESHERBES VIII — 42 66 13 01

THE AGNÈS B CARDIGAN made of brushed cotton has a detailed little flap on either side and, according to the designer, was conceived as a T-shirt you can unbutton. Every season she changes the 12 colours, but white and black are always included in the range.

AGNÈS B   6, RUE DU JOUR I — 40 26 36 87

THE HILDITCH AND KEY SHAWL is made of cashmere voile and printed wool. It is a miracle of feel and weight (at only 35 grams) and is one of the best-selling items at this English firm which opened a Paris branch in 1913.

HILDITCH AND KEY   252, RUE DE RIVOLI I — 42 60 36 09

THE VUITTON LEATHER BUCKET-BAG was originally the means by which you took bottles of champagne to the races.

Thanks to 'shine and colour at the peak of leatherwork' you need not fear scratches and it keeps its shine for ages.
VUITTON   78, AVENUE MARCEAU VIII – 47 20 47 00; 54, AVENUE MONTAIGNE VIII – 42 89 12 88

MANUEL CANOVAS STRIPY CANVAS BEACH BAG was inspired by one he found in New England. It's enormous and always comes with a monochrome printed lining.
MANUEL CANOVAS   30, AVENUE GEORGE-V VIII – 49 52 00 36

LOEWE GLOVES are cut in exceptionally soft suede, dyed in beautiful colours with cuffs inlaid in contrasting colours.
LOEWE   57, AVENUE MONTAIGNE VIII – 42 89 06 61

LAURE WELFLING'S TARTAN BLANKET WITH TASSELS comes in a wonderful variety of colours and designs. You throw it over a bed or a sofa which are immediately transformed.
LAURE WELFLING   30, RUE JACOB VI – 43 25 17 03

PORTHAULT'S VOILE LINEN is woven in France with the finest Egyptian cotton. It is then embroidered (by hand) or printed. The most famous motif is the club which was designed by a former customer, the writer Louise de Vilmorin.
PORTHAULT   18, AVENUE MONTAIGNE VIII – 47 20 75 25

THE FILOFAX You can now buy almost 500 different inserts – a diary, a blotter, an envelope, composition paper, drawing paper, tracing paper, graph paper, an underground map of Paris or London or New York, memo pads for businessmen or housewives, notepaper in bright colours or plain colours or stripes or squares, scorepads for bridge enthusiasts or golfers, credit-card holders and even a super-slim calculator. All of these fit into rings set into a leather or vinyl binder.
FILOFAX   58, RUE DE BABYLONE VII – 45 55 53 34

THE MONTBLANC PEN In black or wine crowned with a white star, model No. 4810, with its golden quill, reminds you of the great altitude of France's highest mountain. Made by hand, it comes with a pretty case in a variety of different leathers.
MONTBLANC at ÉLYSÉES STYLOS MARBEUF   40, RUE MARBEUF VIII – 42 25 40 49

THE CROSS BALLPOINT PEN dates from 1946, the centenary year of the American firm. The Century is made of solid silver.
CROSS at ÉLYSÉES STYLOS MARBEUF (as above)

THE AGRY SIGNET RING They engrave the coats-of-arms of the great French families on to gold or lapis-lazuli. These families also have their visiting cards and invitations made up here.

AGRY   14, RUE DE CASTIGLIONE I – 42 60 65 10

CHÂTELAINE BABYWEAR clothes royal babies (and others) in embroidered ruffs and knitted bootees. Every item is handmade and can be commissioned with a new arrival's first name or with a particular design of your choice.

LA CHÂTELAINE   170, AVENUE VICTOR-HUGO XVI – 47 27 44 07

THE BARBOUR You wear it in the countryside all year round. You also see people wearing them in the city. Made of oiled canvas, it has a velvet collar and enormous pockets.

BARBOUR at CYRILLUS   104, AVENUE DE VILLIERS XVII – 47 66 43 17; at KINETON 40, RUE VITAL XVI – 45 04 67 21

JEAN LAFONT TORTOISESHELL GLASSES are light and come in different shapes to suit different eyes whether they be brown, hazel, blue, green or olive.

JEAN LAFONT   11, RUE VIGNON VIII – 47 42 25 93

BOOKPLATES FROM CASSEGRAIN take their motifs from books in the Bibliothèque Nationale (the French National Library). The refinement consists in having these engraved with your monogram or initials.

CASSEGRAIN   422, RUE SAINT-HONORÉ VIII – 42 60 20 08

BARGAIN BASEMENTS AND SALE SHOPS

Nothing is more chic than buying a bargain or dressing yourself from top to toe in goods with designer labels at knockdown prices. All the Parisians are at it: rummaging around in warehouses, discount stores and bargain basements and still managing to look a million dollars for next-to-nothing!

BETTY In the pretty square called the Place d'Aligre the flea market and the second-hand furniture shops are no longer worth visiting but a little shop with scant regard for its appearance draws well-off women from all over Paris. It specializes in ex-designer-label clothes and sells them at unbeatable prices. It's worth a detour.

BETTY   10, PLACE D'ALIGRE XII – 43 07 40 64

ANNEXE DES CRÉATEURS All the designer labels are here, from Sophie Sitbon to Nathalie Garçon, from Mugler to Beretta, accessories as well as clothes, and all with 40% to 50% off. The designs are new but one season out-of-date. You should try and go in the morning because it gets very crowded in the late afternoons.

ANNEXE DES CRÉATEURS 19, RUE GODOT-DE-MAUROY IX – 42 65 46 40

NINA RICCI You used to have to go down to the basement. Now Nina Ricci has opened a whole shop devoted to her bargain items, next-door to the Ricci Club. There's more room now and the clothes are attractively displayed. They are quite often haute couture designs, a year or two old, and with 60% to 80% off their original prices. You can buy a silk blouse for around 3,000 francs.

NINA RICCI   17, RUE FRANÇOIS-Iᵉʳ VIII – 47 23 78 88

MENDÈS On the first floor of a building with which all the capital rummagers are very well acquainted, Mendès sells the Yves Saint Laurent's 'Variations' and 'Rive Gauche' collections, one season out-of-date and at totally unbelievable prices. But you have to be able to handle the crowds and try the clothes on in front of everyone, because they don't have any fitting-rooms. And there are loads of people. Treat yourself to a luxury item at half its original price.
MENDÈS   65, RUE MONTMARTRE II – 42 36 83 32

ANNA LOWE sells last season's designer clothes. She very often buys these up from stock left over in provincial shops she knows and displays their designer labels with great emphasis. There are Chanel cardigans and Ungaro suits at almost half their original price.
ANNA LOWE   35, AVENUE MATIGNON VIII – 43 59 96 61

STORE SR Translated into English: Sonia Rykiel. This is the most beautiful shop in the Rue d'Alésia. There women tussle over the jersey-knit suits and the towelling coordinates at half their original price. There's a rumour going round that Chantal Goya and Carole Laure are regular customers here.
STORE SR   64, RUE D'ALÉSIA XIV – 43 95 06 13

DOROTHÉE BIS STOCK This is a very calm, neat shop with a large selection of sizes and design from last season. There are also super-bargains from two years ago. At the end of June, summer clothes have an extra 50% knocked off their price tags, as do the winter clothes at the end of January. They've had the rather neat idea of dividing the shop into two, with summer clothes at one end and winter clothes at the other.
DOROTHÉE BIS STOCK   74, RUE D'ALÉSIA XIV – 45 42 17 11

SOLDE TROIS There are two shops, one for men and one for women, but they both sell Lanvin clothes. All his designs from the haute couture to the ready-to-wear are here with 50% discounts or even more if they're over one season old. You can find silk handkerchiefs for 50 francs and wallets for 100 francs. Two or three times a year they have special promotions (they'll tell you when if you telephone the shop). Some articles cost next-to-nothing.
SOLDE TROIS   3, RUE DE VIENNE VIII – 42 94 93 34

LE MOUTON À CINQ PATTES A must for all bargain-hunters. For more than 30 years women have been coming here to buy that once-in-a-lifetime bargain. But they have to come right at the beginning of the season and know how to scrummage through packed clothes rails. But the sheer ecstasy they experience when they find a Joseph label makes the whole experience worthwhile! Don't forget to pay a visit to the shop at No. 18 where they sell end-of-the-line goods from the other shops at crazy prices.

♡ ♧ **LE MOUTON À CINQ PATTES** 8, 18 and 48, RUE SAINT-PLACIDE VI — 45 48 20 49

AZZEDINE ALAÏA A rather bourgeois establishment, a discreet entrance upstairs on the first floor and a rather uninviting welcome don't stop them selling end-of-the-line Alaïa clothes at half their original prices.

AZZEDINE ALAÏA   60, RUE DE BELLECHASSE VII — 47 05 13 18

CENTRE DE LA MODE EN GROS All the jumpers in all the colours with a 50% reduction. And, in particular, an incredible selection of cashmere jumpers from around 1,000 francs.

♡ **CENTRE DE LA MODE EN GROS**   101, RUE RÉAUMUR II — 42 36 68 53

BRIGITTE CASSEGRAIN also sells Longchamp luggage retail (although she is the manufacturer as well). It's well worth a visit for the sale corner with its permanent 50%-off selection of discontinued lines.

BRIGITTE   CASSEGRAIN 21,   BOULEVARD   RICHARD-LENOIR   XI — 43 38 59 00

DIDIER LUDOT is actually more of an antique clothes dealer. You have to ring on the doorbell for them to let you in, just like an expensive jeweller's. Lovers of the past come for original Chanel suits, Saint Laurent shoes from 1965, Cardin dresses of '67 and original 50s' Dior and Balmain wedding dresses.

DIDIER LUDOT   24, RUE MONTPENSIER JARDINS DU PALAIS-ROYAL I — 42 96 06 56

You can also get very cheap designer shoes in special sale shops if you can be bothered to trudge your way to their rather obscure locations:

BALLY   156, RUE DE RIVOLI I — 42 60 22 46

KAMMER at BEAUBOURG   59, RUE DE BEAUBOURG III — 42 77 78 85

MANSFIELD at BARIGAMS   47, RUE SAINT-PLACIDE VII — 40 49 03 96

Another cheap alternative to bear in mind is the clothes exchange. Introduced 20 years ago, it has become a way of life for some women. The idea is that you take designer clothes you no longer wear along to a shop which will sell them for you, as long as they're in good condition. Nowadays it's not just the poverty-stricken who do this. You'll find business executives, journalists, lawyers and doctors. A whole new generation of customers is springing up among college students who want to find a dress to wear to their next event, since the women who go there to sell their clothes invariably end up buying others with the money.

CHLOROPHYLLE is where it's at for avant-garde designers. You'll find Lolita Lempicka, Kenzo, Ventilo and Montana.
CHLOROPHYLLE   2, RUE DU SABOT VI – 45 44 02 44

DÉPÔT-VENTE DE PASSY This used to be called 'Catherine Baril' and there are two shops in the same street. It is very chic indeed. At No. 14 you will find genuine Chanel suits which sell like hot cakes and Yves Saint Laurent. At No. 25 they sell Georges Rech.
DÉPÔT-VENTE DE PASSY   14, RUE DE LA TOUR XVI – 45 20 95 21; 25, RUE DE LA TOUR XVI – 45 27 11 46

TROCADE This establishment which is patronized by everyone who lives in the 17th arrondissement constantly restocks with clothes, from the decorative Saint Laurent suit (at around 1,500 francs) to the wild creations of Junior Gaultier, via the Chloé jacket and the Myrène de Prémonville ensemble. Chic customers come to buy top-of-the-range products.
TROCADE   9, AVENUE DE VILLIERS XVII – 42 67 80 14

RÉCIPROQUE is a veritable institution of a shop where Nicole Morel keeps an eye on clothes brought to her premises by the wives of the captains of industry, film stars and members of the jet-set, who all want to make a few bob. There is also a real shop with impressive trade prices. You can only bring goods in by appointment (telephone them on 47 04 82 24).
RÉCIPROQUE   95, RUE DE LA POMPE XVI – 47 04 30 28

CAMÉLÉON They sell accessories like Chanel scarves and small leather goods. They also have the odd nice thing from Hermès and Céline. You have to find it yourself.
CAMÉLÉON   142, RUE DE LA POMPE XVI – 44 05 03 04

GRIFF TROC Media and show-biz types love it here, as do sophisticated provincial women. It's the best place to go for woolly tops, parkas, shawls and Hermès scarves. You can also buy Prada bags and Lacroix's jersey dresses.
GRIFF TROC   17, BOULEVARD DE COURCELLES VIII – 42 25 86 07

LA MAISON DU BONHEUR is the kingdom of the accessory from the Hermès Kelly bag to the Chanel quilted one and there's a vast selection of silk scarves.
LA MAISON DU BONHEUR   55, AVENUE DE SUFFREN XV – 45 67 63 74

SELECTED ADDRESSES

Fashion journalists, media types, business women and shrewd young misses all meet up at certain shops that know how to use their good taste and their talent to select the signs of the times: here are the addresses of the 'clued-in' women of fashion.

VICTOIRE Françoise Chassagnac, the famous talent-spotter, never stops looking for new staff for her five Parisian shops. The Victoire style consists of very simple, easy-to-wear clothes with the distinctive hallmark of creativity. Françoise has a particular soft spot for the Italian designers Moschino and Dolce Gabbana, the Belgian designers behind Anvers, Hartford's T-shirts and embroidered silk shirts, and the American designer Donna Karan. She has five shops in Paris including:

♡ **VICTOIRE   12, PLACE DES VICTOIRES II – 42 61 09 02**

MARIA LUISA Maria Luisa set up shop in a rather 'couture' area more or less by accident since this young passionate Venezuelan is more of a 'street chic' sort of girl. Her selection of clothes and accessories are with-it but not over-the-top. She sells: Italien Costume National, the young avant-garde designer Olivier Guillemin, Marcel Marongiu for his restrained daring, Corinne Cobson, Martine Sitbon and an awful lot more. An impressive detail is the warm welcome you receive as you come into the shop even if you're just asking the way to somewhere else.

MARIA LUISA   2, RUE CAMBON I – 47 03 96 15

ABSINTHE A pretty woman whose small pale face is framed in a mass of black curls, and who has a 'now' look, Marthe Desmoulins is a true original. Her shop is none the less so, with its natural wood floor, armchairs and purple velvet sofas which

Map labels:

R. DES JEUNEURS

2

BOURSE

TEMBRE
STIN

CLERY

RUE D

ALBERT

RUE DE

R. VIVIENNE

BOURSE

BIBLIOTHÈQUE
NATIONALE

R. DE LA BANQUE

RUE REA...

RUE SENTIER

RUE DU MAIL

RUE D'ABOUKIR

ST SAUVEUR

R. DES Pts CHAMPS

PLACE
DES
VICTOIRES

ABOULT

RUE MONTMARTRE

RUE MONTORGUEIL

RUE GRENETA

PALAIS
ROYAL

BANQUE
DE
FRANCE

RUE ÉTIENNE MARCEL

R. TIQUETONNE

R. DE VALOIS

R. ROUSSEAU

R. DU JOUR

TURBIGO

1

R. DU LOUVRE

ST
EUSTACHE

R. TURBIGO

R. CROIX des Pts CHAMPS

R. J. J.

BOURSE
DU
COMMERCE

LES HALLES

R. ST DENIS

SEBASTO POL

RUE ST HONORÉ

FORUM

R. DE RIVOLI

QUARTIER
PLACE DES VICTOIRES Iᵉʳ

Victoire
12, place des Victoires Iᵉʳ

Agnès B
6, R. du

Absinthe
74-75, Rue Jean-Jacques Rousseau Iᵉʳ

t. Mugler
10, Place

Christian Louboutin
19, Rue Jean-Jacques Rousseau Iᵉʳ

Kenzo
3, Pla

Sibylla
62, Rue Jean-Jacques Rousseau Iᵉʳ

Yohji
25, R

En Attendant les Barbares
50, Rue Étienne Marcel IIᵉ

Comm
42,

Maria Luisa
2, Rue Cambon Iᵉʳ

Moke
18,

are highlighted in lime green: a startling mixture of avant-garde hats and clothes.

♡ **ABSINTHE**   74–76, RUE JEAN-JACQUES-ROUSSEAU I – 42 33 54 44

HÉMISPHÈRES Years of sophisticated fashion gleaned from around the world. Embroidered T-shirts, chambray shirts, exquisite women's blouses, skin-tight, very well-cut trousers.

HÉMISPHÈRES   22, AVENUE DE LA GRANDE-ARMÉE XVII – 42 67 61 96

LIGHT This is a funny place, full of clutter, muddle and tourists, just as you often find with shops on the Champs-Elysées. Rather mysterious is the way the shop is always full. This organized chaos conceals couturiers' slightly cheaper clothes, the best designs from Kookaï and a very good selection of cocktail dresses. The really astute business decision was to maintain a permanent sale corner including clothes from all the best designers.

♧ **LIGHT**   92, CHAMPS-ÉLYSÉES VIII – 43 59 83 72

MARINA DE BOURBON The Princess Marina de Bourbon-Parme, a former antique-dealer, and her partner, Jean-Pierre Lopez, took a commercial gamble by opening a shop that only sells things to their own taste, particularly given that they are both mad about art, unusual objects and travel. By a stroke of good luck their taste coincided with that of their customers and includes classic parkas and 'keds', the sandals designed in 1920 that Katharine Hepburn wears.

MARINA DE BOURBON   112, BOULEVARD DE COURCELLES XVII – 47 63 42 01

MEREDITH Barbara Gwast is the daughter of the Merediths, the owner of the avant-garde fashion shop in the Rue de Passy. Following in the family tradition, her charming shop with its marble floor, decorated with a hand-painted floral pattern, shelters the talents of young designers. The clothes are easy to wear.

MEREDITH   354, RUE SAINT-HONORÉ I – 42 60 42 24 and, of course, the parent shop at 14, RUE DE PASSY XVI – 42 88 08 20

APC Discreet initials (Atelier de Production et de Création) indicate, not a stone's throw from the Luxembourg Gardens, the definitive shop for today's fashion victims. These clothes pros have rigorously selected their stock, which includes jackets, narrow-fitting trousers, parkas and T-shirts made of soft materials in quality cuts and sophisticated colours. They have exclusive fabrics.

♡ **APC**   4, RUE DE FLEURUS VI – 42 22 12 77

IRIÉ An ex-Kenzo boy, Irié, who is also Japanese, was the pioneer and pet of the Rue du Pré-aux-Clercs. Without ever having to sell himself to the media, he has been able to make his personal style felt on the street and in magazines. Followers of avant-garde fashion regularly come to his white marble shop to buy well-cut jackets, soft matching skirts and viscose T-shirts. Low prices, perfect tailoring.

♡   **IRIÉ   8, RUE DU PRÉ-AUX-CLERCS VII − 42 61 18 28**

CHEZ PEINTURE Anita Saada has been selling Liberty prints forever and the public never grows tired of them. But she also sells wool-lace shawls and cotton shawls knitted in Nottingham in 45 different shades.

CHEZ PEINTURE   18, RUE DU PRÉ-AUX-CLERCS VII − 45 48 18 52

KASHIYAMA This Japanese firm founded in 1927 sells clothes from all over the world. While it has always remained on the original site in the Boulevard Saint-Germain, the directors have grafted very pure décor on to their superb location. The architect was Colombe Stevens. The manageress buys in all the most fêted of the current crop of international designers, including Rifat Ozbek and Sybilla, and their clothes hang side-by-side with the works of young painters.

KASHIYAMA   147, BOULEVARD SAINT-GERMAIN VI − 46 34 11 50;
22, BOULEVARD RASPAIL VI − 46 34 11 50

ZENTA With distressed stucco on the walls, white wood on the floor, beech furniture and comfortable fitting-rooms, Isabelle Hébey, the designer, has manipulated space and light to create a shop which sells the work of a dozen designers hung from grey clothes rails. 'I wanted to offer women as representative a selection as possible of each designer', explains the director.

ZENTA   6, RUE DE MARIGNAN VIII − 42 25 72 47

L'ÉCLAIREUR There's no doubt about it, Armand Hadida is a good businessman with a great feel for fashion. Arriving from Morocco by way of Jerusalem in the 70s, he began his career as a shop assistant at Tati. Today he sells the creations of the Belgian avant-garde designers like Ann Demeulemester, which are quite as beautiful as Hamilton Hodge's jewelry-bags.

L'ÉCLAIREUR   49, AVENUE FRANKLIN-D.-ROOSEVELT VIII − 45 62 49 15;
84, AVENUE DES CHAMPS-ÉLYSÉES VIII − 45 62 18 76

And also:

RIVER   68, RUE BONAPARTE VI − 43 26 35 74

L'OBSERVATOIRE   70 BIS, RUE BONAPARTE VI − 43 54 43 06

NADINE SAMSON   52, RUE DE PASSY XVI − 46 47 85 57

Key money for premises is exorbitant, which is why more and more young designers are setting up studios, showrooms and shops in their own apartments.

MARIOT-CHANET Two pros hide behind this trade name – Michèle Meunier and Olivier Chatenet. They design with a pure eye for line, and work on detail and in trompe-l'oeil. Michèle was trained by Karl Lagerfeld at Chanel and Olivier by Alaïa and Mugler. They've opened their first showroom-shop up a staircase in a designer space set up in a former clothes' manufacturing studio which looks like something between a fitting-room and a fashion show arena. There are rag-rolled walls, painted by Andrée Putman, and 50s' chairs. But do keep your eyes open, because there's no sign on the door. In the evening and at weekends you have to key in 0134A to attain the privilege of climbing the two flights of stairs.

MARIOT-CHANET   32, RUE DE L'ÉCHIQUIER X – 48 24 37 37

PARVINE FARMANFARMAÏN Parisians don't hesitate to climb the 73 steep stairs that make up the four floors that lead to the most beautiful silk shirts and dressy blouses in Paris. Parvine updates her collection every two months and if you don't like the print she'll make it up for you from a different batch but for the same price. You can also select a skirt.

♡   **PARVINE FARMANFARMAÏN   15, RUE ROYALE VIII – 47 42 48 21**

BLANDINE D'ALTON has gained an enormous following for her waisted or belted suits. She studied at the École de la Chambre syndicale de la Couture (fashion school) before a whistlestop stay with Hanaë Mori. It is difficult to park near the Place de la République when visiting her second-floor studio.

BLANDINE D'ALTON   39, RUE VOLTA III – 40 29 94 27

CORNILLE-LÉOTARD You have to walk down 19 stairs to get to the designs of Valérie Cornille and Dominique de Léotard. At the far end of a courtyard in the Muette district, their doll's house is worth the detour to find daywear outfits that should be worn as ensembles but may be hired as separates. They have a particular fondness for making up the same design repeatedly but in differing fabrics and colours.

CORNILLE-LÉOTARD   8, RUE GUICHARD XVI – 45 20 28 02

ISABELLE ALLARD The beautiful Isabelle and her sister Dominique de Tournemire receive customer-friends in their show-room. Isabelle shows two collections annually; her specialities are wrap-over sheath dresses and evening ensembles.

ISABELLE ALLARD   420, RUE SAINT-HONORÉ VIII – 47 03 49 58

ANNE DE THÉZY An ex-biologist, she has always been fascinated by chiffon. In her workshop she primarily works in silk but she also designs wedding dresses.

ANNE DE THÉZY   28, RUE ERNEST-RENAN XV – 45 67 27 63

MADE TO MEASURE

In the old days everything was made to measure. From shoes to tablecloths, from dresses to plates. Nowadays it's a real luxury, not least because of the fact that it takes a very long time to have the things made. But what a joy to have something that no one else has, in your own colour, your own measurements or even with your own initials! The personalized gift is always a winner with the 'person who has everything' but you should always get an estimate before you commission anything.

NOUEZ-MOI and **LA MAISON BLEUE** embroider first names, figures or sayings on all your household linen at very reasonable prices.

♡ ♧ NOUEZ-MOI   27, RUE DES SABLONS XVI – 47 27 69 88

LA MAISON BLEUE   58 BIS, RUE FRÉDÉRIC-CLÉMENT 92380 GARCHES – 47 01 18 32

L'ARTISANAT MONASTIQUE and **LE TRÈFLE BLEU** are just as happy to personalize household linen as crockery or glasses.

♧ L'ARTISANAT MONASTIQUE   68 BIS, AVENUE DENFERT-ROCHEREAU XIV – 43 35 15 76

LE TRÈFLE BLEU   2, RUE LARGILLIÈRE XVI – 45 27 80 15

PORTHAULT, LA CHÂTELAINE and **PÉNÉLOPE** embroider tablecloths with the same motif as your dinner plates and decorate pillowcases, sheets, bathrobes and towels with your first name or your initials. The cost is dear but the fabrics divine.

♡ **PORTHAULT**   18, AVENUE MONTAIGNE VIII – 47 20 75 25

LA CHÂTELAINE   170, AVENUE VICTOR-HUGO XVI – 47 27 44 07

♡ **PÉNÉLOPE**   19, AVENUE VICTOR-HUGO XVI – 45 00 90 90

LE LIT NATIONAL will tailor your bed, your duvet and your pillows to fit your dreams.

LE LIT NATIONAL   2, PLACE DU TROCADÉRO XVI – 45 53 33 55

GUERLAIN engraves initials on the very beautiful bee-shaped bottle that holds the 'Eau Impériale' cologne, and you can then have your own bottle refilled.

♡ **GUERLAIN**   68, AVENUE DES CHAMPS-ÉLYSÉES VIII – 47 89 71 00

FLEURS ET PAYSAGES will dress the head of a bride with wreaths of artificial flowers or fruits for her wedding day, and they will do the same for the bridesmaids. You can also select your bouquets in the shop.

FLEURS ET PAYSAGES   116, RUE DU BAC VII – 45 44 62 45

LE SORBIER will make up bouquets of dried flowers to match the fabric samples you bring to the shop. And then they will arrange them for you in your own vases or window boxes.

LE SORBIER   70, RUE VIEILLE-DU-TEMPLE III – 48 87 69 72

MONTBLANC will engrave your pen with your initials (and supply a leather case for it). **CARTIER** will do the same thing with your signature.

MONTBLANC   at   **CASSEGRAIN** 422,   RUE   SAINT-HONORÉ   VIII – 42 60 20 08

CARTIER   51, RUE FRANÇOIS-Iᵉʳ VIII – 40 74 60 60

DIDIER LAMARTHE sews his bags and his luggage in the leather of your choice. His speciality is two-tone or even multi-tone.

DIDIER LAMARTHE   219, RUE SAINT-HONORÉ I – 42 97 44 46

LA FAÏENCERIE DE GIEN keeps up the ancient tradition of the monogrammed dinner service. There are six different colours with various border patterns. The more pieces you order, the cheaper it becomes. Do it as a family so long as you can bear to have the same crockery as your sister-in-law or your mother-in-law!

♡ **LA FAÏENCERIE DE GIEN**   18, RUE DE L'ARCADE VIII – 49 24 07 77

LA MANUFACTURE DU PALAIS-ROYAL will paint your china for you. Dominique Paramythiotis has very good taste and does the designs himself.

LA MANUFACTURE DU PALAIS-ROYAL   172, GALERIE DE VALOIS, JARDINS DU PALAIS-ROYAL I – 42 96 04 24

KAOLA executes made-to-measure designs and monograms on plates (you can even bring your existing ones to the shop). They will also make up copies of cracked pieces from your service.

KAOLA   38, RUE POUSSIN XVI – 46 51 41 44

CHRISTOFLE engraves his silverware to your design or, naturally, with your initials.

CHRISTOFLE   9, RUE ROYALE VIII – 49 33 43 00

SCHWEITZER will faithfully copy all crystalware (and repair broken pieces).

SCHWEITZER   84, QUAI DE JEMMAPES X – 42 39 61 63

CHEVALIER is a planisher, that is, he works in silver and pewter. He will also repair your favourite teapot.

CHEVALIER   26, RUE DES GRAVILLIERS III – 42 74 18 11

GUÉNOT prolongs the life of very beautiful pieces of silverware, and often works for museums.

GUÉNOT   79, RUE DES ARCHIVES III – 48 87 81 79

DEVAUCHELLE is a bookbinder and saves our favourite volumes from total disintegration, which enables us to read and reread them constantly.

DEVAUCHELLE   98, RUE DU FAUBOURG POISSONNIÈRE X – 48 78 67 12

PASCALE LAURENT is an illustrator. She will transform the references you give her into a visual image, which she can do in watercolour or in quite charming little trompe-l'oeil images. What a talent!

PASCALE LAURENT at JACQUES LEGUENNEC   14, RUE DE SEINE VI – 43 26 28 24

BOUCHERON sculpts gold medals engraved with your child's first name which are worn on a chain round your neck or hanging from a chain bracelet. It has been the favourite piece of jewelry of mothers with large families since time immemorial.

♡   BOUCHERON   26, PLACE VENDÔME I – 42 61 58 16

HUGUES DE PAILLETTE is a jeweller who will fix a gemstone in a gold setting and then engrave it with a word or a name.

HUGUES DE PAILLETTE   16, BOULEVARD RASPAIL VII – 45 48 51 56

LA LETTRE D'OR will draw your country cottage, your dog or your coat-of-arms on your trays, table mats, packs of cards, matchboxes, or whatever, and it's very reasonable.

♣   LA LETTRE D'OR   214, RUE DE GRENELLE VII – 47 05 99 18

CLAIRE DE GRAMONT and **ÉLISABETH LABOURET** make frames from the strips of pine that they tint themselves in order to match the wood perfectly with the engraving or painting that you've brought in.

CLAIRE DE GRAMONT and **ÉLISABETH LABOURET** by appointment on 42 65 08 14

RAPID'CADRE guarantee a one-hour emergency framing service. Otherwise the job can take up to a week. There are 350 kinds of frame to choose from, which means that you can get exactly what you're looking for.

RAPID'CADRE   7, RUE DU COMMANDANT-RIVIÈRE VIII – 42 56 06 08; 60, BOULEVARD MALESHERBES VIII – 42 93 75 50

MAUNY has been making wallpaper since 1933 and has a fantastic collection of old patterns in stock that you can have made up in the colours of your choice. The friezes are particularly splendid but the prices match the top quality of the goods.

MAUNY at PRELLE   5, PLACE DES VICTOIRES II – 42 36 67 21

ÉTOFFE ET MAISON, L'ATELIER AUX ÉTOFFES and **LA TOILE DE MAYENNE** are all general tapestry manufacturers. They make curtains, bedspreads and duvet covers.

ÉTOFFE ET MAISON   74, RUE DE RENNES VI – 45 48 93 18

L'ATELIER AUX ÉTOFFES at the CENTRE COMMERCIAL LES 4 TEMPS 92800 LA DÉFENSE – 47 73 55 90

LA TOILE DE MAYENNE   6, RUE MEISSONIER XVII – 47 63 96 26

RODIN sells more than 5,000 different patterns of upholstery fabric, from which they will make up regular curtains, net curtains and duvet covers.

RODIN   36, AVENUE DES CHAMPS-ÉLYSÉES VIII – 43 59 58 82

LE COMPTOIR SUD-PACIFIQUE sells perfume samples in little metal bottles. You can have your own scent made up, with added vanilla or a slightly more floral bouquet, for example.

LE COMPTOIR SUD-PACIFIQUE   17, RUE DE LA PAIX II – 42 61 74 44

DESTAILLES They make shirts and blouses to measure with the aid of a computer. They take your measurements and then you have to choose the material, the shape of the collar and the cuffs. The information is programmed into the computer by the boss. You can also have your initials embroidered. It takes three weeks but is not overly expensive.

DESTAILLES   240, RUE DU FAUBOURG SAINT-HONORÉ VIII – 45 63 43 13

CHARVET is the best made-to-measure men's shirt tailor. You can choose between all the different shades of blue (of which there are over 50) or green, and different-sized stripes. This is a shop for women who like wearing perfect blouses.

♡   **CHARVET**   20, PLACE VENDÔME VIII – 42 60 30 70

SABBIA ROSA makes the prettiest strapless tops, the most sophisticated bodies and the lowest-cut nighties.

SABBIA ROSA   71–73, RUE DES SAINTS-PÈRES VI – 45 48 88 37

CADOLLE After multiple fittings and a three-week wait, you will be the proud owner of the most beautiful swimming-costume or bikini in Paris.

CADOLLE   14, RUE CAMBON I – 42 60 94 94

LA SOIE DE PARIS Here's lightning, seamless service for a skirt, a dress or a top in stretch-jersey, lycra, lurex or silk. And all made to measure.

♡   **LA SOIE DE PARIS**   14, RUE D'UZÈS II – 45 08 12 21

REPETTO will put slippers and Gainsbourg-style lace-up shoes on your feet.

REPETTO   22, RUE DE LA PAIX II – 47 42 47 88

ADIDAS with its special instep and the seven points of support for the feet can be bought in the Adidas-Styles shops.

ADIDAS   3, RUE DU LOUVRE I – 42 60 34 83

AUBERCY sell perfect leather or lizard pumps in all the colours under the sun.

AUBERCY   34, RUE VIVIENNE II – 42 33 93 61

LOLITA LEMPICKA In her design salons, with their walls hung in red quilted material, she sells a collection that is cut and sewn in the studio below her showroom. Go there for very low-cut dresses made of embroidered ottoman or one-off wedding dresses.

LOLITA LEMPICKA   78, AVENUE MARCEAU VIII – 40 70 96 96

JEAN DOUCET A former pupil of the haute couture school in the Rue Saint-Roch, he set up shop not a stone's throw from the Bastille. He only sells made-to-measure party dresses, with two fittings for the pattern and then two more once the material has been cut out. For women who want a totally unique outfit.

JEAN DOUCET   8, AVENUE DAUMESNIL XII – 43 43 79 84

BEHIER-GALLIC is the front for two designers: Stéphane Behier and Roland le Gallic who have relaunched the concept of the small couture fashion house. They show about 15 different designs to selected guests three times a week. The customers order the prototype of their choice and then, after a rough cut and two fittings, they end up with a made-to-measure suit or evening dress.

BEHIER-GALLIC 79, RUE DU CHERCHE-MIDI VI – 42 22 14 86

LA FEMME ÉCARLATE specializes in making up evening or cocktail dresses to measure. The customer arrives with a drawing or a photo cut out of a magazine, and has her dream outfit made up with only three fittings.

LA FEMME ÉCARLATE 42, AVENUE BOSQUET VII – 45 51 08 44

MANCINI creates shoes in half-sizes and gives quotations. You can order particular colours, heels, widths or insteps.

MANCINI 20, RUE DU BOCCADOR VIII – 47 20 18 93

CATHERINE PUGET Besides her famous wedding dresses, Catherine Puget supplies escapist fantasies with a line of summer dresses that she sells all year round. Clients come for something special. Each customer is measured carefully, can change the shape of the design to suit her own tastes and can choose the material. You might meet the Duchess of Württemberg there, since she pays a visit every time she comes to Paris.

CATHERINE PUGET 58, RUE BONAPARTE VI – 46 34 60 04

And also:

For lampshades, see the section on LAMPS.

All the Parisian stores have a department where you can have a wide variety of objects personalized.

The great jewellers of the Place Vendôme will all make up a jewelry design that you've sketched or copy one of your own jewels for you if you want to give one to your daughters, your grand-daughters or, for that matter, your daughters-in-law.

The great stationery-engravers (see the STATIONERY section) will take orders and can decorate your stationery with a sketch of your weekend cottage or your country house.

Carpets and rugs can be woven to your colour and size specifications (see the CARPETS section).

HOUSEHOLD ARTS

INTERIOR DESIGNERS

Their job description consists of having long chats with their clients, carefully inspecting the flats or houses that they're going to decorate and calmly thinking over proposals. Another aspect of their work is the continual search for material, wallpaper, carpets, furniture and tasteful pieces of art, which some even design themselves as well, and which they may sell separately in shops of their own. They hold these shops dear as brainstorming centres, places to network and priceless showcases.

LAURE WELFLING studied fine art and did the textile designs for the top Parisian couturiers before starting her own interior design business in 1980. She is an expert in trompe-l'oeil and will make any furniture you like to order. She works superbly in wrought iron in a Baroque or geometric spirit, or even imitating passementerie. Her particular talent is a daring blend of colour and material, which she displays in the windows of her ochre and black shop, adding some wonderful piece she's picked up somewhere on her travels.

♡ **LAURE WELFLING   30, RUE JACOB VI – 43 25 17 03**

YVES ET MICHELLE HALARD opened their first shop 40 years ago in the Faubourg Saint-Honoré. They now have a shop in the Boulevard Saint-Germain which is dominated by their sofas and armchairs, which are upholstered by Michelle and designed for Lauer, the publisher, and the look is finished off with a particularly noteworthy line of furniture that they call 'Les Petits'. A doting grandmother, Michelle Halard also finds the time to design sheets, tablecloths, silverware for Plasait and glasses for Quartz and Sèvres. She also frequently displays the work of other young designers in whom she has faith, and she never makes mistakes about that sort of thing.

♡ **YVES ET MICHELLE HALARD**   252 BIS, BOULEVARD SAINT-GERMAIN
VII – 42 22 60 50

CHRISTIAN BENAIS is multi-talented. He started out illustrating women's magazines and then became a men's fashion stylist (for Lanvin and Dior) before launching a brilliant career as an interior designer and an upholstery-textile designer (for Chotard and Brochier). His shop, which is in the 16th arrondissement, gathers together all his 'little finds' and he has a particular thing about the 19th century and about Italy, from where he imports upmarket household linen from a firm called 'Jesurum'.

♡ **CHRISTIAN BENAIS**   18, RUE CORTAMBERT XVI – 45 03 15 55

FIRST TIME is the shopfront for all the designs of the handsome Didier Gomez, the director of the Yves Saint Laurent shops all over the world. For a number of years now, he's been designing perfect sofas, chairs and tables, which he displays in this enormous shop.

FIRST TIME   27, RUE MAZARINE VI – 43 25 55 00

ÉTAMINE is the kingdom of Francine Royneau who has gathered all her own designs as well as everything else she likes in one large shop on two levels. Wallpaper and fabrics are in the basement, furniture and decorative pieces on the ground floor. The window displays are so perfectly thought out that people sometimes buy them straight off, just as they are.

ÉTAMINE   63, RUE DU BAC VII – 42 22 03 16

NOBLESSE OBLIGE was named as a tribute to Alec Guinness by the designer Catherine Colé, who thought the famous film title was an apt one for her line of business – in which you are constantly forced to take on new roles. The ambience is very 'New England' and, in the shop, you will find pretty furniture that she designs or has updated, and linen, hemp and Tuscan cotton fabrics.

NOBLESSE OBLIGE   27 BIS, RUE DE BELLECHASSE VII – 45 55 20 43

DAVID HICKS is the best known of the English designers. His Parisian offshoot, which was opened in 1973, is run by Christian Badin and Barbara Wirth, who decorate their clients' homes in the same spirit as their famous mentor and share out the work among themselves according to individual taste and talent. Christian Badin designs some of the fabrics and furniture with a rather contemporary feel, while Barbara Wirth selects the objets d'art and the rest of the furniture, which she sometimes has copied when the pieces are old, as, for example, she did with the perfect, classic, brass reading-lamp that customers have been fighting over for years.

DAVID HICKS   12, RUE DE TOURNON VI – 43 26 00 67

CHRISTIAN LIAIGRE is a horse-riding enthusiast and designs wonderful leather furniture, which is as perfectly built as the most beautiful of saddles. His design is bright and strong, just like his shop.

CHRISTIAN LIAIGRE   122, RUE DE GRENELLE VII – 45 55 16 42

And also:

JOYCE PONS DE VIER   64, GALERIE VIVIENNE II – 42 96 32 18
FRÉDÉRIC MÉCHICHE   4, RUE DE THORIGNY III – 42 78 78 28
ARCASA   37, RUE GAMBETTA 92100 BOULOGNE – 46 05 55 99

THE GOOD OLD DAYS

Their window displays are magnetic, you are drawn to them and, then, you just have to go inside. Once you are inside you feel good, as if you're ten again, surrounded by those hundred and one familiar objects that were always there at your grandma's house when you were a child. You will also be drawn to the shops by your sense of the aesthetic, for the delight of hearing the tales of the women who 'hustled' in these long-lost goods and to share in the artistry of people who know how to manufacture objects using traditional techniques.

AU FOND DE LA COUR In season they have white hydrangeas and, all year round, they have Marie-Laure de l'Ecotais's cane and bamboo furniture. The kind of thing they had in winter gardens at the turn of the century and which she's brought back into fashion for Parisian drawing-rooms as well as for country houses. She also sells metalware and pottery in the shape of birds and flowers, and shellfish sculptures. It's sheer poetry.

♡ AU FOND DE LA COUR   49, RUE DE SEINE VI – 43 25 81 89

À LA BONNE RENOMMÉE opened amid the antique panelling of an old hardware shop in the Marais district and in a workshop in Saint-Germain-des-Prés. Catherine Legrand and Elisabeth Gratacap sew their wonderful patchwork with its braiding and its ribbons, imaginatively intertwined with delightful fabrics to make bedspreads, peasant tops, hippy skirts, circular purses, tablecloths and berets. The touch of Titania.

♡ À LA BONNE RENOMMÉE   26, RUE VIEILLE-DU-TEMPLE IV – 42 72 03 86; 1, RUE JACOB   VI – 46 33 90 67

LA GALERIE DU PASSAGE shelters the 'findings' of Pierre Passebon. An ex-publisher, his passion for 19th-century literature has led him to the design of the period. From the Drouot district and the flea market, excursions to the countryside and trips abroad, he comes back laden with furniture and precious goods which the greatest of interior designers all turn up to buy from him. He has just opened a shop in the delightful Véro-Dodat shopping gallery, near the Palais-Royal, which contains a daring blend of wares.

♡ LA GALERIE DU PASSAGE 20–22, GALERIE VÉRO-DODAT I – 42 36 01 13

DIPTYQUE For the last 30 years all the sophisticated Paris intellectuals have been buying things at this shop, in which Desmond Knox-Leet and Yves Coueslant sell fabulous scented candles (in 32 different odours), eaux-de-toilette and pâte-de-verre necklaces. It's a very special place.

♡ DIPTYQUE   34, BOULEVARD SAINT-GERMAIN V – 43 26 45 27

LES PUCES DU CHÂTEAU aim to sell goods from the 30s, 40s and 50s, including artwork and small items of furniture at prices that are still reasonable. They have a pretty selection of light-fittings.

LES PUCES DU CHÂTEAU   125, RUE DU CHÂTEAU XIV – 43 20 49 89

TINKER TAILOR Mary Cook, a second-hand furniture dealer from Lincolnshire, used to sing this nursery rhyme as she travelled round her native country picking up old china and silver cutlery to take back to Paris. Teapot collectors will be simply thrilled by the selection in this tiny boutique.

TINKER TAILOR   110, RUE DES ENTREPRENEURS XVI – 48 42 46 77

JUSTE MAUVE because mauve is Anne-Marie de Ganay's favourite colour. She has done up her shop to look like her version of an English home, with chintz, floral pot-pourris, turned-wood and fabric-covered furniture, cane armchairs, cross-Channel delicacies and all backed by the solid advice of a real pro.

♡   **JUSTE MAUVE**   29, RUE GREUZE XVI – 47 27 82 31

ANNE VIGNIAL collects, piles up, hooks and hangs frames over every inch of her shop. A real goldmine for women who collect photos, portraits, drawings, watercolours and even mirrors. It's a whole new kind of patchwork. She also sells pretty furniture and objets d'art.

♡   **ANNE VIGNIAL**   8, RUE DE COMMAILLE VII – 42 22 44 39

ANNE GAYET thinks of her antique shop as a home. Customers like Christian Lacroix turn up regularly – and leave smiling.

ANNE GAYET   3, RUE DE LUYNES VI – 45 44 79 85

MICHEL LORENZI Just like his father and grandfather (who started in the year 1871), Michel makes 'antiques', which the current trend for the neo-classical has brought right back into fashion. The bas reliefs of fruit in white or light colours are perfect for decorating the kitchen walls in your country house.

MICHEL LORENZI   19, RUE RACINE VI – 43 26 38 68

CORINNE K is a self-taught artist who paints furniture, hidden away down a little passage. You can bring her what you will and she will restore and decorate it, however you choose, from a sophisticated floral pattern to a naive design.

CORINNE K   44–46, RUE DE L'OUEST XIV – 43 22 99 60

ÉLISABETH BUSSON copies furniture and objets d'art with a gentle sheen. There are little grandma chairs, hand-painted crockery and toile de Jouy cushions.

ÉLISABETH BUSSON   20, PLACE DE LA MADELEINE VIII – 42 65 24 06

À L'ÉPI D'OR They will repair or replace the wonderful bathroom accessories that were once only found in palatial surroundings.

À L'ÉPI D'OR   17, RUE DES BERNARDINS V – 46 33 08 47

SEMAINE sells a happy mixture of Madame Petit's 'little finds' and the creations of her son Patrice Collet: pleated lampshades, cushioned armchairs, painted screens. You can bring your own material.

♡ ⚲   **SEMAINE**   20, RUE NICOLO XVI – 45 20 06 69

LA MAISON IVRE is a reference to a boat owned by Arthur Rimbaud, the 19th-century poet and particular favourite of Sylvine Nobécourt. She collects pottery and particularly things she finds on trips to Provence. She also sells very beautiful baskets made of coconut shell and rope, as well as the delightful varnished wood and straw furniture designed by Bruno Carles.

LA MAISON IVRE   34, AVENUE NIEL XVII — 47 66 05 72

VIVEMENT JEUDI As its name ('Lively Thursday') suggests, this shop is only open on the fourth day of the week. Dominique Bénard-Dépalle was a full-time antique-dealer and her husband, Pierre, worked in advertising. Nowadays they both scout around all over the place to fill their delightful shop with a completely different selection of items every week, a rule they stick to rigidly.

VIVEMENT JEUDI   52, RUE MOUFFETARD V (under the archway) — 43 31 44 52

The **GALERIE SAMIA SAOUMA**   has regular exhibitions of the greatest photographers, living and dead. They handle black and white with mastery and sensitivity.

♡   **GALERIE SAMIA SAOUMA**   16, RUE DES COUTURES-SAINT-GERVAIS III — 42 78 40 44

And also:

♡   **TERRITOIRE**   30, RUE BOISSY-D'ANGLAS VIII — 42 66 22 13

♡   **FORESTIER**   35, RUE DURET XVI — 45 00 08 61

LES IMPRESSIONS   29, RUE DE CONDÉ VI — 43 26 97 86

SOULEÏADO   78, RUE DE SEINE VI — 43 54 62 25

ANNICK CLAVIER   32, RUE DE VERNEUIL VII — 42 61 08 39

POIDS DE SENTEUR   8, RUE DU BOURG-TIBOURG IV — 42 77 10 02

ROBIN DES BOIS   15, RUE FERDINAND-DUVAL IV — 48 04 09 36

AU PASSÉ RETROUVÉ   30, GALERIE MONTPENSIER I — 42 96 09 45

ANNA JOLIET   9, RUE DE BEAUJOLAIS I — 42 96 55 13

♡   **GRAIN DE BEAUTÉ**   9, RUE DU CHERCHE-MIDI VI — 45 48 07 55

KIN LIOU   81, RUE DU BAC VII — 45 48 80 85

HARD, PURE, CONTEMPORARY DESIGN

There are women who never follow fashion, either in the things they wear or in the design of their houses. Women who challenge the style of the times, looking for something that will mark them out from other people. Certain designers have the same alternative ideals, which create extraordinary results but, my goodness, they're interesting! Top of the pops, no doubt, in the year 2000 and showrooms that look like something from the 22nd century. You have to have a look, even if you know you'll never buy a thing.

LA FICELLERIE Christian Astuguevieille's shop harbours furniture and objects with a story, which their inventor tells us with the aid of string and rope, hemp and cotton. In plain, painted or golden shades, these fabulous designs are veritable works of art, in limited editions or as one-offs, displayed in a beautiful, wax-coated décor that creates a very green atmosphere. The master of the house seems to be inviting you to enter the kingdom of Vertumnus. All power to the imagination!

♡ **LA FICELLERIE   42, GALERIE VIVIENNE II – 42 60 10 70**

COUR/INTÉRIEUR is seven years old. Gérard Saint-Fort Paillard designs himself – but far too rarely – and takes great interest in other designers' work: Lison de Caunes and her straw mosaics, Alexis de La Falaise and his classic furniture, François Privat, the specialist in piano stringing, Augustin Granet and his brushed-metal furniture, and not forgetting Stéphane Herbelin, Isabelle Munoz, Claire Illiouz, Monica Mariniello, who all held their first shows in his white-tiled gallery and have, subsequently, had tremendously successful careers. The charming courtesy of the owner can be experienced at his superb two-storey space at the far end of one of the courtyards in the Marais district, where you will find both a harmonious display and a superb demonstration of talent.

COUR/INTÉRIEUR   109, BOULEVARD BEAUMARCHAIS III – 42 77 33 10

EN ATTENDANT LES BARBARES welcomes the most avant-garde designers under the watchful eyes of Agnès Belbeau and Frédéric de Luca. A few years ago the movement was led by the super-talented team of Elisabeth Garouste and Mattia Bonetti, but the tribe has now expanded without ever dropping its original contributors, and now includes the work of Patrick Rétif, Eric Schmidt, Jean-Philippe Gleizes, Pascale Laffay and others, who all know how to combine both poetry and precision in a design. The eponymous barbarians continually surprise us, constantly seduce us.

♡ **EN ATTENDANT LES BARBARES   50, RUE ÉTIENNE-MARCEL II – 42 33 37 87**

VIA are the initials in French for the Association for Innovation in the Art of Furniture Design and its aim is to demonstrate the multiplicity of creative talent on the French contemporary scene. For 13 years Jean-Claude Maugirard and Aline Fouquet have been playing the matchmaker between design and industry, and the flower of French design has thus been supported, published, exhibited and even exported through this channel. The showroom in Saint-Germain-des-Prés is a superb building containing furniture and objets-d'art specially designed by Jean-Claude Maugirard himself, but also by Yamo, Abdi, Philippe Starck, Daniel Pigeon, Tom Tilleul, Garouste and Bonetti, Andrée Putman, Marc Berthier, Mounir Chaïbi, Sylvia Corrette, Jean-Pierre Caillères, and many others. VIA is a veritable treasure trove of design.

♡ **VIA   4–6–8, COUR DU COMMERCE-SAINT-ANDRÉ (130, BOULEVARD SAINT-GERMAIN) VI – 43 29 39 36**

NESTOR PERKAL is a designer and architect, both on his own account and on behalf of the stable of young designers whose work he exhibits in his gallery. Particularly stunning is the collection of contemporary silver for the dining-room, which harmonizes to perfection with the antique silverware.

NESTOR PERKAL   8, RUE DES QUATRE-FILS III – 42 77 46 80

AXIS sells objects with which you will either fall in love at first sight or which will make you fall about laughing. For 20 years Laurence Dumaine has been collecting these pieces from all over the world. One of the constant best-sellers has been a line of teacups balancing on little legs, as well as the designs of the Catalonian firm Mariscal, the Spanish firm Juma, Combas and the Di Rosa brothers. Laurence, who is a Tintin fan, has also produced carpets and crockery inspired by the designs of Hergé, Tintin's creator. He is a highly imaginative fellow.

AXIS 18, RUE GUÉNÉGAUD VI – 43 29 66 23; 13, RUE DE CHARONNE XI – 48 06 79 10

JÉRÔME SEGUIN has covered the length and breadth of Indonesia over the years and now imports for other people the kind of fabulous objects with which he has decorated his own flat. There are enormous batik urns, gigantic conch shells, terracotta water jars, roughly hewn pieces of wooden furniture, branches in strange warped shapes, dugout canoes. Souvenirs of a journey that most people will never make themselves.

JÉRÔME SEGUIN 13, RUE TITON XI – 43 48 05 10

GLADYS MOUGIN says that her 'raison d'être' is to be an agent for contemporary artists. In order to fulfil her aim, she has opened a very beautiful gallery-showroom and exhibits one-off pieces. Her protégés are more than talented and include André Dubreuil, Christian Astuguevieille, Tom Dixon, Paul Belvoir. They work in iron, bronze and silver, creating designs that are both astonishing, and yet at the same time poetic.

GLADYS MOUGIN, ART DÉCORATIF 30, RUE DE LILLE VII – 40 20 08 33

ARTELANO initially imported Italian designs from the 70s, then Samuel Coriat began to manufacture the designs of his compatriots, including the work of Marie-Christine Dorner, the Pagnon-Pelhaître partnership, Pascal Mourgue, Olivier Gagnères and Gérard Van den Berg. This year he has shown the perfect furniture designs of Richard Peduzzi and Michelle Halard's tables. Precision rules Samuel Coriat's choices and rightly so.

♡ **ARTELANO** 4, RUE SCHOELCHER XIV – 43 22 48 01

ÉCART ought to have taken the name of its founder, Andrée Putman. The modesty of this grand old lady of the design world is only equalled by her prodigious talent. She reissues the designs of Mallet-Stevens and Eileen Gray but she also designs her own furniture. One of her most recent creations for a museum in Bordeaux is a teak, high-backed bench which is now available to the general public. An interesting advance, moving between series production and one-offs, but always with the purity of line characteristic of her style.

ÉCART 111, RUE SAINT-ANTOINE IV – 42 78 79 11

NAÏADE belongs to the fashion designer Irié, who has a passion for marble, alabaster and glass and who designs a whole range of household objects in these materials: vases, candlesticks and little dishes. If the shop is closed, go across the road to the Irié boutique and ask for the key. You'll have a good time looking at the clothes in the boutique, in any event.

NAÏADE   9, RUE DU PRÉ-AUX-CLERCS VII – 42 61 18 28

GALERIE DIFFÉRENCES is owned by Ulle and Jean-Pierre Lorence, who know how to dig out great, undiscovered talent. Yamo, Marco de Gueltz and Carole Jouffroy were all unknowns when they exhibited at this enormous showroom in the Marais district. Now fame has caught up with them all.

GALERIE DIFFÉRENCES   11, RUE DU ROI-DORÉ III – 48 87 38 13

HILTON McCONNICO,   the exquisite moustachioed poet born in Memphis (Tennessee), has brought together all his creations within a turquoise décor beneath a domed ceiling ornamented with gold leaf. Objects and furniture are dotted with leaves, cactus, kiwis, cats or lobsters. Makers include Daum, Kotska, Drimmer, Toulemonde-Bochart and Point à la Ligne. Everywhere humour and colour. Adorable.

♡   **HILTON McCONNICO   28, RUE MADAME VI – 42 84 32 22**

ARTISTES ET MODÈLES copies pieces of furniture designed in the 20s and manufactures the designs of Jean-Claude Maugirard and those of his daughter, Charlotte, who transforms pots and pans into candlesticks and light-fittings. They also sell the work of others on the cutting edge of design, including Tom Tilleul and Abdi.

♡   **ARTISTES ET MODÈLES   1, RUE CHRISTINE VI – 46 33 83 20**

NÉOTU Pierre Staudenmayer's gallery unveils the future stars of the design world. We are already indebted to him for discovering Garouste and Bonetti, Martin Szekely and, more recently, Olivier Vedrene. What's more, the directors of the French pavilion at Seville's Expo '92 entrusted him with the design of the showcase shopfront. He engaged 22 of his designer pals to assist him in the creation of a Gallic-Hispanic style with a contemporary feel to it.

♡   **NÉOTU   25, RUE DU RENARD IV – 42 78 96 97**

CHAUMETTE ET POIRIER Their first names are Marie and Patrick and they are two interior architects who work in wool, cotton, silk and linen to create geometric motifs with which they decorate screens, blankets, cushions and household linen. It is all terribly sophisticated stuff.

CHAUMETTE ET POIRIER   68, RUE VIEILLE-DU-TEMPLE III – 42 71 04 33

PERSONA Arlette Pérez's shop gathers together the furniture of very well-known designers like Oscar Tusquets, Gino Brini and Ettore Sottsass and the glassware of Boris Sipek. These are objects with which you will fall head-over-heels in love and they'll never go out of fashion.

PERSONA   47, RUE DE L'UNIVERSITÉ VII – 45 48 85 83

MURMURES gathers together the remarkable selection of furniture and contemporary pieces that Danièle Feigenbaum, a former newspaper researcher, has picked up at furniture show-rooms. This includes the work of Gilles Derain, Pascal Mourgue and copies of the work of Ecart International, Tebong and Transfert. An unclassical sale format in a very 'bon chic, bon genre' (the Paris equivalent of the Sloane Ranger) district.

MURMURES   158, RUE DE COURCELLES XVII – 42 67 07 09

And also:

AVANT-SCÈNE   4, PLACE DE L'ODÉON VI – 46 33 12 40

DUO SUR CANAPÉ   3, RUE DE TURBIGO I – 42 33 37 12

ÉDIFICE   27 BIS, BOULEVARD RASPAIL VII – 45 48 54 60

M.F.I.   55, RUE DE LA GLACIÈRE XIII – 43 36 26 20

SENTOU   GALERIE   18–24, RUE DU PONT-LOUIS-PHILIPPE IV – 42 71 00 01

ASPHALTE   35, RUE JUSSIEU V – 43 29 99 59

DIAGONALE INDIGO   52, RUE DES MARTYRS IX – 48 78 75 95

ABSOLUTE   22, RUE DES SAINTS-PÈRES VII – 42 96 18 03

Addresses at which to find the truly surprising piece of work:

BAÏKAL looks on to the enormous public garden that now stands where the Ménilmontant abattoirs used to be. Its owners, Thierry de La Salmonière and Michel Monlaü, criss-cross the United States to bring back something unexpected and different, and the history of which they will recount with great panache. They sell birdcages from New England and knives made of fossilized stone, along with Zuñi fetishes made of quartz and other gemstones, found in the Indian reserves of Utah and Nevada. This is an original and truly charming selection.

♡ ♧   **BAÏKAL   15, RUE LACHARRIÈRE XI – 43 06 00 37**

PYRAMIDE moved to La Grande-Motte before becoming a big hit with everyone in Paris. Martial Pons and Roger Sarrailh sell a humorous mixture of items that they find in 'gift shops' around the world, which might be for the home, for the office, for the garden or for children.

PYRAMIDE   97, RUE DE COURCELLES XVII – 46 22 14 36

LA CHAISE LONGUE has a selection of 'funny' decorative pieces as well as copies of household objects from the 30s through to the 50s.

**LA CHAISE LONGUE   20, RUE DES FRANCS-BOURGEOIS III – 48 04 36 37;
30, RUE CROIX-DES-PETITS-CHAMPS I – 42 96 32 14**

TOBIA specializes in avant-garde designers like Sabine Charoy and Ronald Cecil Sportes and contemporary designers like Jean Luce who all concentrate on accessories and household objects like light-fittings, bathroom linen, crockery and small pieces of furniture.

TOBIA   71, BOULEVARD RASPAIL VI – 45 49 33 05

And also:

♡ **L'ENTREPÔT   50, RUE DE PASSY XVI – 45 25 64 17**
PYLÔNES   7, RUE TARDIEU XVIII – 46 06 37 00

WOMAN'S WORK

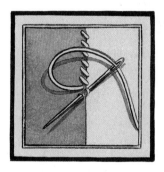

There are women who can barely manage to sew on a button – although this particular act can make all the difference to the look of a suit. There are women who collect pretty ribbons to tie in their hair or round their waists. There are also women who enjoy working with a needle, embroideresses and seamstresses. Two famous novelists, Régine Desforges and Geneviève Dormann, have both written an entire best-seller about their communal consuming passion for petit point stitching. And The Encyclopaedia of Women's Work *(L'Encyclopédie des ouvrages de dames), written in the 19th century by Thérèse de Dillmont, is regularly reprinted.*

LA DROGUERIE is heaven for pearls, buttons, ribbons and lace. Anne Laguillaumie was one of the pioneers of the Les Halles shopping centre. Now permanently swamped by girls in

mini-skirts and trendy young things, her shop has doubled in
size over the last 15 years and is now a real Ali Baba's cave.

♡ **LA DROGUERIE** 9, RUE DU JOUR I – 45 08 93 27

MOKUBA is a considerable Japanese company specializing in
selling ribbons to Parisian women with 22,000 different types in
stock including braids and trimmings. They have spotted ribbons
and tartan ribbons, stripes and gathers, pleats and prints,
colour-contrasts and moiré, embossed, seersucker, lace and
patterned. It's all enough to do your head in, as will the prices!

MOKUBA 18, RUE MONTMARTRE I – 45 08 80 02

ALICE IN RIBBONLAND displays kilometres of ribbon
draped from railings. They come in all sizes and colours and
some women use them for weaving delightful cushions.

ALICE IN RIBBONLAND 1, COUR DU COMMERCE-SAINT-ANDRÉ VI –
43 26 19 65

IRIS is the Parisian outlet for a Japanese company that makes 5
million buttons a day! In a wooden décor, 900 drawers open to
reveal buttons made of mother-of-pearl, horn, leather, pearl,
china, plastic, gilt or silver-plate. They also sell gemstones in
different colours, in enamel, engraved and printed. An incredible choice with a wide price range.

IRIS 350, RUE SAINT-HONORÉ I – 42 61 53 75

LOGOBROD will undertake orders in a vast range of colours.
They will machine-embroider your initials, coats-of-arms,
crowns, flowers, horsemen and golfers, so necessary on sheets,
tablecloths, pillowcases, sweaters and T-shirts or whatever you
happen to bring in. It takes about a week.

LOGOBROD 61, RUE DE PONTHIEU VIII – 43 59 86 41

LE COMPTOIR DES OUVRAGES This is the world of two
experts, Laurence Roque and Monique Lyonnet, who design
delightful tablecloths, sheets, alphabet samplers, towels, and so
on, and who sell the kits for you to make them yourself, whether
you are a beginner or a real expert. You will also find a vast range
of specialist materials that allow you to count the stitches on
canvas, cottons and wools. And there is also a good reference
section. In the basement of their shop, they sell very beautiful
linen embroidered in Brazil. They also give courses for those who
haven't yet quite mastered the art.

♡ **LE COMPTOIR DES OUVRAGES** 69, RUE SAINT-MARTIN IV –
42 72 22 12

CLAUDINE BRUNET designs tapestry frames with old and
contemporary motifs. A passionate believer in her art, she will
dispense good advice to all and sundry, create a design for you

with an estimate of the cost and she will also reproduce any design you bring to the shop in the dimensions you specify.
CLAUDINE BRUNET   128, GALERIE DE VALOIS I – 42 61 44 41

CASA LOPEZ This carpet dealer also sells very pretty cushion kits which come in petit point or in a style known as 'Bargello'. You can embroider flower baskets, Chinese vases, playing cards, little dogs, nests, and so on. A particular joy is the 'footstool' kit that comes complete with the necessary material and wool.
♡   **CASA LOPEZ   32–36, GALERIE VIVIENNE II – 42 60 46 85**

LE BONHEUR DES DAMES or 'the happiness of women', as this shop is called, consists, according to the owners of this charming place, in using a needle. There are alphabet samplers and wreaths of fruit and flowers that come in a variety of soft colours, and an avalanche of needlepoint kits.
LE BONHEUR DES DAMES   8, PASSAGE VERDEAU IX – 45 23 06 11

VOISINE The owners are also tapestry and embroidery enthusiasts, and they import Elizabeth Bradley's superb 'Victorian Collection' kits from England. She has, incidentally, also written an excellent book on the subject. Once you've finished you can frame it, make it into a cushion cover or even a rug or a doormat. The good advice comes free.
VOISINE   12, RUE DE L'ÉGLISE   92200   NEUILLY-SUR-SEINE – 46 37 54 60

L'ATELIER D'ANAÏS is now 35 years old and, to celebrate, Anne-Marie Giffard has written a book called *Le Petit Point*, published by Editions Jean-Claude Lattès. 'Tapestry shouldn't be a form of punishment but of relaxation', she says.
L'ATELIER D'ANAÏS   23, RUE JACOB VI – 43 26 68 00

LES PATCHWORKS DU ROUVRAY 20 years ago, this shop and its founder, Diane de Obaldia, introduced Parisian women to these bedcovers, made from small scraps of material by the first North American immigrants. In the shop you can admire fabulous old examples or you can buy the necessary equipment to make your own. They also sell books on the subject and you can take classes there.
LES PATCHWORKS DU ROUVRAY   1, RUE FRÉDÉRIC-SAUTON V – 43 25 00 45

MALBRANCHE designs beautiful hand-embroidered household linen. For the most gifted seamstresses they sell patterns that you can take home and embroider yourself. For beginners or women who want to improve their skills, they give embroidery lessons: painting with a needle.
MALBRANCHE   17, RUE DROUOT IX – 47 70 03 77

KELL'S CORNER has now reopened. A delightful American lady called Kell Kelly introduced the art of petit point to the Parisians (and to some 'beautiful people' like Hubert de Givenchy) some years ago. They shed tears the day she left. She also used to design rather lyrical tapestry frames. Her partner, Marie-Françoise d'Amiens, has taken up the torch. She creates all the patterns and also gives courses for beginners as well as for experts.

♡   KELL'S CORNER   82, RUE DU CHERCHE-MIDI VI – 45 48 36 12

And also:

The HABERDASHERY departments of BON MARCHÉ and SAMARITAINE

MARIETTE   15, RUE DES BELLES-FEUILLES XVI – 45 53 02 61

LE GANT D'OR   118, AVENUE VICTOR-HUGO XVI – 47 27 06 46

IMAGINE   40, RUE DE PONTHIEU VIII – 42 25 10 02

TAPISSERIES DE LA BÛCHERIE   7, RUE DE LA BÛCHERIE V – 40 46 87 69

LA BOUTIQUE DES OUVRAGES   72, RUE ROCHECHOUART IX – 48 74 48 57

BROD'LINE   71, RUE FONDARY XV – 45 77 18 53

MODES ET TRAVAUX   10, RUE DE LA PÉPINIÈRE VIII – 46 62 20 50

LOGNON   33, RUE BOISSY-D'ANGLAS VIII – 42 62 25 33

LA PERLOTTE   12, RUE VAVIN VI – 43 54 87 09

AU BON GOÛT   1, RUE GUICHARD XVI – 42 88 61 68

IMAGINE-YVINE   87 TER, RUE DIDOT XIV – 40 44 98 77

By mail order: very beautiful tapestry kits designed by

HERVÉ LELONG   43, RUE DE CHÂTEAUDUN 28000 CHARTRES – (16) 37 21 01 04

HOUSEHOLD BASICS

SOFAS, ARMCHAIRS AND BOOKCASES

One sits down to relax, to chat, to have tea, to write, to read, to gaze out of the window, to play cards or to sew. An awesome range of activities for which a comfortable seat is indispensable. After years of sofas that look pathetic and feel like a pile of stacked-up pillows, it is high time to return to solid frames and reassuring structures, which are both aesthetic and comfortable.

YVES HALARD is the top Parisian specialist in sofas and armchairs, made up, if you so desire, in very beautiful fabrics designed by Michelle Halard. She was the first to relaunch loose covers, which she makes in very haute couture styles. The collection they call 'Les Petits' is particularly alluring since all the chairs are miniatures. They also sell the perfect pouffe and the perfect stool. This is the address with a capital 'A'.
♡ **YVES HALARD 252 BIS, BOULEVARD SAINT-GERMAIN VII –** 42 22 60 50

ROCHE-BOBOIS has been an institution in the world of furniture for more than 30 years. The brothers, Roche and Chouchan, have been using the chair-designing talents of Hans Hopfer for many years now and he firmly beliefs that comfort is of the essence. The firm's strong point is the leather sofas which make up 75% of their total sales. If you're after a more old-fashioned feel, they have the chaise longue design they call 'Liseuse' ('reader'), which forms part of the Provincial range. You can also buy cane or wooden furniture.
♡ **ROCHE-BOBOIS 207, BOULEVARD SAINT-GERMAIN VII –** 45 48 07 61

FIRST TIME harbours the very beautiful chairs designed by Didier Gomez. Unusual wood and sophisticated materials combine harmoniously with comfortable designs. From this year's collection, we particularly liked a chaise longue which was sophistication itself.

♡   **FIRST TIME   27, RUE MAZARINE VI – 43 25 55 00**

ÉTAT DE SIÈGE exhibits more than 200 designs from Louis XIII (17th century) to the year 2000. For all locations and all styles.

ÉTAT DE SIÈGE   1, QUAI DE CONTI VI – 43 29 31 60; 94, RUE DU BAC VII – 45 49 10 20

COLLECTANIA sells furniture designed by top names over almost 1,500 square metres of shopfloor. Their best-seller is a leather sofa designed by De Sede.

COLLECTANIA   168, RUE DE RIVOLI I – 42 97 01 30

ROSET has been working in wood for 130 years and was converted to the contemporary chair more than a quarter of a century ago when it formed a partnership with another firm, CINNA, and began to select French and foreign designers. The 'Saint-James' armchair designed by Jean Nouvel is particularly ethereal in conception, since its back and armrests look as if they are perching on the tubular frame.

ROSET   5, AVENUE MATIGNON VIII – 42 25 94 19

CINNA 134, BOULEVARD DIDEROT XII – 43 42 12 66

ÉDIFICE furnishes the homes of the enthusiasts of contemporary style, who all adored Philippe Starck's 'Costes' chair and made it a best-seller.

ÉDIFICE   27 BIS, BOULEVARD RASPAIL VII – 45 48 53 60

CAP offers sofas at very reasonable prices that simply have to be looked at if you're thinking about buying one.

CAP   1, AVENUE DE FRIEDLAND VIII – 42 89 15 23

PERSONA and its director, Arlette Perez, have always dared to offer the work of designers at the cutting edge of style: Philippe Starck, Oscar Tusquets and Borek Sipek. The best-selling item in this pretty shop in the 7th arrondissement is a large sofa-stool designed by Zanotta.

PERSONA   47, RUE DE L'UNIVERSITÉ VII – 45 48 85 83

ARREDAMENTO likes the Italian version of alternative style. The 'Tuscana' chair designed by Saporiti is perfect for bridge-players, since it supports the back at all points with its curved, wooden backrest. They also sell the 'Pigalle' chair designed by Pier Angelo Casaramia which comes in a rainbow of bright Alcantara colours.

ARREDAMENTO   18, QUAI DES CÉLESTINS IV – 42 74 33 14

UN FAUTEUIL POUR DEUX will deliver the chairs to your home before you've paid for them. Then you can try them out for comfort and to see the all-round effect, which is one hell of a service.

UN FAUTEUIL POUR DEUX   9, RUE CORNEILLE VI – 43 29 74 32

PACIFIC COMPAGNIE grasped the idea that its customers often received unexpected guests and thus became one of the market-leaders in sofa-beds, now selling over 30 models. As a general guideline, prices start at 3,600 francs. They are made in the best-quality fabrics (often with detachable covers) and there are matching armchairs and pouffes. You can even have curtain lining made up in the same material, all according to individual choice.

PACIFIC COMPAGNIE   63–65, AVENUE DE LA BOURDONNAIS VII – 47 53 76 77; 18, AVENUE MAC-MAHON XVII – 47 64 43 84

M.D. has only recently completed its selection of furniture, which is made up exclusively of sofas and armchairs. Solid wooden frames and cushions with washable leather covers in 38 colours or in Alcantara (50 different shades).

M.D.   85, RUE DU BAC VII – 45 44 38 84; 254, BOULEVARD SAINT-GERMAIN VII – 42 22 43 33

ÉQUATION sells the work of the Designer of the Year of 1992, Kristian Gavoille, and various other designers. Classics like the 'Coventry' and 'Cardiff' sofas stand alongside the old-fashioned 'Cottage' bergère which is decorated with piping. They also sell the 'Baccara', which is very 20s, while 'Icare' and 'Hermès' are made of leather and 'Kouros' is covered in a kilim fabric which is particularly fashionable now.

ÉQUATION   12, RUE DU QUATRE-SEPTEMBRE   92130   ISSY-LES-MOULINEAUX – 40 95 13 59

MANUEL CANOVAS now designs a small collection of sofas, of which he always has two on show in his beautiful shop. He covers these, naturally, in his own wonderful prints.

MANUEL CANOVAS   30, AVENUE GEORGE-V VIII – 49 52 00 36

INTERDÉCOR is a specialist in reasonably priced leather sofas. Removable covers, sofa-beds, they're all here. You can choose the colour and you have to wait around four to five weeks. Watch out though, because they aren't always open and it's best to telephone before you pay a visit.

♙ INTERDÉCOR   93, RUE DE STALINGRAD   93100   MONTREUIL – 48 59 09 19

JEAN-CLAUDE THÉODORE is an impressive weaver who can make up any pattern from the simplest to the most complicated. Top Parisian designers constantly make use of his talents.

JEAN-CLAUDE THÉODORE   8, RUE DE PONTOISE V – 46 33 00 08

DESIO manufacture classic, comfortable sofas, stuffed with Bultex, and, of course, all the covers are removable. All the cushions are reversible since they use double-sided fabrics, or you can supply your own fabric, if you so desire.

DESIO   42, RUE POUSSIN XVI – 40 71 99 93

L'UNIVERS DU CUIR makes every single one of its 75 sofas with matching armchairs, in ten different colours, dyed with aniline. They have every imaginable style and you must surely find the one you're looking for. The prices are reasonable.

♠ L'UNIVERS DU CUIR   46, RUE DU FAUBOURG SAINT-ANTOINE XII – 43 43 87 60

And also:

VIA   4–6–8, COUR DU COMMERCE-SAINT-ANDRÉ VI – 43 29 39 36

COUR/INTÉRIEUR   109, BOULEVARD BEAUMARCHAIS III – 42 77 33 10

NÉOTU   25, RUE DU RENARD IV – 42 78 96 97

COSTE   11, RUE DE RIVOLI I – 42 78 54 34

POLTRONA FRAU   242 BIS, BOULEVARD SAINT-GERMAIN VII – 42 22 74 49

HUGUES CHEVALIER   17, RUE DU CHERCHE-MIDI VI – 45 48 69 55

ACTUA   42, BOULEVARD SAINT-GERMAIN VI – 43 54 96 90

CASSINA   168, RUE DU FAUBOURG SAINT-HONORÉ VIII – 45 63 91 01

GUERMONPREZ   18–20, BOULEVARD EDGAR-QUINET XIV – 43 20 87 79

MARWAY   11, RUE DU BAC   VII – 42 61 22 28

MEUBLES ET FONCTIONS   135, BOULEVARD RASPAIL XIV – 45 48 55 74

STEINER   67, BOULEVARD RASPAIL VI – 45 48 94 61

Bookcases

Even if you're not a literary critic with your living-space literally taken over by books, as a civilized member of society you will inevitably wake up one day to find piles of jumbled books all over your flat. The only thing for it is to reorganize your whole shelving system and to call in an expert. Besides, with the dawning of the age of the compact-disc and the video-cassette, new pieces of furniture specially designed for storing these items have become essential lifestyle objects.

ROCHE-BOBOIS sells component units, which are often designed by Luigi Gorgoni, the Italian designer. Two recent designs are units in white-leaded veneer, which come in a natural wood or slate-coloured, and, for CDs and videos, a small revolving unit made of dyed, synthesized resin. This firm, which is now 30 years old, offers a wide variety of furniture: contemporary, provincial, colonial and British, but all of which include sensible shelving systems for books.

ROCHE-BOBOIS   207, BOULEVARD SAINT-GERMAIN VII – 45 48 07 61

ARTELANO now sells a well-balanced blend of the hyper-modern and the designers more tuned-in to the quality of life. So, you will find that the 'Colonnades' display units designed by Pascal Mourgue with two long dyed-mahogany legs supporting two large panes of glass can be combined with the theatre designer Richard Peduzzi's intelligently designed shelving units for CDs and videos.

ARTELANO   4, RUE SCHOELCHER XIV – 43 22 74 91

LE BIHAN has had a shop in the Faubourg Saint-Antoine for a quarter of a century. In his four floors of space, Roger Le Bihan blends the designs of the great European names with his own. His best-selling item is a shelving system which Jacques Gourvenec designed for him.

LE BIHAN   25, RUE DU FAUBOURG SAINT-ANTOINE XI – 43 43 06 75

M.D. is the absolute expert in component unit furniture. It is frankly impossible to describe the hundreds of different ways to put together the bookcases and the shelving units, so you had better just go and see for yourself. Our favourite is made up of polished cherrywood panelling and is called the 'Littera'. The prices are calculated according to the required lengths of shelving.

M.D.   85, RUE DU BAC VII – 45 44 38 84; 254, BOULEVARD SAINT-GERMAIN VII – 42 22 43 33

MARAIS INTERNATIONAL manufactures numerous pieces

Map labels:

R. DU TEMPLE
R. des QUATREFILS
ARCHIVES
ARCHIVES NATIONALES
TOURELLE CHARLOT
SOURDIÈRE
RUE
R. de POITOU
3
R. du TEMPLE
DU TEMPLE
RUE
ROI DORÉ
R. St CLAUDE
DE TORENNE
ANASTASE
PLACE de THORIGNY
R. des BL. MANTEAUX
RUE DES
VIEILLE
BARBETTE
R. PARC ROYAL
R. St GILLES
St CROIX BRETONNERIE
MOUSSY
R. des ROSIERS
FRANCS BOURGEOIS
MUSÉE CARNAVALET
SÉVIGNÉ
RUE DE TORENNE
Bg TROURG
R. du ROI DE SICILE
ÉCOUFFES
4
RUE de
R. PAV
MALHER
R. de TURENNE
RIVOLI
St PAUL
PLACE DES VOSGES
RUE St ANT
RUE St ANT
BRAUL

QUARTIER
LE MARAIS IVe

Azzedine Alaïa
6, Rue de Moussy IVe

Popy Moreni
13, Place des Vosges IVe

Issey Miyaké
3, Place des Vosges IVe

L'Art du Bureau
47, Rue des Francs-Bourgeois IVe

Le Bihan
25 Rue du Fbg Saint-Antoine XIe

A la bonne Renommée
26, Rue Vieille-du-Temple IVe

Mariage Frères
30, Rue du Bourg-Tibourg IVe

of plexiglass furniture, which are now very well-known, but they also sell furniture in other materials, including the combined video-CD unit in dyed and polished 'premium', designed by Pierre Vandel. Recently, Bernard and Xavier Bertet have become the distributors of the 'Efa', a modular furniture range, which is good to bear in mind.

MARAIS INTERNATIONAL at **CASA DESIGN**   16, AVENUE VICTORIA I – 42 33 84 84

LUNDIA is an expert in spruce. The bookcases can be sanded, varnished or dyed, which will enable you to install them anywhere in your house.

♧ **LUNDIA**   6, RUE DE FOURCROY XVII – 42 67 62 42

INITIAL   Paul Michel's shop sells the work of young designers. At the last Annual Paris Furniture Exhibition, they exhibited a tall column called the 'Big Band', made of glossy pearwood and matt black lacquer to hold 144 CDs. There is also a stacker containing units for hi-fi, video machine, records and cassettes. Both were designed by the Zebulon group. Torck and Noirot designed a special video unit they call 'Duke', with a variety of shelving trays made in shiny black lacquer.

INITIAL at **ADS RÉVOLUTION**   61, RUE DU FAUBOURG SAINT-ANTOINE XI – 43 47 49 50

YAMAKADO gives his designs funny names. Particularly interesting are the shelving units he calls 'Virages Dangereux' (dangerous bends) and 'l'Entrecôte', which is tall and thin and holds a variety of small objects.

YAMAKADO at **GALERIES LAFAYETTE**

MARIE-CHRISTINE DE LA ROCHEFOUCAULD is a passionate reader and started off designing for herself. Now she manufactures her designs, which often contain trompe-l'oeil effects of bound books (made in painted wood), on the uprights of her bookcases, her little staircases and her coffee tables. She also makes carpets with designs of book bindings.

MARIE-CHRISTINE FOUCAULD   16, RUE DE L'UNIVERSITÉ – 42 86 02 40

EVER WOOD makes the 'small items of furniture' intelligently designed by Catherine Painvin, in dyed or plain oak or elm. You can view them in a superb loft space.

♡ ♧ **EVER WOOD**   9, RUE DUVERGIER XIX – 40 38 42 18

And also:

VIA   4–6–8, COUR DU COMMERCE-SAINT-ANDRÉ VI – 43 29 39 36

HABITAT   35, AVENUE DE WAGRAM XVII – 47 66 25 52

The DECORATIVE ARTS departments of **GALERIES LAFAYETTE, BON MARCHÉ, PRINTEMPS** and **SAMARITAINE**

CARPETS

The first carpets were woven several thousand years before we were born, by the nomadic tribes of Central Asia, a continent which continues the tradition. Closer to home, in the year 1443, one Jean Gobelin, a dyer who specialized in the colour scarlet, set up business at Saint-Marcel, near Paris. Later, Henri IV and Louis XIV made the Gobelins factory carpet-weavers by appointment to the King, and with that came fame and fortune. In the 20th century, painters, architects, interior designers and fashion designers have all taken up the art of carpet design.

CASA LOPEZ Spanish and Portugese craftsmen weave from cartoons drawn by Bernard Magniant – whose wife has nick-named him Bernard the Carpet! The patterns look like off-white Irish knitted jumpers or very florally patterned ones in demi-point stitching. They also have pretty nest and vase motifs sewn in petit point, or even in ribbed wool. More recently they have produced the two-coloured, low-priced carpet and the two-coloured tasselled coconut rug. Their wool-jute combination is simply perfect and creates a very special damask effect. They also sell a selection of matching cushions which can, if you are a real expert, be bought in self-assemble kits. This is a modern, sophisticated showroom.

♡ **CASA LOPEZ 32–36, GALERIE VIVIENNE II – 42 60 46 85; 58, AVENUE PAUL-DOUMER XVI – 45 03 43 75; 27, BOULEVARD RASPAIL VII – 45 48 30 97**

TOULEMONDE-BOCHART Sells both hand and machine-woven work by the great designers like Andrée Putman, Jean-Michel Wilmotte, Christian Duc, Pascal Mourgue, Didier Gomez and Hilton McConnico. Some designs have become part of the permanent exhibitions at museums like the Decorative Arts galleries in Paris and Lausanne, the Pompidou Centre, the Cooper-Hewitt in New York and the Kunstindustrimuseet in Oslo. For real fans of made-to-measure items, you can have sisal made up in your desired size and colour and then have it embroidered with a matching or contrasting edging.

♡   **TOULEMONDE-BOCHART**   10, RUE DU MAIL II – 40 26 68 83

JULES FLIPO has been one of the great specialists in rugs and carpets since 1867, and originated in the north of France. The styling department draws its inspiration from designs they have collected over many years and some, like the 897 and the 1308, are best-sellers. You can also choose from among the incredible range of stock, and have a particular border or motif incorporated to create a carpet that is almost made-to-measure. Designers like Patrick Frey, Manuel Canovas and Andrée Putman also have their drawings made up there.

JULES FLIPO   8, RUE D'ABOUKIR II – 45 08 47 64

ÉTAMINE This is a fine interior design store which of course sells carpets. Roger Oates has created superb designs for Long Métrage. Woven stripes give an effect of vertical bands in four harmonies of three colours, or of chevrons in three harmonies of four colours.

♡   **ÉTAMINE**   63, RUE DE BAC VII – 42 22 03 16

TAÏ PING CARPETS manufacture the designs of Jean-Charles de Castelbajac, Zofia Rostad and Thierry Blet. They sell the naive, colourful designs of the fashion designer and the household linen expert, or a splendid geographical map set against a deep-black background.

TAÏ PING CARPETS   30, RUE DES SAINT-PÈRES VII – 42 22 96 54

TISCA has a wonderful selection of comic cartoons woven into carpets. Naturally, they only sell limited editions of work by Moebius, Tardi, Franck Margerin and Martin Veyron, famous cartoonists one and all.

TISCA   46, RUE DE GRENELLE VII – 42 22 84 23

GÉOMÉTRIE VARIABLE sells the designs of LC Collection, which calls on the skills of, amongst others, Nemo and Gilles Derain. Very handsome, modern work.

GÉOMÉTRIE VARIABLE   28, RUE DE CHARONNE XI – 43 38 60 59

ARTCURIAL aims to publish the works of the great artists of our century. These are numbered. They do the same for the carpets, which are all made individually, by hand. They held their first collection in 1977, with a wonderful Sonia Delaunay (followed by nine others). Since that date, 15 artists have had their drawings made into carpets: Da Silva Bruhns, Piero

Dorazio, Natalia Dumitresco, Gilioli, François-Xavier Lalanne (a delightful herd of sheep), Le Parc, Matta, Meurice, Alicia Penalba (four patterns), Anne and Patrick Poirier, Rougemont, Schöffer, Valmier, Van Der Leck and Zao-Wou-Ki, whose 'Nocturne' carpet is quite marvellous. Each design is made in a limited edition of 100, and some are available in a variety of sizes. Why not walk on a work of art?

ARTCURIAL   9, AVENUE MATIGNON VIII – 42 99 16 16

ANN SHELTON GALLERY Through Elysées Editions, they produce the work of designers like Marie-Christine Dorner, Philippe Starck and Ettore Sottsass, or painters like Keith Haring and Victor Vasarely, or even an architect like Christian de Portzamparc. In some cases, the designs are only produced in very small quantities.

ANN SHELTON GALLERY   50, BOULEVARD LATOUR-MAUBOURG VII –
45 55 79 35

YVES GASTOU This gallery owner produces the work of his designer pals, who include Shuro Kuramata, André Dubreuil, Olivier Gagnère and Sylvain Dubuisson.

YVES GASTOU   162, GALERIE DE VALOIS JARDINS DE PALAIS-ROYAL
I – 42 61 88 99

SAM LAÏK also manufactures pretty dhurries in pastel colours from sketches designed by people like Mathias, Sylvia Corrette, Jean-Christophe Leclercq and Jacques Luzeau. They sell a floral-motif cashmere rug in cross-stitching and very New England-influenced lattice work.

SAM LAÏK   18, RUE YVES-TOUDIC X – 42 41 13 63

TAPIS D'AVIGNON used to have a factory in the Sorgue valley and were regularly used in churches in the 19th century. They are particularly solidly made in plain threaded or woven wool or Jacquard, and then finished by pressing, scratching and cropping the material so that it lies flat. BVT makes them in wonderful colours.

TAPIS D'AVIGNON DE BVT at ÉTAMINE 63, RUE DU BAC VII –
42 22 03 16

GALERIE CHEVALIER specializes in antique carpets, which are truly splendid.

GALERIE CHEVALIER   17, QUAI VOLTAIRE VII – 42 60 72 68

GALERIE DIURNE imports magnificent carpets from Nepal, made from hand-spun wool, which gives them their incredible colour shades: beige, white, ivory, greyish, bluish, pink, salmon and orangey.

GALERIE DIURNE   45, RUE JACOB VI – 42 60 94 11

BADIET piles up carpets from Iran, China, Pakistan and Russia, so that the shop looks like the Grand Bazaar. It requires stamina to buy something since this involves pulling each carpet out, one by one, and they normally have about 500 in stock, so that everyone is likely to find their heart's content. There are also 200 different kinds of rug, some of which come in a wide range of colours.

BADIET   94, BOULEVARD DE GRENELLE XV — 45 79 92 54

BOBIN doesn't make carpets. Come to that he doesn't sell them either. He cleans them. They'll collect them from your house and give you a quotation, which is a quite priceless service, completed by an SOS-anti-stain emergency telephone service, which can get you out of a nasty fix.

BOBIN   27, RUE DE LA VANNE 92120 MONTROUGE — 46 57 64 00

And also:

ROCHE BOBOIS, four shops in Paris, including: 207, BOULEVARD SAINT-GERMAIN VII — 45 48 07 61

HABITAT, four shops in Paris, including: 45, RUE DE RENNES VI — 45 44 68 74

LES TAPIS DE COGOLIN   3, AVENUE DE L'OPÉRA I — 42 60 61 16

JAB   155, BOULEVARD HAUSSMANN VIII — 43 59 92 50

PATRICK FREY   47, RUE DES PETITS-CHAMPS I — 42 97 44 00

JADE   71, AVENUE DES TERNES XVII — 40 55 02 19

DESCHEMAKER   22, RUE DU MAIL II — 42 33 35 80

NÉOTU   25, RUE DU RENARD IV — 42 78 91 83

NISSIM   32, RUE DU FAUBOURG SAINT-ANTOINE XII — 43 43 78 00

GALERIE ZHAOS 52, RUE DU FAUBOURG SAINT-ANTOINE XII — 43 44 28 10

CARRÉ BASTILLE 74, RUE DU FAUBOURG SAINT-ANTOINE XII — 43 45 48 86

The CARPET departments at GALERIES LAFAYETTE, BON MARCHÉ, PRINTEMPS and SAMARITAINE.

TEXTILES

Giving warmth to your walls and creating a convivial atmosphere make hangings of all kinds valuable household decorations. In the Middle Ages, tapestries were taken with households whenever they moved, from castle to manor house, and used as decoration in the large banqueting halls. Curtains were hung to make bedrooms feel a little warmer and, in summer, these were replaced by lengths of lighter fabric. This is a sophistication that some people still practise today by changing their curtains and loose covers with the onset of autumn, and then, once again, with the first days of spring.

LES IMPRESSIONS Magda d'Auzers's shop combines plain colours and sophistication. Time after time, Magda uses the fabrics of Dominique Kieffer, amongst others. Stripes and small checks are made up in plain, damask-effect material and she also has a soft spot for Anatolian kilims. As well as fabric by the metre and expert advice, she supplies finished items like cushions, little tapestry footstools and sofas.

♡ **LES IMPRESSIONS   29, RUE DE CONDÉ VI – 43 26 97 86**

MANUEL CANOVAS designs his own textiles. For the last 20 years, he has had a particular partiality for flowers. He makes an initial sketch, from something he's seen on one of his country-side excursions, and then he paints it using a wonderful range of colours. In his last January collection, he paid tribute to plain, pure colours (48 shades of a smooth, Egyptian cotton velvet, and 49 shades of silk), since he firmly believes in a return to the 'sophistication of simplicity', as he puts it. In his shop you will also find old documents, which he recolours, as well as striped fabrics and tartans. He was the first designer to make his designs up into ranges of finished products like sheets, tablecloths, crockery, bags and even nightdresses and pretty tops.

♡   **MANUEL CANOVAS**   7, PLACE DE FURSTENBERG VI – 43 25 75 98; 30, AVENUE GEORGE-V VIII – 49 52 00 36

CHOTARD ET BROCHIER   An old Lyons firm, set up in a Parisian town house formerly owned by Colbert (Louis XIV's adviser). Some years ago, Christian Benais, the designer, was engaged as the artistic director, and silk and Jacquard fabrics have become even more prominent under his guidance. You should take a look at the fabulous painted ceiling in the showroom, which is attributed to the School of Le Brun and dates from around 1650.

♡   **CHOTARD ET BROCHIER**   5, RUE DU MAIL II – 42 61 54 94

PIERRE FREY   Patrick Frey, the son of the founder, has been the director of this establishment for some years now, and claims not to be able to draw. But he does know how to uncover hidden talents, or to take very successful motifs from old cushions and lengths of forgotten curtain material found in other people's attics. On the ground-floor of his showroom in the 1st arrondissement, on both sides of an archway-entrance used by the musician Lully, you will find a shop that sells both his household linen and wares made up in his fabrics.

♡   **PIERRE FREY**   47, RUE DES PETITS-CHAMPS I – 42 97 44 00; 5, RUE JACOB VI – 46 33 73 00

SOULEÏADO   contains all the charm of both Provence and the Deméry family, who continue the tradition of the old textiles, by redyeing them and using them in every imaginable way: from curtains to pleated skirts, from crockery to braiding, via tablecloths, tiles and cardigans. They have both classic and modern designs that will never go out of fashion and will fill your days with sunshine.

♡   **SOULEÏADO**   78, RUE DE SEINE VI – 43 54 62 25

RUBELLI   Venice encountered, with its palaces and its gondolas, wreathed in damask and silk! The business, established in the Serenissima for centuries, set up a truly magnificent shop in Paris some years ago.

♡   **RUBELLI**   1, RUE DE L'ABBAYE VII – 43 54 27 77

ÉTAMINE   is directed by Francine Royneau, who adds her own textile collections to those of French designers like Garouste and Bonetti, Belgian designers like Isabelle de Borchgrave, and English ones like Tricia Guild.

♡   **ÉTAMINE**   2, RUE DE FURSTENBERG VI – 43 25 49 83

COMOGLIO   is an old textile design firm which was given a new impetus a few years ago by an antique-dealer called Philippe La Querrière, who is totally enamoured of antique textiles and collects them furiously. In his two-storey shop in the Rue Jacob you will feel as if you're in someone's house in the countryside. Saintes, Crèvecoeur, Linerolles, Bois-le-Roi and Mortagne all have a crazy charm.

COMOGLIO   22, RUE JACOB VI – 43 54 65 86

PANSU has been making textiles since the middle of the 18th century, and in 1911 Jules Pansu had a beautiful building put up in the Faubourg Poissonnière in which to house them, enhanced by a wonderful carved wooden staircase. They are specialists in Jacquard, and have kilims and Hungarian and floral designs in this fabric. Pansu also sells lamps and old-fashioned tapestries made of velvet which you can hang from your walls, and a line they call 'graded furniture', which consists of pieces of pre-cut fabric, which allow you to recover your armchairs, stools and bedheads completely.

PANSU   42, RUE DU FAUBOURG-POISSONNIÈRE X – 42 46 72 45

NOBILIS was founded in 1928 by Adolphe Halard to concentrate on textiles as well as wallpaper. It has become an institution in Rue Bonaparte which has gradually swallowed up all the other textile manufacturers in the area. There are a large number of designs, and some patterns have been selling for a long time because people just keep on asking for them! Designers like Hubert de Givenchy, Alberto Pinto and Jean-Michel Wilmotte have all worked for this old firm.

NOBILIS   38, RUE BONAPARTE VI – 43 29 21 50

And also:

♡ **YVES HALARD   252 BIS, BOULEVARD SAINT-GERMAIN VII – 42 22 60 50**

LAUER   5, AVENUE DE L'OPÉRA I – 42 60 61 16

CASAL   40, RUE DES SAINTS-PÈRES VI – 45 44 78 70

L'ABEILLE   234, RUE DU FAUBOURG SAINT-ANTOINE XII – 43 72 97 00

DOLLFUS-MIEG   3, RUE DE FURSTENBERG VI – 40 46 94 82

♡ **LELIÈVRE   13, RUE DU MAIL II – 42 61 53 03**

FARDIS   6 BIS, RUE DE L'ABBAYE VI – 43 25 73 44

♡ **BRAQUENIÉ   111, BOULEVARD BEAUMARCHAIS III – 48 04 30 03**

CHANÉE-DUCROCQ-D.L.D.   6, RUE DU MAIL II – 42 60 82 01

DESCHEMAKER   22, RUE DU MAIL II – 42 33 35 80

EDMOND PETIT   23, RUE DU MAIL II – 42 33 48 56

SAT   25–27, RUE DU MAIL II – 45 08 07 60

BOUSSAC-ROMANEX   27–29, RUE DU MAIL II – 42 21 83 00

UNION TEXTILE DE L'EST   62, RUE SAINT-LAZARE IX – 42 85 35 36

PRELLE   5, PLACE DES VICTOIRES I – 42 36 67 21

BISSON-BRUNEEL   15, RUE DU MAIL II – 42 96 87 94

♡ **HOULÈS, PASSEMENTIER   18, RUE SAINT-NICOLAS XII – 43 44 65 19**

**LA   PASSEMENTERIE   NOUVELLE   15,   RUE   ÉTIENNE-MARCEL   I –
42 36 30 01**

**CHAMBRE SYNDICALE DES TISSUS D'AMEUBLEMENT (CSTA)   35, RUE
DANIELLE-CASANOVA I – 42 86 04 05**

WALLPAPER

*A rainbow of colours, a plenitude of designs, panoramas, trompe-
l'oeil, friezes, braids and painted paper adorn walls and lay siege
to doors, run along skirting boards and cross ceilings.*

BESSON is the address for wallpaper with a capital 'A'. All
the current designs are on show in big catalogues, enough to
make your head turn, in some people's opinion. The possibilities
are endless, others reply. The assistants give excellent advice.
**BESSON   46, AVENUE MARCEAU VIII – 47 20 75 35; 18, RUE DU VIEUX-
COLOMBIER VI – 45 48 87 62; 32, RUE BONAPARTE VI – 40 51 89 64**

LES DOMINOTIERS is over 20 years old. Monique Martin, a
canny businesswoman, opened the shop in which she not only
chose a perfect selection with a modern flavour, but where she
also, very rapidly, began to produce her own designs. The shop
has maintained an expertise in panoramic patterns.
LES DOMINOTIERS   4, AVENUE DU MAINE XV – 45 48 21 41

LAURA ASHLEY For a long time now, this shop has been
selling wallpaper at very reasonable prices, in the designs that
made it famous: masses of tiny flowers and larger open blooms,
geometric and falsely plain patterns, and very pretty friezes.
♡ ♧ **LAURA   ASHLEY   261,   RUE   SAINT-HONORÉ   I – 42   86   84   13;
94, RUE DE RENNES VI – 45 48 43 89**

FARDIS now distributes, in addition to its own attractive fabrics and wallpapers, the English ranges of G.P. and J. Baker, Osborne & Little, and Nina Campbell.

FARDIS   6 BIS, RUE DE L'ABBAYE VI – 43 25 73 44

And also:

♡   **MANUEL CANOVAS   5, PLACE DE FURSTENBERG VI – 43 25 75 98**

♡   **ÉTAMINE   3, RUE JACOB VI – 43 25 70 65**

NOBILIS   29, RUE BONAPARTE VI – 43 29 21 50

♡   **SOULEÏADO   78, RUE DE SEINE VI – 43 54 15 13**

PIERRE FREY   47, RUE DES PETITS-CHAMPS I – 42 97 44 00

NOBLESSE OBLIGE   27 BIS, RUE DE BELLECHASSE VII – 45 55 20 43

HOUSEHOLD ACCESSORIES

HOUSEHOLD LINEN

'Draw, draw, draw the needle through, my girl,' goes an old French song. In olden days, nice young ladies sewed and embroidered their trousseaux during their brief adolescent years, ending up as very youthful brides. Then came Aristide Boucicaut, who realized that ladies didn't always actually enjoy sewing, and who invented the concept of the 'white sale' in 1868, in his store, Bon Marché. In January, just after the New Year celebrations. But linen is still women's business. The title 'Creator of Tex'Styles 1992' was awarded to Evelyne Julienne last year, and other designers at the top of the popularity league (some of whom don't have their own shops but design for other people) include: Primrose Bordier, Milava Riston for Anne de Solène, the embroiderer from Provence Edith Mézard, Zofia Rostad, Anaïk Descamps, Laurence Laffont, Pauline Courtois for Kachémoi, José (without the normal extra 'e' at the end of her name) Houel, Patricia Fletcher, Marianne Rachline and, last but not least, Michelle Halard (who makes tablecloths).

DESCAMPS chose Primrose Bordier as their designer more than 25 years ago. She revolutionized the sensible, classic white world of household linen by designing sheets and pillowcases covered in floral patterns. She still produces bountiful Gardens of Eden, but she has recently reintroduced the charm of white, harmonizing it with the colour ivory. And her rainbow of plain colours is a wonder. Of course, the duvet covers and the bathroom linen coordinate but then so do the nightdresses. Primrose also designs damask, coloured dining-room and kitchen linen for French Jacquard, which you will find in the Descamps shops. There are many branches in Paris, including:
BOUTIQUE DESCAMPS 44, RUE DE PASSY XVI – 42 88 10 01

PORTHAULT was founded by a lady called Madeleine, whose customers included the Duchess of Windsor, Louise de Vilmorin, Gloria Swanson and Aristotle Onassis. The Kennedys, the Rothschilds and all the top French actresses still come here to be greeted by Marc Porthault and his wife Françoise. The diaphanous voile sheets are incredible and the embroidery and designs magnificent. The shop of this 'linen couturier' is covered in wood panelling and the wares are stocked over two quite exceptional floors of the building.

♡ **PORTHAULT   18, AVENUE MONTAIGNE VIII – 47 20 75 25**

LA MAISON DE RENATA This is dominated by the tastes of its eponymous fashion-designing owner, refined to her fingertips. Her interior design was so renowned among her friends that, one day, she decided to make some money out of her sheets and place-settings specially embroidered for her by the machinists who make up her blouses and dresses. She has added some furniture to the collection, which makes a perfect combination.

♡ **LA MAISON DE RENATA   2, BOULEVARD RASPAIL VII – 45 48 08 58**

NOUEZ-MOI was opened by Eléonore and Jocelyne Poux as a studio. The two sisters-in-law manufactured braided, scalloped and embroidered linen to order. The business went so well that last year they opened up a very pretty shop in which they still sell linen at very reasonable prices. It's refined and accessible.

♡ ♧ **NOUEZ-MOI   27, RUE DES SABLONS XVI – 42 27 69 88**

PÉNÉLOPE was started as a self-help organization in 1949 to assist impoverished, nimble-fingered women. Under the guiding hands of the wonderful Jacqueline Maillard, Pénélope has become the aid organization with which talented people wish to have their names linked. Their biannual show gathers together the trendiest of designers, and their shop, which is hidden away at the far end of a courtyard, is constantly packed with people. The household linen, nightdresses, négligés and smocks are fantastic. They also have embroidered tablecloths with matching china and glassware which are sewn by true needlecraft virtuosi.

♡ **PÉNÉLOPE   19, AVENUE VICTOR-HUGO XVI (at the far end of the courtyard) – 45 09 90 90**

MANUEL CANOVAS started using some of his furnishing textile designs to make sheets. Now he has a whole range of designs, with matching towels. Look out for the heavy quilted coverlets, an American custom that has spread to France. The Manuel shops are masterfully directed by his wife Catherine, who is a very refined lady indeed.

MANUEL CANOVAS   30, AVENUE GEORGE-V VIII – 49 52 00 36; 5, PLACE DE FURSTENBERG VI – 43 26 89 31

OLIVIER DESFORGES uses as stylist Laurence Laffont, who learnt with the renowned Primrose Bordier. Laurence has added to the household linen collection, which although varied is dominated by tartan and stripes, by introducing cushions, nightdresses and matching little children's outfits. There are several Parisian shops, including:

OLIVIER DESFORGES   18, RUE VIGNON IX – 47 42 26 99

SIÈCLE completes its wonderful selection of tableware with magnificent tablecloths embroidered in Portugal, the birthplace of Marisa Osorio-Farinha. They come in white, natural or coloured linen, with needle-point embroidery, 'Richelieu' embroidery, or drawn stitching, and there are matching table sets and napkins.

SIÈCLE   24, RUE DU BAC VII – 47 03 48 03

LE TRÈFLE BLEU is named in honour of Louise de Vil-morin, who always embellished her signature with a drawing of a *trèfle* (clover leaf). The idea behind the shop, which is directed by the writer's two nieces, is to give the stock, and particularly the household linen, a personal touch with the use of embroidery in a distinctive print or with an individual design.

LE TRÈFLE BLEU   2, RUE LARGILLIÈRE XVI – 45 27 80 17

CHRISTIAN BENAIS This designer imports fabulous 'Jesurum' household linen from Italy. Embroidery, openwork, scalloping and lace insets alternate on cotton as diaphanous as Chantilly lace. This is real luxury.

CHRISTIAN BENAIS   18, RUE CORTAMBERT XVI – 45 03 15 55

NUIT BLANCHE is a whole shop given over to sleep and dining, under the watchful eye of Sabine Marchal, the designer. Embroidery, appliqué work and brushwork can all be ordered in every conceivable colour.

NUIT BLANCHE   41, RUE DE BOURGOGNE VII – 45 50 39 29

LA BOUTIQUE DU SOMMEIL was opened 20 years ago by Marianne Giannoli, shortly after she became famous for invent-ing her 'Gadgetière'. At the time, nice people didn't let guests go into the bedroom, which was considered a very private place. Comfort, consequently, suffered from this attitude and Marianne had the idea of devoting a whole shop to the bedroom, and began to search the four corners of the earth to find suitable décor. This was a very far-sighted gamble, which proved to be a real winner.

LA BOUTIQUE DU SOMMEIL   24, AVENUE PIERRE-Iᵉʳ-DE-SERBIE XVI – 47 20 57 36

LA PARESSE EN DOUCE is an invitation to the comforts of idleness. Claudine Bisson and Jeanne Haddad never forget a thing when it comes to the snug joys of evening, night-time and the late morning lie-in. From quilts to dressing-gowns and from curtains to hot-water-bottles, their range is incredible.

LA PARESSE EN DOUCE 97, RUE DU BAC VII – 42 22 64 10

CARRÉ BLANC The shop's motto goes, 'Even our labels are softer', and they stock all the top names in household linen at reasonable prices (Elvé, Bassetti, Cacharel, Move, etc.). They also sell their own designs.

⌘ **CARRÉ BLANC** 33, RUE DE SÈVRES VI – 45 48 66 73; 111 BIS, RUE DE COURCELLES XVII – 42 27 03 25

CHIFF-TIR When it was opened in 1974, the shop advertised with a slogan that loosely translated as, 'All half price and your dreams fulfilled'. 20 years later they still sell bargains, as long as you're prepared to hunt around. There are several shops in Paris, including:

⌘ **CHIFF-TIR** 20 AVENUE DES TERNES XVII – 43 20 08 14

ANAÏK DESCAMPS Her name is synonymous with household linen. She's been a designer for all the famous manufacturers for years, but has recently launched her own collection, using her own first name and a pretty mimosa motif.

⌘ **ANAÏK DESCAMPS** at GALERIES LAFAYETTE, BOULEVARD HAUSSMANN IX

LA MAISON BLEUE Evelyne Rouquette's shop machine-embroiders household linen and related accessories just the way you would want them to. You can even buy by mail order.

⌘ **LA MAISON BLEUE** 58 BIS, RUE FRÉDÉRIC-CLÉMENT 92300 GARCHES – 47 01 18 32

MARIE-LAVANDE This is Joëlle Serres's pretty nickname and she is an expert on the restoration of antique textiles. She dry-cleans even the most fragile of embroidered table linen and includes amongst her clientèle the actress Carole Bouquet, the fashion designer Christian Lacroix and interior decorators like Christian Benais and Jean-Louis Riccardi. She gives quotes.

MARIE-LAVANDE 22, RUE HONORÉ-OURSEL 94290 VILLENEUVE-LE-ROI – 45 97 11 84

And also:

LA CHÂTELAINE 170, AVENUE VICTOR-HUGO XVI – 47 27 44 07
YVES DELORME 153, RUE SAINT-HONORÉ I – 42 97 00 50
KENZO 3, PLACE DES VICTOIRES I – 40 39 72 03
CHRISTIAN DIOR 30, AVENUE MONTAIGNE VIII – 40 73 54 44
LAURA ASHLEY 94, RUE DE RENNES VI – 45 48 43 89
NINA RICCI 39, AVENUE MONTAIGNE VIII – 47 23 78 88
AGNÈS COMAR 7, AVENUE GEORGE-V VIII – 47 23 33 85

AU BAIN MARIE   10, RUE BOISSY-D'ANGLAS VIII – 42 66 59 74

PATRICK FREY   47, RUE DES PETITS-CHAMPS I – 44 77 36 00

The LINEN departments of the big department stores.

Some shops that generally specialize in 'Table Arts' also sell wonderful tablecloths that they design themselves:

GENEVIÈVE LETHU   95, RUE DE RENNES VI – 45 44 40 35

YVES HALARD   252 BIS, BOULEVARD SAINT-GERMAIN VII 42 22 60 50

GÉRARD DANTON   38, RUE DE BELLECHASSE VII – 45 55 21 11

DÎNERS EN VILLE   27, RUE DE VARENNE VII – 42 22 78 83

MURIEL GRATEAU   132, GALERIE DE VALOIS, JARDINS DU PALAIS-ROYAL I – 40 20 90 30

SOULEÏADO   78, RUE DE SEINE VI – 43 54 62 25

TABLE ARTS

This charming term covers every aspect of setting a table, at any time of day, whether for a party or for a simple family meal. There is a whole range of beautiful materials to select from to create your own personal work of art – transparent crystal and coloured glass, heavy silver and brilliant steel, delicate porcelain and painted earthenware. And there is no need – in fact it is no longer fashionable – to serve an entire meal off the same dinner service (a fashion that only began in the 14th century in any case!). The prettiest effects can be achieved by mixing up a couple of dozen entirely different dessert plates, and the same can be done with assorted glasses. Even paper plates can be used for starters and cheese, for example – provided, of course, that they're exquisite! It's all a question of harmony.

LA FAÏENCERIE DE GIEN began in 1821 and has a quite remarkable collection displayed on dressers in their factory in the Loiret area, south of Paris. Pierre and Evelyne Jeuffroy regularly reissue their wonderful designs (including delightful torch-flames in pink and turquoise) and get their inspiration from antique illustrated manuscripts (Magellan with his abundance of birds and exotic flowers, for example). They carry on manufacturing their best-selling lines like the rebus puzzle plates which used to cause howls of laughter among the Dominican monks at the end of every meal. They also commission contemporary designers like Garouste and Bonetti (a Camargue scene, in yellow and turquoise) and Dominique Lalande (an expert on painted landscapes).

♡ **LA FAÏENCERIE DE GIEN BOUTIQUE**   18, RUE DE L'ARCADE VIII – 49 24 07 77

CHRISTOFLE has been a silversmith since 1830 and now has a shop in the very beautiful former home of the Duc de La Rochefoucauld, after having spent more than 80 years resident in the building facing it. This is still a family business, led with a masterly flair by a high-powered brotherly triumvirate comprised of Albert, Henri and Marc Bouilhet (the fifth generation). The stock is displayed in a white wood décor, accentuated with gilded brass, which looks magnificent and even includes a little exhibition of antique pieces in a kind of museum corner. But if you really want to gaze in wonder go to Saint-Denis, north of Paris, where you will find their factory and a harmonious blend of modern technology and traditional handicraft. The silverware collection, often coloured by the use of lacquer, is supplemented by glassware and china, and the most recently designed china dinner service is called 'Orientalys' and is entirely covered in hand-painted blue and red flowers. There is a more classic dinner service on which butterflies and morning glory are superbly spread out on a pink and white background. They also sell the indispensable gloves which make cleaning silver so much less of a chore.

♡ **CHRISTOFLE   9, RUE ROYALE VIII – 49 33 43 00**

HAVILAND ET PARLON is one of the biggest of the Limoges porcelain manufacturers. Out of the inexhaustible archives, Michel Ardant regularly reproduces delicate, precious designs. One of these, 'Pivoine de Vincennes' (designed in 1750), is on sale at the shop in the Museum of Decorative Arts in Paris. Designers like Manuel Canovas (who created 'Les Pivoines de Vincennes' and 'L'Herbier') and Didier Galerne (who designed 'Rome', from old architectural drawings) are also welcomed with open arms.

♡ **HAVILAND ET PARLON   47, RUE DE PARADIS X – 47 70 07 70**

LES CRISTALLERIES DE SAINT-LOUIS was founded in 1586 and, at that stage, it was called Verrerie Lorraine de Munzthal, before becoming the Royal Glassworks of Saint-Louis in 1767 and producing the first crystalware in France some 14 years later. The shop on the Rue Royale has been decorated by Rena Dumas and it is here that you can find exquisite red and green crystal goblets, finely embellished with cable twists which are also made of crystal. They also sell modern ornamental pieces in clear or amber-coloured crystal with which to decorate tables (and which come in five different styles) and, naturally, the old designs are constantly reproduced. Tradition and modernity combined.

♡ **LES CRISTALLERIES DE SAINT-LOUIS   13, RUE ROYALE VIII – 40 17 01 74**

BERNARDAUD chose a modern, celadon and black style of décor to exhibit his collection which is sometimes inspired by the East India Company or by the great manufacturers of Sèvres, Saint-Cloud and Vincennes china. The new designs are by Giovanna Amoruso, Jean-Pierre Hamard and Catherine Pointud. They sell a perfectly designed plate called 'Soleil' (Sunshine).

BERNARDAUD   11, RUE ROYALE VIII – 47 42 82 66

BACCARAT was founded by Louis XV in 1764 and was the supplier to the Elysée Palace from 1878. The crystalworks owns an amazing museum in Paris, whose centrepiece is the figure of 'Lady Baccarat', dressed from head to toe in crystal pendants. There are glasses displayed in cabinets that were made for royalty and heads of state, and there are bottles designed for the world's most famous perfumes, along with more recent models bearing the signature of Robert Rigot, Yann Zoritchak, Ung-No-Lee and Thomas Bastide. One of the less expensive services in the catalogue is the delicately gadrooned 'Flore' service. One of the most popular is the 'Masséna' service. Baccarat is also famous for its delightful paperweights, which come in a variety of shapes – hearts, thimbles, pens, books and balls. The firm has also opened a wonderful shop on the Place de la Madeleine, devoted not just to crystal but also to porcelain and silverware.

♡   **BACCARAT   30 BIS, RUE DE PARADIS X – 47 70 64 30; 11, PLACE DE LA MADELEINE VIII – 42 65 36 26**

DAUM is over 120 years old and continues to play with the transparency of colour. The greatest artists in the field have had their work produced by the firm and, at present, Dalí, César, Lalanne, Fassianos, Hilton McConnico, André Dubreuil, Garouste and Bonetti are all in stock. Charming sidelines are the pâte-de-verre jewels and the evening bags with precious clasps.

♡   **DAUM   4, RUE DE LA PAIX II – 42 61 25 25**

LALIQUE consists of three first names, all of which form a dynasty of great artists: René, Marc and Marie-Claude. Their work is constantly reproduced and sometimes recoloured. You should start collecting the floral perfume bottles and they sell a round ring that changes in colour and is, naturally, made of crystal. As is the late work of J. O. d'Albertville, which consists of medals soberly set in gold, silver and bronze.

LALIQUE   11, RUE ROYALE VIII – 42 65 33 70

PETER This great silversmith-cutler set up in Alsace as early as 1785 but only arrived at the Faubourg Saint-Honoré in 1961. He mounts silver place settings on to jasper, ebony, tiger's-eye and quartz handles, to create truly precious objects.

PETER   191, RUE DU FAUBOURG SAINT-HONORÉ VIII – 45 63 88 00

PUIFORCAT constantly produces the sumptuous silver designs of its founder, the great Jean Puiforcat. Perfection and purity of line, with the addition of exotic wood and gemstones, conjure up magnificent results. Eliane Scali has now also added a beautiful range of jewelry to the collection.

♡   PUIFORCAT   2, AVENUE MATIGNON VIII – 45 63 10 10; 22, RUE FRANÇOIS-Iᵉʳ VIII – 47 20 74 27

AU BAIN MARIE is an immense shop behind the Place de la Concorde. Aude Clément is a specialist in the reproduction of objects that we have always seen in our family homes but which clumsy hands have smashed or inheritances dispersed among many. There are artichoke dishes, asparagus plates and tongs, knife rests, etc. There is also a very pretty range of household linen. An Ali Baba's cave of treasures on two floors and from which you will not emerge empty-handed.

AU BAIN MARIE   10, RUE BOISSY-D'ANGLAS VIII – 42 66 59 74

MOLIN has just been bought up by the Jeuffroys, who already owned the Faïencerie de Gien. The designer, Mathias, has created a wonderful range of gilded plates for them, bordered with little round designs. In the recently opened shop, you will find a screen decorated with tiny dishes of colour which display the entire rainbow of choice. It is vast.

MOLIN   17, RUE DE MIROMESNIL VIII – 42 65 09 00

SÉGRIÈS This is faïence-style ceramic ware from Provence, in which plates from the 'Nénuphar' (Water Lily) range and piles of fruit in large bowls appear in white colours and in relief.

SÉGRIÈS   13, RUE DE TOURNON VI – 46 34 62 56

WEDGWOOD is world-famous for its 'bone china', which is a bisque of coloured porcelain decorated with cameos, intaglios and medallions. The colour ivory and a classical line define the 'Edme' service which is made of Queen's Ware porcelain, and which includes some ornamented pieces. 'Blue Siam' was inspired by a drawing from the Far East.

WEDGWOOD at PRINTEMPS and GALERIES LAFAYETTE

QUARTZ sells the glassware that Emmeline Bauer digs up all over the world, with impressive flair. There are Zébulon fluted goblets with blue or green bases and Guggisberg-Baldwin bowls, coloured and mounted on low legs. There is a range of sand-engraved lamps, chandeliers and glasses. An expert in flower arranging, Emmeline tempts you to buy all her vases.

♡   QUARTZ   112, RUE DES QUATRE-VENTS VI – 43 54 03 00

SIÈCLE or the story of one young couple, Philippe Chupin and Marisa Osorio-Farinha, who design deluxe place settings with heavily worked handles, in the shape of tritons or wickerwork, and made of Surinam leopardwood or Gabonese ebony, or, indeed, horn or fossilized stones, Asian palmwood, sharkskin or inlaid mother-of-pearl.

SIÈCLE   24, RUE DU BAC VII – 47 03 48 03

DÎNERS EN VILLE or the story of two female friends, Blandine de Mandat-Grancey and Chantal de Lussac, who boldy mix old and new on the dining-room table. On a corner, behind a red façade, decorated with matching frothy blinds, you will find one of the most beautiful shops in Paris, devoted to Table Arts. Chantal de Lussac also designs tablecloths at reasonable prices, which are splendid and very tasteful. Perfect items to add to your wedding list.

♡   **DÎNERS EN VILLE   27, RUE DE VARENNE VII – 42 22 78 33**

MARIE-PIERRE BOITARD also combines all the sophistications of the dining-room table. For a long time, she has been the anonymous designer at many of the famous firms. But now she has started designing for herself and happily digs out a few old pieces as well.

MARIE-PIERRE BOITARD 9–11, PLACE DU PALAIS-BOURBON VII – 47 05 13 30

GUNTHER LAMBERT selects magnificent modern objects for the table, and, in particular, those made of silver-plate and glass.

GUNTHER LAMBERT   21, RUE LAS-CASES VII – 45 50 23 62

JEAN-PIERRE DE CASTRO is a 'scavenger'. One of his particular specialities is old silverware (or silver-plate). Renovation or demolition work on old houses are goldmines for him, and you can find regiments of place-settings, battalions of plates and squadrons of vegetable dishes and teapots in his shop. Something to start off your (future) children's inheritance, perhaps.

JEAN-PIERRE DE CASTRO 17, RUE DES FRANCS-BOURGEOIS IV – 42 72 04 00

GEORG JENSEN is Danish. In his shop you will find old-style ceramics from the Royal Copenhagen collection as well as more contemporary designs. And pretty silver jewelry.

GEORG JENSEN   239, RUE SAINT-HONORÉ I – 42 60 07 89

MURIEL GRATEAU In her very individual way, Muriel mixes designs for china plates, Venetian blown-glass and very beautiful damask linen tablecloths.

MURIEL GRATEAU 132, GALERIE DE VALOIS, JARDINS DU PALAIS-ROYAL I – 40 20 90 30

GENEVIÈVE LETHU has curly hair, a pretty face and round glasses. She comes from La Rochelle, near Bordeaux, and, with immaculate timing, realized that Table Arts were about to be transformed. In her shops she gathers together all the necessary accessories, which are all pretty and accessible. Laurence Laffont, the designer, creates her exclusive designs, for crockery as well as for household linen. Don't miss it!

♣ **GENEVIÈVE LETHU   95, RUE DE RENNES VI – 45 44 40 35**

QUIMPER FAÏENCE decorate crockery like they used to in Brittany 300 years ago. With lots of yellow background. One of their classics is the bowl with your name on it.

QUIMPER FAÏENCE   84, RUE SAINT-MARTIN IV – 42 71 93 03

PORTO SANTO Portugal is the place to find crockery decorated with blue and white checks and sometimes punctuated with little florets. That's when the plates and dishes aren't covered in large flowers in bright colours.

PORTO SANTO   7, RUE DU VINGT-NEUF-JUILLET I – 42 86 97 81

BRITISH SHOP brings its crockery over from England. The 'Fresh Fruit' service is particularly charming.

BRITISH SHOP   2, RUE FRANÇOIS-PONSARD XVI – 45 25 86 92

HERMÈS Some time ago, the famous saddler added a Table Arts department to his existing collection, with china plates (manufactured by Haviland and Parlon) decorated in as colourful a way as his famous scarves. More recently, he launched a fabulous crystalware collection: the 'Djerba' range is made of crystal enamelled in white (the lamp is quite wonderful), while the 'Inca' range uses a 19th-century technique known as *macédoine*, which involves mixing the ends of coloured rods together. The result is constantly delightful but the shades aren't always exactly identical.

HERMÈS   24, RUE DU FAUBOURG SAINT-HONORÉ VIII – 40 17 47 17

CARTIER also has a Table Arts department. It is so glamorous that you'll think you're at a jeweller's shop. The silverware is decorated with the famous triple rings, in silver-gilt. The salt and pepper pots, studded with lapis-lazuli cabochons, are small jewels in their own right. The table service is china, dotted with gold. There are crystalware glasses.

CARTIER   51, RUE FRANÇOIS-Iᵉʳ – VIII – 40 74 61 83

ROCHAS is a perfumer and fashion designer and the artistic director, Christian Astuguevieille, believes that accessories really make the 'look', so he supplies enormous hand-painted and gilded china plates, with blown-glass from Biot.

♡ **ROCHAS   33, RUE FRANÇOIS-Iᵉʳ VIII – 47 23 54 56**

SOULEÏADO matches crockery to Provençal fabrics, and Jean-Pierre Deméry, who is a big fan of bullfighting, has designed a wonderful dinner service in sober black and white, decorated with the stylized head of a bull and motifs of cattle brands.

♡ **SOULEÏADO   78, RUE DE SEINE VI – 43 54 62 25**

KALINGER He is an expert in resin jewelry and now designs astonishing place-settings and decanters in the same material, which harmonizes with glass and steel.

KALINGER   60, RUE DU FAUBOURG SAINT-HONORÉ VIII – 42 66 24 39

TAÏR MERCIER Let us introduce Judith and Philippe, a couple who design polypropylene objects in bright or pastel colours. And, also, very beautiful ranges of table sets.

♠ **TAÏR MERCIER   7, BOULEVARD SAINT-GERMAIN V – 43 54 19 97**

LA GADGETIÈRE imports plates from the Metropolitan Museum of Art in New York. They are made of papier-maché (there are matching napkins), and they are reproductions of designs for antique porcelain from China, Japan, France and Germany, all of which are drawn from the museum's vast collection. You will undoubtedly want to start making a collection of your own.

♣ **LA GADGETIÈRE   1, RUE GEORGES-BIZET XVI – 47 50 52 20**

POINT À LA LIGNE is, primarily, a candle specialist, but these have become 'a must' for any well-decorated table. They sell them in a wide range of charming colours and in various sizes, and they come in wonderful shapes forming, among other things, hearts, jewels, palaces, cakes, eggs, flowers, trees and shells. The choice is enormous and there are matching candlesticks and papier-maché plates, as well as paper napkins to match the candles.

**POINT À LA LIGNE   87, AVENUE VICTOR-HUGO XVI – 45 00 96 80;
25, RUE DE VARENNE VII – 42 84 14 45**

SIMON and **LA VERRERIE DES HALLES** are primarily suppliers to a large number of restaurants, brasseries and cafés, who turn up to restock on heavy white china plates; dark green coffee cups with gold edging; small stoneware jugs with fiery or pearly patterns or with traditional Florentine designs (bunches of grapes); and every kind of wine-glass. For Riesling, Bordeaux, Burgundy, Muscadet, port, whisky, vodka, liqueurs and champagne. Individuals who like the bistro style are very well received and the prices are very reasonable.

♠ **SIMON   36, RUE ÉTIENNE-MARCEL II – 42 33 71 65**

♠ **LA VERRERIE DES HALLES   15, RUE DU LOUVRE I – 42 36 86 02**

The *Rue de Paradis* has become the meeting-point for all lovers of china, earthenware, silverware, crystalware and glassware since the day Baccarat opened its Parisian office in this street in 1831. It was soon joined by the Cristalleries de Saint-Louis, Haviland et Parlon and Bernardaud. In 1979, an enormous, super-modern building was put up to house the whole Table Arts profession under one roof but, thank God, the beautiful stone façades of the two prestigious glassmakers were retained. There are many boutique-showrooms all the way down the street, including the one at No. 2, **GÉO MARTEL,** which reproduces the most famous original designs of Moustiers, Rouen, Strasbourg, Nevers and Marseilles (47 70 13 95). No. 12 is the home of **LIMOGES-UNIC,** which specializes in the top-of-the-range products of the famous names (47 70 54 49). At No. 31, **PORCELAINOR** sells Sèvres crystal, as well as Wedgwood and Philippe Deshoulières (48 24 49 30). At No. 34, **MADRONET** is an expert on the great porcelain manufacturers (47 70 34 59) and at No. 38, **LES ÉMAUX DE LONGWY** are enamel manufacturers from Lorraine which began in 1798 with their cloisonné designs. They still make these but, this year, they have introduced magnificent new designs by Hilton McConnico (48 24 40 10). At No. 56, the second **LIMOGES-UNIC** shop sells a selection of more affordable pieces (47 70 61 49).

And also:

MATHIAS 117, RUE DE CHARENTON XII – 43 46 68 68

KAOLA 38, RUE POUSSIN XVI – 46 51 41 44

♡ **CASA LOPEZ** 32, GALERIE VIVIENNE I – 42 60 46 85; 58, AVENUE PAUL-DOUMER XVI – 45 03 42 75

♡ **YVES HALARD** 252 BIS, BOULEVARD SAINT-GERMAIN VII – 42 22 60 50

LANCEL 127, AVENUE DES CHAMPS-ÉLYSÉES VIII – 47 23 66 03

NESTOR PERKAL 8, RUE DES QUATRE-FILS III – 42 77 46 80

PATRICK FREY 47, RUE DES PETITS-CHAMPS I – 44 77 36 00

MANUEL CANOVAS 30, AVENUE GEORGE-V III – 49 52 00 36

♡ **LAURE WELFLING** 30, RUE JACOB VI – 43 25 17 03

JARDINS IMAGINAIRES 9 BIS, RUE D'ASSAS VI – 42 22 90 03

♡ **NUMÉRO 20** 20, PLACE DES VOSGES IV – 42 78 67 74

VILLEROY ET BOCH 21, RUE ROYALE VIII – 42 65 81 84

ROSENTHAL 37, BOULEVARD DES CAPUCINES II – 42 61 58 21

GÉRARD DANTON 38, RUE DE BELLECHASSE VII – 45 55 21 11

L'ENTREPÔT 50, RUE DE PASSY XVI – 45 25 64 17

LA SALLE À MANGER 12, AVENUE MOZART XVI – 45 27 15 22

LA BOUTIQUE CRILLON 17, RUE DE LA PAIX II – 42 61 37 27

UN JARDIN EN PLUS Eight shops in Paris including: 66, AVENUE VICTOR-HUGO XVI – 45 00 07 76

LAURE JAPY 34, RUE DU BAC VII – 42 86 96 97

LA DESSERTE   57, RUE DU COMMERCE XV − 42 50 00 81
BOUTIQUE ELLE   30, RUE SAINT-SULPICE VI − 43 26 46 10
LA VIE DE CHÂTEAU   17, RUE DE VALOIS I − 49 27 09 82
JEANNE GAMBERT DE LOCHE   21, RUE DE VALOIS I − 42 96 04 65
PASSION INTÉRIEUR   117, RUE DE LA CONVENTION XV − 40 60 63 13
NINA RICCI   39, AVENUE MONTAIGNE VIII − 47 23 78 88
CHRISTIAN DIOR   30, AVENUE MONTAIGNE VIII − 40 73 54 44

The marvellous TABLE ARTS departments at **BON MARCHÉ, GALER-IES LAFAYETTE** and **PRINTEMPS**

The sublime collections of paper plates, napkins and tablecloths designed by Primrose Bordier for ♡ ♧ **DEEKO PARTY**, which you will find in supermarkets and in a special area at **PRINTEMPS**.

LAMPS

Every designer will tell you, the important thing is the lighting. If that isn't right, the most artistic of décor is worthless. You've really got to think seriously in a field that has become dominated by long-stemmed lamps and the return of the chandelier in a big way. But a couple of pretty vase-lamps are always pleasant, particularly if they are antiques. And, of course, the right shade is essential, and should be talked over at length with the experts.

CHAUMETTE creates a new lamp and chandelier collection twice a year. Decorated earthenware, earthenware with a sheen or bronze-look, or even worked wrought-iron, make this one of the leading specialists in decorative lamps.

♡ **CHAUMETTE**   45, AVENUE DUQUESNE VII − 42 73 18 54

HABITAT is an expert in contemporary lighting at reasonable prices. It is the perfect place to find those indispensable kitchen spotlights or bedside lamps for guest-rooms. Or if you decide that you simply have to change your lampshades, in a simple, unsophisticated way. Four shops in Paris including:

♣ **HABITAT** 35, AVENUE DE WAGRAM XVII – 47 66 25 52

ATELIER SEDAP skilfully combines plaster and light by using the multiple talents of designers like Yves Blayo. Loïc Beuchet, Luc Peirdo and Michel Tortel. The collection consists of 100 wall lamps, sunken spotlights, a few standard lamps, some table lamps and some hanging fittings. Go and see the whole massive collection in the showroom just outside Paris. The retailers' details are clearly labelled.

ATELIER SEDAP 16 BIS, RUE POTTIER 78150 LE CHESNAY – 39 63 34 48

ÉLECTRORAMA only sells creations from the cutting edge of contemporary design.

ÉLECTRORAMA 11, BOULEVARD SAINT-GERMAIN V – 43 29 31 30

ESPACE LUMIÈRE imports light-fittings by Italian designers. They are occasionally a little bit nutty.

ESPACE LUMIÈRE 167, BOULEVARD HAUSSMANN VIII – 42 89 01 15

VÉRONÈSE is the Parisian harbour for the Murano glass artists. The flowered stem chandeliers are miracles of lightness and copies of the ones that decorate the palaces of Venice. They can be made to measure for the ceilings from which they will hang. There are also various regular wall lamps and handsome old-fashioned mirrors conjured up by Venetian artisans.

♡ **VÉRONÈSE** 184, BOULEVARD HAUSSMANN VIII – 45 62 67 67

GÉRARD DANTON makes earthenware vase-shades in bright colours or with stripes. They come in all shapes and sizes with matching candlesticks and even ashtrays. As he designs and produces tablecloths as well, you can make everything match.

GÉRARD DANTON 38, RUE DE BELLECHASSE VII – 45 55 21 11

MARWAY This excellent specialist in English furniture has just created a very pretty collection of candlestick-lamps in turned wood, with sophisticated lampshades.

MARWAY 10 and 26, RUE DE RICHELIEU I – 42 96 26 56; 11, RUE DU BAC VII – 42 61 22 28

DAVID HICKS has been making the most perfect of reading lamps for a number of years now, which are supposed to be fixed behind one's sofa. They are made of gilded brass and have become an absolute fashion essential which has been heavily imitated by all and sundry, always the price of success.

DAVID HICKS 12, RUE DE TOURNON VI – 43 26 00 67

LE BAZAR D'ÉLECTRICITÉ set up in the Bastille district in 1886 and now has one of the largest selections of light-fittings in Paris displayed over three floors. There is something for everyone, including that indispensable item, the pocket torch. The electrical general strike is a frightening reality! So you'd better come here when you're all out of ideas.

LE BAZAR D'ÉLECTRICITÉ   34, BOULEVARD HENRI-IV IV − 48 87 83 35

CRISTAUX ET BOBÈCHES inscribed the words 'Articles for candlelight' on his shopfront in 1875. In the wonderful décor of the period, lit by chandeliers of all sizes, lamp frames are arrayed in glittering crystal drops and faceted spheres. For those of us who have ever smashed a trinket, a candle-ring or a candelabrum, this is a precious address indeed. And those of you who wish to observe 'one of Paris's special little areas of skill' had better beat a path straight there.

♡ **CRISTAUX ET BOBÈCHES, GRANDIÈRE FRÈRES   12, RUE MARTEL X − 47 70 65 98**

DELISLE is situated in the marvellous Canillac building, one of the pink houses of the Marais district. The former supplier to the European monarchies, specialist in lighting, has recently taken on the fittings at the Opéra, the Château de Versailles and the Ritz Hotel. He also produces the contemporary designs of people like Christian Duc. A most fortunate cross-fertilization.

DELISLE   4, RUE DU PARC-ROYAL III − 42 72 21 34

CHARLES The first of the name was christened Emile-Albert. He was a craftsman of bronze and, for four generations now, the torch has been taken up by his descendants. Chrystiane Charles and her son Laurent are now in charge and they are acutely aware of how to manufacture reproductions of classic designs and yet, at the same time, commission modern designers like Arman, Didier La Mache, Jacques Pierrejean, Christian Duc and Sylvain Dubuisson. The 'Stockholm' lamp, which won a prize at the last annual Paris light show, is particularly wonderful.

CHARLES   34, RUE BONAPARTE VI − 43 25 60 04

JACQUES LEGUENNEC normally makes neo-classical-style lamps which are accompanied by matching pieces of furniture. They have an excellent selection of lifestyle and decorative arts books and watercolours by Pascale Laurent.

♡ **JACQUES LEGUENNEC   14, RUE DE SEINE VI − 43 26 28 24**

And also:

DES LAMPES   9, RUE DE VERNEUIL VII − 40 20 02 58

DRIMMER   30, BOULEVARD SAINT-GERMAIN V − 46 33 60 22

LUMIÈRES DE PARIS   26, BOULEVARD RASPAIL VII − 45 48 36 77

VOLT ET WATT   29, BOULEVARD RASPAIL VII – 45 48 29 62
BAGUÈS   37, AVENUE PIERRE-I⁻ᵉ-DE-SERBIE XVI – 47 20 61 17
ROCHE-BOBOIS   18, RUE DE LYON XII – 43 44 18 18
CHRYSALIDE   82, RUE JOUFFROY XVII – 43 80 02 10
ARLUMIÈRE   8, AVENUE VICTORIA IV – 42 71 23 42
AXIS   18, RUE GUÉNÉGAUD VI – 43 29 66 23

There are a number of in-house designers who, having created light-fittings for their own studios, considered these to have been so successful that they decided to market them:
FIRST TIME   27, RUE MAZARINE VI – 43 25 55 00
LAURE WELFLING   30, RUE JACOB VI – 43 25 17 03
NOBLESSE OBLIGE   27 BIS, RUE DE BELLECHASSE VII – 45 55 20 43
YVES HALARD   252 BIS, BOULEVARD SAINT-GERMAIN VII – 42 22 60 50
EN ATTENDANT LES BARBARES   50, RUE ÉTIENNE-MARCEL II – 42 33 37 87
LA GALERIE MAISON ET JARDIN   120, RUE DU FAUBOURG SAINT-HONORÉ VIII – 45 61 93 30
The LIGHTING departments of the big department stores.

Specialists in lampshades
These are true lamp stylists. They have designs in their shops which they can make up, however you like, to your own specifications. Pleated, braided, fringed, spotted, laced, stencilled, embroidered, garlanded, made of paper (bookbinder's, kraft, glazed, handmade, parchment, etc.) or of material (silk, chintz, cambric, velvet, canvas, taffeta, etc.). Come provided with lamp base, swatches from objects surrounding the lamp and a description of the piece of furniture you're going to place it on. It's all a question of balance and harmony and it's therefore crucial to consult an expert.

♡ **CLAIR OBSCUR**   2, RUE DU CAPITAINE-OLCHANSKI XVI – 42 24 48 42
♡ **SEMAINE**   20, RUE NICOLO XVI – 45 20 06 69
CAPELINE   144, AVENUE DE VERSAILLES XVI – 45 20 22 65
BEL OMBRE   32, RUE GUSTAVE-COURBET XVI – 47 27 96 57
L'IMPROMPTU   8, RUE GUSTAVE-FLAUBERT XVII – 42 27 62 99
ISABELLE ROUTIER   9, RUE DE SAVOIE VI – 46 33 36 58
MARIE ET CATHERINE GOUNY   5, RUE DE CHARONNE XI – 48 07 23 48
ANTICA   88, RUE DE VERNEUIL VII – 42 61 28 86
BOUCHARDEAU   13, RUE DE L'ARSENAL IV – 42 72 86 95
L'ATELIER DE L'ABAT-JOUR du BHV 52, RUE DE RIVOLI IV – 42 74 90 00
MILLER ET BERTAUX   27, RUE DU BOURG-TIBOURG IV – 42 77 25 31

COOKING UTENSILS

The most fashionable people now give dinner parties in the kitchen, which has become an important room in its own right. It is, therefore, as important to get the right look in your kitchen as to be furnished with the right kind of cooking utensils.

LA CARPE has been selling kitchen equipment for a long time. From caviar dishes to elegant folding trolleys, from the most efficient corkscrew to gadgets that stop serving spoons and forks slipping into the dish, from cappuccino machines that make real Italian espresso to the pretty fruit and vegetable bowl made of white wood and supplied with three separate racks. For all these reasons a visit to this shop is obligatory. Their best-selling items are a crusher and strainer for making fruit jellies, an old-fashioned purée-press and an oyster holder for opening the oysters without hurting yourself. There is a small catalogue you can consult.

LA CARPE   14, RUE TRONCHET VIII – 47 42 73 25

FRANCE MASSÉNA is directed by Hélène Maury, who criss-crosses the world in search of useful kitchen gadgets or manufactures her own, including melamine crockery, funny little mats and rubbish-bins with swivel-lids.

FRANCE MASSÉNA at L'ENTREPÔT   50, RUE DE PASSY XVI – 45 25 64 17

GENEVIÈVE LETHU is as much of an expert in kitchen utensils as she in Table Arts. She has even designed a very pretty collection of kitchen furniture made of painted wood.

♡   **GENEVIÈVE LETHU   95, RUE DE RENNES VI – 45 44 40 35**

KITCHEN BAZAAR has always been the Mecca of kitchen utensils, set up in a minimalistically designed shop. From A for appliance-hooks to W for wok, this shop contains every possible

kind of saucepan, vast quantities of knives with handles made in
sycamore wood or tough rubberized material, all kinds of cooking
tins, pretty kettles and clever bottle-openers. Just next-door to
the Kitchen Bazaar shop you will see the annex, which is called
AUTREMENT and is 'a new collection of natural objects, often
hand-made by artisans, which add a touch of colour, rural
delight and history to your kitchen décor'. Wooden place-
settings, wickerwork, tin-plated baskets, fish grillers, muslin
food-cloches – you'll find them all in the shop which has a sort of
environmentally aware feel to it.

♡   KITCHEN BAZAAR   11, AVENUE DU MAINE XV – 42 22 91 17;
142, RUE DE COURCELLES XVII – 43 80 77 37; AUTREMENT 6, AVENUE
DU MAINE XV – 45 48 89 00

CULINARION has two shops in Paris, one in Boulogne, one in
Vincennes and another in Suresnes. Non-rust metal, chromium-
plated brass, glass and coloured melamine all harmonize to make
up intelligent, functional items.

CULINARION   99, RUE DE RENNES VI – 45 48 94 76; 83 BIS, RUE DE
COURCELLES XVII – 42 27 63 32

GALERIE LA CORNUE has been making wonderful kitchen
units since 1908. This is old-fashioned style moulded into
marvels of cast-iron, copper, bronze and enamel that are only
made to order, and you have to be prepared for a wait. They look
simply divine in enormous country kitchens and they come
complete with gas and electricity connections. To match the
kitchen-ranges, they also make saucepans, frying-pans and non-
rust or copper cooking utensils, racks to hang these from,
baskets, knives, aprons, linen cloths and cast-iron scales. A
treat to behold.

GALERIE LA CORNUE   18, RUE MABILLON VI – 46 33 84 74

MARIAGE FRÈRES has been importing tea since 1854. But
because you need the right container for the goods, they also sell
an incredible selection of teapots, teaspoons and tea caddies in
their two Paris shops.

♡   MARIAGE FRÈRES   30, RUE DU BOURG-TIBOURG IV – 42 72 28 11;
13, RUE DES GRANDS-AUGUSTINS VI – 40 51 82 50

FAGUAIS He's a confectioner but he also sells a wonderful
espresso machine and a bachelor's coffee service (cafetière, cup,
saucer and sugar-bowl). There is a pleasing selection of coffee
storage jars made of aluminium.

FAGUAIS   30, RUE DE LA TRÉMOILLE VIII – 47 20 80 91

FRANCIS BATT sells a selection of very pretty 'Cook Line'
designs. They've got wooden clocks with naive cut-out designs,

aluminium baskets, utensil racks and articles of painted metal plate.

FRANCIS BATT   180, AVENUE VICTOR-HUGO XVI – 47 27 13 28

And also:
The COOKING UTENSIL departments of the big department stores, as well as:

DEHILLERIN   18–20, RUE COQUILLÈRE I – 42 36 53 13

MORA   13, RUE MONTMARTRE I – 45 08 19 24

LA BOVIDA   36, RUE MONTMARTRE I – 42 36 09 99

SIMON   48, RUE MONTMARTRE I – 42 33 71 65

GARDEN FURNITURE

Specially treated to withstand the rigours of wet weather, garden furniture looks equally good in the garden, on the terrace, on the veranda or even in the living room. If you locate it in the latter, you will believe spring has arrived when autumn chills are creeping in.

DESPALLES   The old seed and bulb merchant was called 'Aux bonnes semences' (at the house of good seed) when it opened in 1843. Now there are three Paris shops where you can buy very beautiful garden furniture, selected by Laurence, the wife of the boss, Philippe Brunon. Some people are particularly fond of the English turn-of-the-century furniture which is made of white lacquered iron. Kim Moltzer, a gentleman-farmer with a gift for design, also creates blue, wrought-iron furniture for them, including items like armchairs and huge garden benches. An antique-dealer-cum-decorator from Avignon called Hervé Baume sells his designs in the shop and these encompass sofas, circular tables and folding metal chairs as well as wonderful terracotta and varnished red clay pots.

♡ **DESPALLES   5, RUE D'ALÉSIA XIV – 45 89 05 31; 76, BOULEVARD SAINT-GERMAIN V – 43 54 28 98; 87, AVENUE NIEL XVII – 47 66 52 99**

HUGONET sells the designs of Didier Gomez, which include a range of lacquered aluminium armchairs and chaises longues, with rope-bound feet and cushions made up in a vast range of material. As for the designer Pascal Mourgue, he has created a couch from solid iroko and lacquered metal, hung with vinyl polyester canvas.

HUGONET   63, RUE LA BOÉTIE VIII – 43 59 14 26

LE CÈDRE ROUGE has two addresses where you can find the distinctive wooden furniture which gave its name to the label. The garden bench made like a little house is exquisite and is an ideal place for trysts and secluded rendez-vous! There are rococo pieces of worked rattanware in woven strips and they sell chairs, armchairs, pedestal tables and a steel console table, all painted with anti-rust substances and then varnished. They have a magnificent slab of enamelled lava fashioned into a table and a charming crockery service with which to lay the table, decorated as it is with painted radishes, petits pois, lettuce, peppers and other vegetables.

LE CÈDRE ROUGE   22, AVENUE VICTORIA I; 5, RUE DE MÉDICIS VI – 42 33 71 05

TECTONA is a specialist in teak from Indonesia. They sell a sun-lounger on wheels with a detachable tray that hooks on to one side in order to balance a coffee cup after lunch or a glass of sangria before dinner. They have circular tables and tables on wheels in the same material and, for croquet lovers, they sell the sets that have been manufactured by a firm called Jacques, in London, since 1795. These consist of mallets made of exotic wood from Haiti and ringed in brass, heavy balls, and steel or cast-iron hoops.

TECTONA   3, AVENUE DE BRETEUIL VII – 45 55 28 24

HABITAT As you would no doubt expect, Habitat has a large collection of garden furniture at very reasonable prices. The Chilean chairs and the coloured canvas deckchairs are particularly well-built and the colours vary year by year. There are matching parasols and they also sell folding chairs, armchairs and benches made of plain or lacquered metal. They have a pretty selection of black wrought-iron candlesticks.

♧ **HABITAT   35, AVENUE DE WAGRAM XVII – 47 66 25 52**

JARDINS IMAGINAIRES This shop is owned by Cléophée

de Turkheim and Guillaume Pellerin, and its name means 'imaginary gardens'. These imaginary gardens are admirably furnished with teak and cast-iron, lacquered wrought-iron and rattan, and have an old English comfort and style to them which is enhanced by the owners' talents as landscape gardeners, whether in winter or summer. You should try and take a look at the oxidized-iron collection designed by Caroline Odinet.

♡ **JARDINS IMAGINAIRES   9 BIS, RUE D'ASSAS VI – 42 22 90 03**

GALERIE MAISON ET JARDIN now produces furniture in wrought-iron, lacquered black or white, or with a green patina, and in 50s' wood. There's a Traineau chaise longue in a highly amusing design, an armchair with a matching pouffe, sofas, high tables and coffee tables. After the incredible response they received for a 19th-century colonial-style English sofa, they have now started selling a series of pieces of furniture decorated with knots and wicker interlacing. In the same shop you will find a delightful and permanent basketry collection, in both old and modern styles, flowerpot-holders and watering cans made of painted iron and light-fittings in all sizes. Dominique Menvielle-Bourg, the in-house designer, is a passionate antique-hunter, so it's worth popping in every now and then to see his most recent finds.

GALERIE MAISON ET JARDIN   120, RUE DU FAUBOURG SAINT-HONORÉ VIII – 45 61 93 30

And also:

UN JARDIN EN PLUS   222, BOULEVARD SAINT-GERMAIN VII – 45 44 18 67

FLEURS ET PAYSAGES   116, RUE DU BAC VII – 45 44 62 45

YVES HALARD   252 BIS, BOULEVARD SAINT-GERMAIN VII – 42 22 60 50

GARDEN JARDIN   25, RUE DE VARENNE VII – 42 22 97 33

GUNTHER LAMBERT   21, RUE LAS CASES VII – 45 50 23 62

OLARIA   114, RUE DE LA TOUR XVI – 45 04 18 87

LA DESSERTE   57, RUE DU COMMERCE XV – 42 50 60 71

ALLIBERT, GROSFILLEX, FERMOB, TRICONFORT and **RESISTUB** in the department stores and, particularly, in **BHV** and **SAMARITAINE.**

FLOWERS

We adore them in bouquets, and we also love them dried – it's all the rage on the other side of the Atlantic. Some even like them everlasting and silky.

Fresh cut flowers

MARIANNE ROBIC is as exquisite as one of her bouquets. A former assistant of Liliane François, she opened her own shop in an antique fish-merchant's, where she discovered beams and stone dating from the 18th century, which form an incredible backdrop to her wares. Her flowers are bunched together by colour, and her idea is to highlight the beauty of the flowers by an object or a branch, carefully placed next to them. Primrose Bordier and Catherine Canovas, the wife of the textile designer, were among her first customers and, 'They surely brought me good luck', swears Marianne.

♡ **MARIANNE ROBIC** 41, RUE DE BOURGOGNE VII – 44 18 03 47

CHRISTIAN TORTU is the all-round favourite florist for grand evening occasions, both Parisian and international. Nowadays he works alone and without a show-window. His bunches of anemones and red amaryllis tangle with sprays of apple blossom and privet berries twisted round with ivy. His book *Fleuriste* (published by Michel Aveline) is a must.

♡ **CHRISTIAN TORTU** 9, RUE CHRISTINE VI – 43 25 46 79

In the shops that bear the Christian Tortu name, the teams that he has trained carry on his work in the spirit of the master. The identifying trade-mark is the kraft paper in which the bouquets are wrapped and the raffia that ties them.

CHRISTIAN TORTU 6, CARREFOUR DE L'ODÉON VI – 43 26 02 56;
13, RUE SAINT-FLORENTIN VIII – 42 86 94 69

GUILLON FLEURS is run by two sisters, Laurence and Brigitte, who both adore white to such a degree that their two shop windows permanently show a sublime display in white. But, of course, they also sell pink, yellow, red and blue.

♡ **GUILLON FLEURS   120, BOULEVARD RASPAIL VI – 45 48 96 16**

MOULIÉ-SAVART His first name is Henri and he's set up shop next to the national parliament building. He doesn't work in politics but successive Prime Ministers of the Republic have all, inevitably, become his customers. 'A bouquet', he says, 'is a moment of desire'. It is thanks to him that interesting variations of foliage have replaced the once inevitable asparagus fern. His baskets of flowers are a 'must'.

MOULIÉ-SAVART   8, PLACE DU PALAIS-BOURBON VII – 45 51 78 43

LILIANE FRANÇOIS really likes foliage. 'It's an indispensable complement which gives a wild, flowing touch to the bouquet.' This florist doesn't have a moment's creative hesitation about intermingling fruit, flowers and vegetables.

LILIANE FRANÇOIS   119, RUE DE GRENELLE VII – 45 51 73 18

LHUILLIER have had a shop in the Place Vendôme for more than 100 years, and create poetry with their little bouquets of flowers. You should also take a look at the exquisite little stall they've opened in the famous Ritz corridor, which runs through the hotel and enables one to emerge on the other side of the Rue Cambon. They will still make up delightful buttonhole sprigs for you, and Americans go there for corsages, which are tiny bouquets that you pin at a lady's heart when you take her out for dinner.

♡ **LHUILLIER   2 and 15, PLACE VENDÔME I – 42 60 29 71/42 60 52 15**

LACHAUME is almost 150 years old and set up shop opposite that famous Paris restaurant Maxim's during those heady turn-of-the-century days we call 'La Belle Epoque'. Duchesses and sweethearts were made to blossom here by their admirers and Marcel Proust stopped by every morning to buy the orchid that he always wore in his buttonhole. A word of advice to plagiarists – they still sell them! In the window there are enormous vases containing 400 tulips, 150 roses, 100 snapdragons, and the single-colour displays of sweet peas at the beginning of May are simply staggering.

LACHAUME   10, RUE ROYALE VIII – 42 60 59 74

PATRICK DIVERT is both a horticulturist and a florist. This former inhabitant of Normandy prefers wild flowers to exotic ones and mixes wild grasses and herbs together in big Greek vases that spill out charmingly on to the Place de Mexico. A year ago, he took over the 'Des Fleurs' shop in the 7th arrondissement where his best-sellers are objects entirely wrapped in moss: apples, bears, ducks, crowns, etc, and little plants in pots that are also covered in moss. It all looks very poetic.

♡ **PATRICK DIVERT** 7, PLACE DE MEXICO XVI – 45 53 69 35; 4, RUE SAINT-DOMINIQUE VII – 42 22 22 46

PAYSAGE was set up in what used to be a restaurant by a graduate in horticultural studies from Provence called Christian Villemin. 'I don't have any particular style', he says, 'I just do whatever I feel like on the day'.

PAYSAGE 56, RUE AMELOT XI – 47 00 58 96

JEAN VASSAL comes from Aveyron and will enthusiastically tell you that there are 3,000 kinds of flowers on the Aubrac plateau in that area. Around ten years ago, it was he who launched the trend for hanging-baskets which he filled, quite simply, with campanulas, wild carrots and scabious. In season he goes home to look for that rare bloom, the black iris.

JEAN VASSAL 28, RUE DU BAC VII – 42 61 28 88

LUC GAIGNARD has a penchant for bright colours, as much for the decoration of his shop as for his bouquets. He boldly mixes together orchids and ears of corn, dried fruit and fresh flowers.

LUC GAIGNARD 13, RUE DU BOULOI I – 43 21 42 00

AU NOM DE LA ROSE doesn't belong to a certain well-known Italian writer but to the singer Dani, who sells not only roses but also all the other possible varieties and colours. People from showbiz, naturally, are among her clientèle.

AU NOM DE LA ROSE 4, RUE DE TOURNON VI – 46 34 10 64

AGAPANTHES All you have to do is ring and she'll come and make your home bloom – either just the once or on a regular basis. Marie-Ange Moreuil is wildly talented and drives all over Paris to deliver her compositions, which she makes up in her garden in the city suburbs.

AGAPANTHES – 46 04 36 66 (no shop)

THALIE is located in the Saint-Jacques du Haut-Pas district. In a prettily decorated salmon-pink shop covered with hexagonal red tiles which was used as a setting for the film *La Discrète*, Pascale Leray and Philippe Leclerc make up their simple, sophisticated bouquets, in which they harmonize all that nature generously offers up to us. There are bunches of pine-cones, ears of wheat and armfuls of laurel on a background of moss or branches of kumquats and lilies.

THALIE 223, RUE SAINT-JACQUES V – 43 45 41 00

JACQUES BARRAINE makes up extraordinary arrangements in his studio. Humble white flowers poke out from behind clumps of magnolia; arum lilies and hydrangeas wind round miniature clipped box-trees. It's an astonishing sight. Gawpers who aren't necessarily going to buy are greeted with a warm welcome and are sure to return when they have some money.

JACQUES BARRAINE 5, RUE MÉDÉRIC XVII – 42 27 96 97

And also:

À FLEUR DE POT 5, RUE DE MÉDICIS VI – 40 51 82 90

COMME À LA CAMPAGNE 29, RUE DU ROI-DE-SICILE IV – 40 29 09 90

PIERRE DECLERCQ 83, AVENUE KLÉBER XVI – 45 53 79 21

RENÉ VEYRAT 168, BOULEVARD HAUSSMANN VIII – 45 62 37 86

AU JARDIN SAINT-HONORÉ 36, RUE DE WASHINGTON VIII – 42 89 09 22

LE LIEU-DIT 21, AVENUE DU MAINE XV – 42 22 25 94

VOGEL-LAGNEAU 2, RUE DE MARIGNAN VIII – 47 23 42 67

LES MILLE FLEURS 2, RUE RAMBUTEAU III – 42 78 32 93

Dried flowers

JULE DES PRÉS is the pretty woman who really brought about the renaissance of dried flowers with her enthusiasm for the rural idyll: miniature trees made up of roses; baskets of sage and lavender; tableaux composed of oats, barley and wheat. A fragile form of art, pricey and much imitated. She remains the top of her field.

♡ JULE DES PRÉS 19, RUE DU CHERCHE-MIDI VI – 45 48 26 84; 46, RUE DU ROI-DE-SICILE IV – 48 04 79 49

UN TEMPS POUR ELLES A kingdom ruled by Catherine Rousse: a counter made of white pine, a ceiling hung with pale dried flowers, a little old fashioned, fragrantly scented. Sheaves and wreaths, garlands and baskets are all produced in front of your very eyes.

UN TEMPS POUR ELLES 10, RUE BOIS-LE-VENT XVI – 40 50 86 06

BOIS LACTÉ A shop-studio, a veritable chaos with an exquisite scent. The flowers are dried on site before use, while every day, outside, Yves Germain hangs up baskets full of everlasting flowers, little roses, delphiniums, hydrangeas and daisies. You can bring him your own vases or baskets, or even a straw hat to dress (which takes about a week).

BOIS LACTÉ 106, RUE DU CHÂTEAU XIV – 43 22 65 73

And also:

LE SORBIER DES OISELEURS   70, RUE VIEILLE-DU-TEMPLE III – 48 87 69 72

CAPUCINE   78, RUE DE CHARENTON XII – 43 43 68 23

CAMÉLIA BLANC   113, ROUTE DE LA REINE 92100 BOULOGNE – 46 04 45 76

CHAUFFOUR   45, AVENUE HOCHE VIII – 45 63 21 07

Silk flowers

TROUSSELIER cuts out his marvellous flower forms in the back of his shop, from velvet, silk or taffeta. Expert craftspeople, armed with delicate tools, immaculately model petals, pistils, stems and leaves.

TROUSSELIER   73, BOULEVARD HAUSSMANN VIII – 42 66 97 95

And also:

GUILLET   99, AVENUE DE LA BOURDONNAIS VII – 45 51 32 98

EMILIO ROBBA   52, RUE CROIX-DES-PETITS-CHAMPS I – 42 36 08 01

MAXIM'S FLEURS   5, RUE ROYALE VIII – 47 42 88 46

Rare plants

DESPALLES has been a regular meeting-place for botanists for the last 150 years. They know they'll find informed, knowledgeable staff and a catalogue with over 15,000 entries, which is one of their bibles. In the shop there are living plants, seeds and all kinds of bulbs, and there are also a horticulture bookshop and all the tools you'll ever need to become an amateur gardener or even a semi-professional.

♡   **DESPALLES**   76, BOULEVARD SAINT-GERMAIN V – 43 54 28 98; 5, RUE D'ALÉSIA XIV – 45 89 05 31; 87, AVENUE NIEL XVII – 47 66 52 99

STATIONERY

Crumpled paper, coloured paper, flecked paper, openwork paper, nowadays we constantly fax each other bits of paper and take down long phone messages on others, but when it comes to the written word, we still take a great deal of pleasure in writing on attractive stationery. Stationers dig into the wellsprings of their creative forces to create inviting designs and desires.

PAPIER + was the first shop to home in on our epistolary desires in 1976. A very cultivated gentleman, Laurent Tisné, who used to be in publishing, has been selling paper by the weight since that date. The scales, which have highly polished copper pans, reign supreme and you can choose between three grades of paper in 20 different sophisticated colours. They even have matching cards and envelopes. There are blank books, bound in linen, or on gilt-edged bible paper, and bundles of pretty-coloured pencils that come complete with a really good detachable rubber. They also sell excellent photograph albums. The shop next-door is devoted exclusively to drawing, but they are both characterized by colour and top-quality goods.

♡ ♧ **PAPIER +   9, RUE DU PONT-LOUIS-PHILIPPE IV – 42 77 70 49**

MARIE-PAPIER is the nickname of Marie-Paule Orluc, the beautiful lady with curly hair who packages the paper with the skill of a top couture designer. She sells it by the leaf or by the half-centimetre thickness and it comes in puckered, grease-proof, crystal, graded, Ingres, embossed, goffered, vellum, kraft cloudy, parchment, and so on. The leaves are made up into little notebooks, larger exercise books and albums, and the wrapping paper makes a wonderful gift in its own right.

♡ **MARIE-PAPIER   26, RUE VAVIN VI – 43 26 46 44**

MAGNA CARTA was opened in 1991 by an American lady called Libby d'Ennery. She imports cards and paper both from her native country and from Great Britain. At Christmas time the choice is incredible, which can be explained by the fact that the sending of greeting cards at this time of year is a real Anglo-Saxon tradition.

♡   **MAGNA CARTA   101, RUE DU BAC VII – 45 48 02 49**

MÉLODIES GRAPHIQUES imports the traditional and sublime marbled paper from Florence. This was invented by one of Louis XIII's bookbinders, Macé-Ruette and the technique was rediscovered by a Florentine called Francesco Giannini, for 'Il Papiro'. In all the colours of jewels and with motifs inspired by peacock feathers, these sheets of paper cover a thousand and one accessories around the office: exercise books, notebooks, desk blotters, letter holders, pencils, etc. Souvenirs of Tuscany.

MÉLODIES GRAPHIQUES   10, RUE DU PONT-LOUIS-PHILIPPE IV – 42 74 57 68

CALLIGRANE is also situated in the Rue du Pont-Louis-Philippe. Ingres paper in 16 colours, striped paper in 6 shades and marbled paper are completed by excellent pencils (Karisma Graphite or Blackhead). For the environmentally aware, they sell recycled paper. The shop next door sells pens: Omas, Spalding, Rohering, Montblanc, and so on. The grey Waltraud is a particularly chic model.

CALLIGRANE   4–6, RUE DU PONT-LOUIS-PHILIPPE IV – 48 04 31 89

LE MUSÉE DE LA POSTE has, like a lot of its colleagues, opened a shop, which was decorated by Christian Duc, and commissioned several designers to style some writing paper. Missives with a cultural connotation.

LE MUSÉE DE LA POSTE   34, BOULEVARD DE VAUGIRARD XV – 42 79 23 45

CASSEGRAIN has been printing writing paper since 1919 and also the visiting cards of the most nobly born members of Parisian society. These are shot through with colour and matching typography, coats-of-arms, too, when they're appropriate. You will also find exquisite little notebooks from Smythson, made in Bond Street: a triple address book for London, Paris and New York; the reversible 'Social and Business' diary; and the 'Don't Forget' notebook. They have desk accessories made in leather.

CASSEGRAIN   422, RUE SAINT-HONORÉ VIII – 42 60 20 08; 81, RUE DES SAINTS-PÈRES VI – 42 22 04 76

FILOFAX An English diary invented in 1921 which generated numerous imitators, but the original is called the 'organizer'. The multiple leaves enable computer programmers, musicians, mathematicians, writers and Uncle Tom Cobley to make up their own individualized binder, with complimentary underground maps for capital cities. They have leather binders (lamb, calf, crocodile, lizard and ostrich) and even vinyl ones for the less well off. There's even a specially designed slide-in pen called the 'Yard O-Led', as well as a range of handbags and briefcases with external pockets in which to store your Filofax. But the trendiest way to carry it is under your arm, and you should then leave it on the table in front of you, very nonchalantly, when you sit down.

♡ **FILOFAX 58, RUE DE BABYLONE VII – 45 55 53 34**

LEFAX is Filofax's main commercial competitor and they also have a shop in Paris.

LEFAX 32, RUE DES FRANCS-BOURGEOIS III – 42 78 67 87

THIERRY PERRIER sells a very pretty selection of writing paper (which you can have printed in the studio in the basement), cards and general stationery.

THIERRY PERRIER 24, RUE BARBET-DE-JOUY VII – 45 50 33 24 (by appointment)

BEAUVAIS This stationer and engraver celebrated his centenary two years ago and has just been bought out by Alain Varrier who continues all the traditions and sells an incredible selection of 400 kinds of ink!

BEAUVAIS 14, RUE DU BAC VII – 42 61 27 61

L'HOMME DE PLUME This is the kingdom of Françoise Leray, the antique-dealer, who has devoted it to office supplies 'which have been a little bit neglected', she says. To the pretty furniture she hunts out from all over the place, she adds appropriate accessories (such as paper knives, magnifying glasses, pencil boxes, etc.) and she's even designed a complete range of stationery.

L'HOMME DE PLUME 18, RUE DURET XVI – 45 01 93 87

GET A PEN is entirely devoted to writing instruments. There are almost 1,000 permanently in stock at all prices. Go there and explore!

GET A PEN 30, RUE DAUPHINE VI – 46 33 32 50

L'ART DU BUREAU cultivates the art of writing (paper and pens), the art of filing (albums, filing cabinets, diaries) and the art of décor (very beautiful furniture).

L'ART DU BUREAU 47, RUE DES FRANCS-BOURGEOIS IV – 48 87 57 97

BENNETON This worthy engraver still receives his customers in a fabulous wood-panelled room. Here stones can be seal-engraved.

BENNETON   75, BOULEVARD MALESHERBES VIII – 43 87 57 39

LE RÉVEIL QUI SONNE They have no shop in Paris, but their recycled paper, in the colours of Siennese soil or in pastel shades, is a must. Jean-Louis Bardon has, moreover, explained that he wanted to recreate a feel for bygone days in the designs, which he does by getting his designers to draw old-fashioned tradesmen, like butchers and grocers. Environmentally sound.

♡ ♧ LE RÉVEIL QUI SONNE at SAMARITAINE and at SUPERLATIF 86, RUE DU BAC VII – 45 48 84 25

LE JOUR & L'HEURE chooses the greatest names in English stationery, from Filofax personal organizers to solid-silver 'Yard O-Led' pens, and from Smythson writing-cases to the same maker's famous little leather notebooks.

LE JOUR & L'HEURE   3, RUE PERONNET VII – 45 44 40 01

And also:

ARMORIAL   26, AVENUE VICTOR-HUGO XVI – 45 01 69 01; 98, RUE DU FAUBOURG SAINT-HONORÉ VIII – 42 65 08 18

VENDEL-A   SHAKESPEARE   109,   BOULEVARD   HAUSSMANN   VIII – 42 65 28 92

SENNELIER   3, QUAI VOLTAIRE VII – 45 08 86 45

ADAM   11, BOULEVARD EDGAR-QUINET XIV – 43 20 68 53

LAVRUT   52, PASSAGE CHOISEUL II – 42 96 95 54

DUPRÉ-OCTANTE   141,   RUE   DU   FAUBOURG   SAINT-HONORÉ   VIII – 45 63 10 11

JOSEPH GIBERT   30, BOULEVARD SAINT-MICHEL VI – 43 29 67 50

LETTERBOX   7, RUE D'ASSAS VI – 42 22 40 03

SACRÉS PAPIERS!   20, RUE YVONNE-LE-TAC XVIII – 42 54 54 96

SHIZUKA   49, AVENUE DE L'OPÉRA II – 42 61 54 61

L'ENTREPÔT   50, RUE DE PASSY XVI – 45 25 64 17

KIMONOYA   11, RUE DU PONT-LOUIS-PHILIPPE IV – 48 87 30 24

BOUTIQUE COLBERT in the BIBLIOTHÈQUE NATIONALE   6, RUE DES PETITS-CHAMPS II – 47 03 81 77

ACT 9   27, AVENUE DE MAC-MAHON XVII – 40 54 94 88; 5, RUE D'ABOUKIR II – 42 33 28 47

L'ÉTIQUETTE   18, RUE SAINT-SULPICE VI – 43 25 54 66

THE WHOLE WORLD IN PARIS

Paris has always attracted foreigners who come for a holiday but end up staying permanently. Some of them launch shops with weird-sounding (to the French) foreign names, which is a way for their compatriots to find a little corner of the homeland and a way for Parisians to discover objects and customs from across borders and from overseas, without ever having to show a passport or change money. As an alternative, some French citizens who travel far and wide return home with 'souvenirs' and sell these themselves.

BRITISH STYLE

*Tweed, tartan, cardigans, polo-neck jumpers, tea, footstools . . .
and, indeed, Burberry raincoats, are always part of the Parisian
scene.*

BURBERRYS has been the symbol of upmarket street chic
since it first opened in 1850 when the young Thomas Burberry,
then aged 21, started a business in Hampshire. The shop on the
Boulevard Malesherbes has been open since 1910, and its walls
are covered in teak and decorated with engravings of sailing
boats, like a club in the Isle of Wight. They still sell the 'gent's
walking Burberry' a raglan raincoat, designed in 1856. The most
chic versions are made of cotton, the most practical in a
polyester-cotton mix. The famous trenchcoat is also very, very
popular, designed, as it was, for infantrymen in the First World
War. There are three shops in Paris, including:

BURBERRYS   8, BOULEVARD MALESHERBES VIII – 42 66 13 01

AQUASCUTUM is a Latin word meaning watershield, Since
the Siege of Sebastapol, the British soldier has been comfortably
equipped with 'a shield against water', the raincoat. Famous
clients have included Lord Raglan (who, because he lost an arm
in the Battle of Waterloo, invented the sleeve that bears his
name), Humphrey Bogart and Sir Edmund Hillary. For the
handsomest trenchcoats in Paris go to:

AQUASCUTUM   10, RUE DE CASTIGLIONE I – 42 60 09 40

SCAPA In this shop they sell the most beautiful cable-knit
pullovers in the capital with soft, matching printed skirts as well.
The collection, which is designed by Brian Redding, also
includes many slightly waisted blazers and pretty blouses.

♡   **SCAPA   71, RUE DES SAINTS-PÈRES VI – 45 44 18 50/45 48 99 44**

MARKS AND SPENCER Since it opened in France in 1975, Marks and Spencer hasn't sat on its laurels as the most important shop for tea and knickers in the capital; it has also developed into an entire department store with 6,200 square metres of floor area. Don't miss out on the muffins, the smoked salmon, the bacon, the underwear department and the men's and women's jumpers. A little piece of England in the heart of Paris.

♡ ♣ **MARKS AND SPENCER   6–8, RUE DES MATHURINS VIII –** 42 66 56 57 / 47 42 42 91

LAURA ASHLEY Everything started in 1953 with the English countryside as a canvas backdrop. Laura Ashley, who was in fact Welsh, designed motifs in her kitchen, which her husband Bernard printed on scarves in a traditional kind of way. We all know what happened next in this particular success story. Today, the heirs have re-formed the 'Ashley' empire, from clothes to wallpaper and from living-room furniture to perfume. For reasonable prices and all the charm of an English country cottage.

♣ **LAURA ASHLEY   261, RUE SAINT-HONORÉ I – 42 86 84 13**

AUX LAINES ÉCOSSAISES Started in 1897, the firm still imports around 20 kinds of tartan from Scotland, with which they make ties, blankets and dressing-gowns. The house speciality is lambswool knitwear from the Shetlands, which they stock in more than 20 colours. And viyella shirts (in cotton and wool).

AUX LAINES ÉCOSSAISES   181, BOULEVARD SAINT-GERMAIN VII – 45 48 53 41

IRELAND WAY A friendly hotch-potch. A large selection of Aran jumpers and cable-knit sweaters made of mercerized cotton.

IRELAND WAY   32, BOULEVARD RASPAIL VII – 45 48 25 21

OLD ENGLAND More than 100 years ago, Alexandre Henriquet, a hosier from the Ardennes, and his Irish partner used to sell tea, whisky, plum puddings and made-to-measure gabardine raincoats for gentlemen's chauffeurs. Their successors in the business have retained the oak staircase, the Cuban mahogany display shelves and the shop windows, but now they sell only clothes. Of course, what you would buy here are cashmere sweaters, Chester Barrie Shetland wool jackets with leather buttons and even the famous polished-shell top hats made by Christy.

♡ **OLD ENGLAND   12, BOULEVARD DES CAPUCINES IX – 47 42 81 99**

DAKS is synonymous with the most beautiful blazers and skirts with adjustable waists and pleats in the front. The house-check is a beige tartan which has been officially recognized by the Scottish Clan Tartan Society. They also manufacture genuine duffle-coats, made from an extraordinarily supple and dense woollen material.

DAKS 269, RUE SAINT-HONORÉ I – 42 60 22 19

HILDITCH AND KEY is an institution for superb, enormous scarves (140 centimetres), made of a silk-wool mix and entirely printed and hemmed by hand, with incredible lightness of touch. The exclusive designs are inimitable and always conceived with a touch of the Orient in mind. And, of course, they have the made-to-measure shirts and the cashmere knits in unusual colours.

HILDITCH AND KEY 252, RUE DE RIVOLI I – 42 60 36 09

ALFRED DUNHILL For the most stylish of horsewomen there are saddles, boots and barrel bags. And there are acid-coloured shirts with plain white collars sewn in a cotton as fine as any silk.

ALFRED DUNHILL 15, RUE DE LA PAIX II – 42 61 57 58

LA CORDONNERIE ANGLAISE Brick-red walls, rugs on waxed parquet flooring and little curtains for privacy. Here they sell and they repair any leather, hand-sewn items, with a special expertise in beautiful shoes.

LA CORDONNERIE ANGLAISE 28, RUE DES ARCHIVES IV – 48 87 11 43

ASHFORD Two pals had the bright idea of importing waterproof brogues, moccasins and court shoes, with leather linings and hand-sewn soles, all made of the softest leather. There are no middlemen, just a very simple décor, self-service sale and low prices.

ASHFORD 24, RUE DE CHÂTEAUDUN IX – 42 80 43 72

CHURCH The most famous shoes of the firm that was founded by Thomas Church in Northampton in 1873 are called the 'Balmoral', like the Queen's Scottish residence, and the 'Grafton', named after a fashionable pack of foxhounds. Both of these are classically styled and incredibly durable. There are four shops in Paris including:

CHURCH 4, RUE DU DRAGON VI – 45 44 50 47

MADELIOS Derek Rose's pyjamas are made of cotton with British regimental stripes, and they sell these in the shop alongside the Pantherella slippers, the woollen, super 100, ultra-light suits and the cashmere suits. They also have an exceptional selection of ties conjuring up the British version of luxury in their new premises.

MADELIOS   23, BOULEVARD DE LA MADELEINE I – 42 60 39 30

BETJEMAN AND BARTON and **TWINING** are naturally sorry that Parisians aren't quite such habitual tea-drinkers as the English. But you can go there to prepare for a real British tea with their selection of lapsang-souchong, orange pekoe, keemun and dozens of other varieties, all sold in pretty metal tins to keep the tea fresh.

**BETJEMAN AND BARTON   23, BOULEVARD MALESHERBES VIII –
42 65 35 94; TWINING 76, BOULEVARD HAUSSMANN VIII – 43 87 39 84**

LE TEA CADDY Behind their cups of tea and their scones and muffins, generations of lovers have sheltered in a desirably intimate atmosphere.

♡   **LE TEA CADDY   14, RUE SAINT-JULIEN-LE-PAUVRE V – 43 54 15 56**

GALIGNANI Under the First Empire (1804–15), this was a reading-room which published a literary gazette for English-speaking Parisians, later becoming the publisher of Byron, Thackeray, Sir Walter Scott and others. In 1856 Galignani set up in the Rue de Rivoli. The bookshop still belongs to the direct descendants of the founder, and it remains an international meeting-place for bibliophiles who are passionate about *belles lettres* and works on the fine arts.

GALIGNANI   224, RUE DE RIVOLI I – 42 60 76 07

W. H. SMITH AND SON and **SHAKESPEARE AND CO** Their primary concern is to nurture Parisians' English literary tendencies. You can place orders and, although you will have to wait a long time, the books will eventually get to you.

**W. H. SMITH AND SON   248, RUE DE RIVOLI I – 42 60 37 97
SHAKESPEARE AND CO   37, RUE DE LA BÛCHERIE V – 43 26 96 50**

WILLI'S WINE BAR was founded, and is now owned, by a charming Englishman called Mark Williamson, who has created one of the premier Parisian wine-bars.

WILLI'S   13, RUE DES PETITS-CHAMPS I – 42 61 05 09

MARWAY furnishes its customers in a comfortably English kind of way. They sell Chesterfield sofas and club sofas, glazed bookshelves and small revolving bookcases. The footstools are perfect for tired huntsmen who want to rest their weary bones after a long day while taking a sip of an old malt whisky. For rainy days they have an incredible selection of umbrellas.

**MARWAY   26, RUE DE RICHELIEU I – 42 96 23 33; 11, RUE DU BAC
VIII – 42 61 22 28**

BRITISH SHOP is situated on both sides of a narrow street in the 16th arrondissement. Chantal Lasserre is half-English and she sells earthenware pottery seconds there, as well as Wedgwood, Mason's and Johnson Brothers' bone china.

BRITISH SHOP   1 and 2, RUE FRANÇOIS-PONSARD XVI – 45 25 86 92

MARTIN BOLTON has a shop in Paris (Table Arts, decorative objects and furniture) and a warehouse in Asnières (furniture), which is only open on particular days of the year. You have to subscribe to his mailing list in order to receive regular news of his acquisitions. He can also track down individual items on request.

MARTIN BOLTON   48, RUE DES ARCHIVES IV – 42 72 27 19; 40, RUE MICHELET 92600 ASNIÈRES – 47 33 71 85

CRABTREE AND EVELYN sells perfume as well as ginger biscuits. The fragrant pot-pourri gives the shop a very distinctive scent.

CRABTREE AND EVELYN   177, BOULEVARD SAINT-GERMAIN VI – 45 44 68 76

COPPERFIELD, LA COMPAGNIE ANGLAISE, LE LOFT, ENGLISH ANTIQUES and **LE COMPTOIR ANGLAIS** all import furniture from England. In natural or painted pine, and in mahogany. Antique or modern, either with old wood or new (you only have to ask). You can also find painted rattan armchairs in glossy colours and the whole effect is very pretty, particularly in a country cottage.

COPPERFIELD   7–13, RUE DE TOLBIAC XIII – 45 85 84 16

LA COMPAGNIE ANGLAISE, ANCIENNE GARE D'AUTEUIL, PLACE DE LA PORTE D'AUTEUIL XVI – 46 51 04 36

LE LOFT   17 BIS, RUE PAVÉE IV – 48 87 46 50

ENGLISH ANTIQUES   14, RUE LINNÉ V – 47 07 54 44

LE COMPTOIR ANGLAIS   143, RUE DE PICPUS XII – 43 42 08 74

TIMOTHY OF SAINT-LOUIS happily mixes a variety of English products: 'Penhaligon' and 'Floris' eaux-de-toilette, sweet goodies from Crabtree and Evelyn and earthenware crockery like 'Calico', with little sky-blue and white flowers as well as ivory Creamware.

TIMOTHY OF SAINT-LOUIS   5, RUE DES DEUX-PONTS IV – 43 54 31 79

ALIETTE MASSENET regularly roots around from Land's End to John O'Groats to find silver-plated photo frames, cake slicers, crockery, etc.

ALIETTE MASSENET   169, AVENUE VICTOR-HUGO XVI – 47 27 24 05

HABITAT The first shop opened in London in 1964, and was founded by the designer, Terence Conran. Since that date he has received a knighthood and Sir Terence crossed the Channel in 1973, with tremendous success. Some people furnish their entire houses there, from the curtains to the kids' toys.

♧ **HABITAT**   35, AVENUE DE WAGRAM XVII − 47 66 25 52; 45, RUE DE RENNES VI − 45 44 68 74; 17, RUE DE L'ARRIVÉE XV − 45 38 69 90; 12, BOULEVARD DE LA MADELEINE IX

CHEZ PEINTURE (or 'at the home of painting') hasn't sold a single picture for a very long time. Anita Saada sells Liberty prints by the metre, from the lightest cotton to the heavier furniture fabric, from diaphanous net to wool-cotton mixes. The famous prints are many and the colours divine. There are matching gossamer wool shawls in different sizes, which are also knitted in England and are ideally suited to new-born babies, doting grandmothers and fragile throats of all ages.

♡ **CHEZ PEINTURE**   18, RUE DU PRÉ-AUX-CLERCS VII − 45 48 18 52

BRITISH STOCK imports all its jumpers from Scotland. They are knitted in 50 different shades of lambswool and two-ply cashmere. At more than reasonable prices.

♧ **BRITISH STOCK**   10, RUE GUICHARD XVI − 45 25 25 52; 15, RUE TRONCHET VIII − 49 24 99 44

CONRAN SHOP   Sir Terence, the creator of Habitat, has returned to Paris's Left Bank and installed his new universe in a former warehouse constructed in metal by Gustave Eiffel. The furniture and objects are a veritable melting-pot of everything, from anywhere in the world, that appeals to this architect-designer. He also puts his name to his own models and gives over a huge space, called the Conservatory, to the garden. It just has to be visited.

CONRAN SHOP   117, RUE DU BAC VII − 42 84 10 01

And also:

FILOFAX and its diaries   58, RUE DE BABYLONE VII − 45 55 53 34
DESIGNER'S GUILD and the fabric and wallpaper of the beautiful Tricia at ÉTAMINE   2, RUE DE FURSTENBERG VI − 43 25 49 83
MULBERRY COMPANY and its leather   14, RUE DU CHERCHE-MIDI VI − 42 22 95 05; 45, RUE CROIX-DES-PETITS-CHAMPS I − 40 41 07 69
TINKER TAILOR and its old-fashioned charm   110, RUE DES ENTRE-PRENEURS XV − 48 42 46 77

ITALIAN STYLE

They are the luxurious manufacturers of chiffon and the Viscontis of elegance. With collections that are as sparkling on the catwalk as they are at evening parties, the transalpine designers have created a place of honour for themselves in the world of Parisian fashion. They indulge their taste for beauty and their skill with the deluxe because they love them both.

MISSONI Optical-geometric prints, tachist artwork, pointillist designs, for the last 40 years Ottavio and Rosita Missoni have remained faithful to their way of mixing all the colours and designs in both their knitwear and their clothes. Irresistible and, unfortunately, exorbitantly priced.

MISSONI 43, RUE DU BAC V – 45 48 38 02

ETRO All the elegant women in the jet-set know Gimmo Etro, the Italian mill owner, who is famous for his cashmere printed textiles. They can buy them in Paris in a luxurious shop whose wood panelling and furniture were bought at Christie's to give a Victorian framework to the indoorwear, the luggage and the household linen. Our favourites are the enormous shawls and the sheets.

ETRO   66, RUE DU FAUBOURG SAINT-HONORÉ VIII – 40 07 09 40

GIANNI VERSACE is the superstar of Italian fashion with his spectacularly printed shirts and his sequinned evening tops which are as famous as the ballet costumes he created for Béjart. For the vamp women he clothes, he has created one of the most beautiful shops in Paris, festooned with frescoes, brand-name furniture, mosaics and glassware. On the first floor, the walls are as dramatic as if you were in a theatre, laden as they are with wistaria and roses hand-painted by an Italian artist. The fitting-rooms are draped with opera curtains, designed by the scene-painter from La Scala. Dazzled by the splendour, you will hesitate between dyed jeans, printed silk shirts and sequinned extravagances. Unaffordable.

GIANNI VERSACE 62, RUE DU FAUBOURG SAINT-HONORÉ VIII – 47 62 88 02

GIORGIO ARMANI It's futile to introduce Giorgio Armani, who symbolizes, everywhere in the world, the elegance of exclusive wool and the long, soft, perfect jacket. Beige, camel, apricot and moleskin grey add a discreet good taste, but without being boring. The ultimate is the result of Armani's research. His universe of *raffinatissima*, like his clothes, must be discovered in silence. But, on a more tangible note, Giorgio is the king of the loose-fitting blazer, cut from his own fabrics.

♡   **GIORGIO ARMANI   6, PLACE VENDÔME I – 42 61 55 09**

VALENTINO has celebrated 30 years in fashion surrounded by his famous clients from Marie-Hélène de Rothschild to Ivana Trump, from Elizabeth Taylor to Monica Vitti, which can be accounted for by the fact that this one-time assistant to Guy Laroche and Jean Dessès designs perfect, elegant fashion, with added charm. The sumptuous boutique with its marble floor is rather intimidating but the welcome is warmer.

♡   **VALENTINO   17–19, AVENUE MONTAIGNE VIII – 47 23 64 61**

CERRUTI 1881 On 1 August 1881 the three Cerruti brothers founded a textile workshop in Biella (in Piedmont). Antonio, alias Nino, their grandson and great-nephew, started his collection with male ready-to-wear designs. Which is why, when he launched a ladies' collection in 1976, he was most impressive with his perfectly cut jackets, his trousers that make one look thin and his impeccable suits.

CERRUTI 1881 FEMMES   15, PLACE DE LA MADELEINE VIII – 47 42 10 78

ROMEO GIGLI It's a former printworks that Romeo Gigli has transformed into a Venetian extravaganza. The entrance is set back and edged with small shrubs and, under an enormous glass roof, rugs are thrown across the floor. The court-coats are exhibited like works of art. The cashmere jumpers harmonize in subtle colourings. The shirts with their over-long sleeves, just as the master decrees, are cut in silk, velvet and jersey. A timeless space. A mysterious beauty. But are you in a fashion shop or in a faraway temple ?

ROMEO GIGLI   46, RUE DE SÉVIGNÉ III – 42 71 08 40

MAX MARA is for elegant women at all hours of the day and night. The diversity of shapes and choice of colours are enormous and the prices are affordable, because Dr Achile Mara Motti is the owner of one of the biggest ready-to-wear factories in Emilia-Romagna.

MAX MARA   265, RUE SAINT-HONORÉ I – 40 20 04 58; 37, RUE DU FOUR VI – 43 29 91 10; 100, AVENUE PAUL-DOUMER XVI – 40 50 34 05

BENETTON There's no need to do a sales pitch for the 'United Colours of Benetton' any more. Their highly controversial advertising campaign has done quite enough for them already. The saga of Luciano and his brothers and sisters forms part of the golden mythology of knitwear. Fashion, joie de vivre and reasonable prices. What more can one ask for? Our favourite shop is:

♣   **BENETTON   63, RUE DE RENNES VI – 45 48 80 92**

PRADA For years now, Parisian women have been fighting over the black reinforced-nylon quilted bag with its gold-chain strap. The collection has grown to include shopping-bags, pochettes and pouches decorated with silk tassels. They also sell pumps for a rich Cinderella, bags that are quilted as well as sophisticated and even a few cashmere jumpers in unusual colours.

♡   **PRADA   5, RUE DE GRENELLE VI – 45 48 53 14**

MARINA RINALDI dresses large women (sizes 14 to 28) with her well-cut suits, her silk blouses and her sun-bathing robes which will expose broader shoulders without giving them a complex.

MARINA RINALDI   56, RUE DU FOUR VI – 45 48 61 57

ERMENEGILDO ZEGNA opened his weaving factory in 1912 with a distinct aim in mind: to make wool as beautifully as the English. He succeeded. The third generation of Zegnas have more than 2,000 employees and their particular speciality is the super-light wool suit. Women who go there to help their husbands shop will find the most exquisite shawls made of wool, silk, cashmere and Parisian mohair.

ERMENEGILDO ZEGNA   10, RUE DE LA PAIX II – 42 61 67 61

GUCCI is one of the most visible shops in Paris since its recent face lift by Dawn Mello. Inès de la Fressange rushes over to buy their famous flat elasticated moccasins in all different colours. A successful come-back for the master saddler born in Florence more than a century ago, and whose saddles were characterized by their striped girths of green, red and green – the colours that have become house-style.

GUCCI   21, RUE ROYALE VIII – 42 96 83 27

MOSCHINO Pronounced 'Moskino', he's the Italian Gaultier.

A designer who mixes daring and classical style, wit and the avant-garde. With a wink at established designers, he's unpredictable but also amusing.

MOSCHINO at L'ÉCLAIREUR   49, AVENUE FRANKLIN-D.-ROOSEVELT VIII – 45 62 49 15; 3 TER, RUE DES ROSIERS IV – 48 87 10 22

KRIZIA (which is actually the designer Mariuccia Mandeli) is known for a penchant for spectacular, bright colours and high spirits. She set up shop on both the Right and Left Banks.

KRIZIA   27, RUE DU FAUBOURG-SAINT-HONORÉ VIII – 42 66 95 94; 35, RUE DE GRENELLE VII – 45 48 40 81

ENRICO COVERI This exuberant, talented Florentine is no longer alive but regulars know they will still find the prettiest summer T-shirts, bra-dresses and his famous sequins in the tiny shop.

ENRICO COVERI   2, RUE VIDE-GOUSSET II – 42 36 86 23

For the last 25 years Italian design has been making itself felt in France with its constantly fermenting talent and creativity.

RUBELLI comes from Venice and is spell-binding with his damask, silk, moire, velvet and lace.

♡   **RUBELLI   6 BIS, RUE DE L'ABBAYE VI – 43 54 27 77**

VOGHI comes from Como, the centre of the Italian textile industry, particularly for silk. The décor in the shop is by Gérard Gallet, who is Italian in spirit.

VOGHI   21, RUE BONAPARTE VI – 43 54 85 44

POLTRONA FRAU was established in Turin in 1912 by a Sardinian called Renzo Frau. All the chairs are made of leather, padded with feathers and there's an incredible rainbow of 100 colours made from the finest skins dyed overall with pure aniline. The greatest Italian designers work with them, or have worked with them: Gió Ponti, Mario Bellini, Marco Zanuso, Michele de Lucchi, Franco Rosi and others . . .

POLTRONA FRAU   242 BIS, BOULEVARD SAINT-GERMAIN VII – 42 22 74 49

ARREDAMENTO is synonymous with furniture for anyone from the Italian side of the Alps. The designers here are called Tobia Scarpa, Cini Boeri, Gae Aulenti, Achille Castiglioni, etc.

ARREDAMENTO   18, QUAI DES CÉLESTINS IV – 42 74 33 14

DANESE FRANCE specializes in functional items: glasses, place settings, frames, vases and office supplies. Most of these are designed by Bruno Munari and Enzo Mari.

DANESE FRANCE   174, BOULEVARD VOLTAIRE XI – 43 56 34 94

ALESSI commissions the top designers, primarily Italians, but others as well. His most recent collection, which was called 'Memory Containers', was designed by women. Cecilia Cassina, Christina Cappelli and Carla Ceccariglia are Italians, the others are English, American, Spanish and Argentinian. All of them work in stainless steel to create a range of dishes, fruit-bowls, centre-pieces, hot-plates, trays, goblets and boxes in unusual shapes.

ALESSI in the big department stores

ARTEMIDE, FLOS ARTELUCE and **TARGETTI** specialize in light-fittings in sober, rigorous shapes, designed by their compatriots.

ARTEMIDE   6, RUE BASFROI XI – 43 67 17 17

TARGETTI   100, RUE DE TOCQUEVILLE XVII – 42 27 48 46

FLO ARTELUCE   23, RUE DE BOURGOGNE VII – 45 51 40 62

VÉRONÈSE and the **GALERIE SAN MARCO** With very great thoughtfulness, they import chandeliers, wall lamps and mirrors from the glassmakers of Murano. The prices reflect the miraculous work of these craftsmen. But you can just go in and have a look.

VÉRONÈSE   184, BOULEVARD HAUSSMANN VIII – 45 62 67 67

GALERIE SAN MARCO   25 BIS, RUE FRANKLIN XVI – 45 53 56 72

GALERIE FARNÈSE scavenges for beautiful ceramic tiling in all the Italian houses they can find that are being pulled down. Chantal and Mario Di Donato also regularly reissue numerous old patterns with great skill. Moreover, you will encounter the finest designers on their premises, since this is a trademark that never makes a mistake.

GALERIE FARNÈSE   47, RUE DE BERRI VIII – 45 63 22 05

BUCCELLATI works in gold and precious stones like a lacemaker. Each one of his jewels is almost transparent, a small miracle. He was born in Milan, and since 1919 his windows at the corner of the Place Vendôme have been a pleasure to behold. He also makes magnificent silverware.

♡   BUCCELLATI   4, PLACE VENDÔME I – 42 60 12 12

BULGARI set up by the Trinità dei Monti in Rome in 1889 and in Paris in 1979. Specialities are medals and intaglios, mounted on necklaces and rings.

BULGARI   41, AVENUE MONTAIGNE VIII – 47 20 70 48

MARINA B is a relative of the above. A big fan of jewelry (it runs in the family), she has managed to put her famous initials to use in very geometric designs that can be used as multi-purpose objects: earrings that become brooches, for example.

MARINA B 18, AVENUE MONTAIGNE VIII – 40 70 16 17

POMELLATO is a Milanese jeweller whose caskets are grey and shut by a band of red elastic. To his jewelry he has now added a very beautiful collection of silver tableware, in very modern designs.

POMELLATO 66, RUE DU FAUBOURG SAINT-HONORÉ VIII – 42 65 62 07

REPOSSI This jeweller from Turin has had a Parisian outpost since 1985. In the Place Vendôme, naturally. He is famous for his dog-collars, his bows and his hearts.

REPOSSI 6, PLACE VENDÔME I – 42 96 42 34

NAJ OLEARI makes clothes, accessories and ornaments in very pretty materials inspired by naive motifs taken from the worlds of botany, flowers and animals (chickens, butterflies, cats, etc.).

NAJ OLEARI 130, AVENUE VICTOR-HUGO XVI – 47 55 67 45; 1 BIS, RUE DU VIEUX-COLOMBIER VI – 40 46 00 43

PERLIER has copied the yellow décor of his Milanese shop, and here in Paris he sells his wonderful body-products, scented with honey.

PERLIER 8, RUE DE SÈVRES VII – 45 48 48 05

LA MAISON DU LIVRE ITALIEN and **LA TOUR DE BABEL** sell a wide selection of Italian books. In the former you can order some of the exhibition catalogues of shows in Venice, Rome, etc.

LA MAISON DU LIVRE ITALIEN 54, RUE DE BOURGOGNE VII – 47 05 03 99

LA TOUR DE BABEL 10, RUE DU ROI-DE-SICILE IV – 42 77 32 40

ROUND EUROPE WITHOUT LEAVING PARIS

SPAIN

We were already 'au fait' with paella, bullfighting, flamenco dancing, tapas, Picasso and Dalí, but, since Expo '92 has focused the media spotlight on Seville, Hispanic designers have descended, en masse, on the Parisian scene.

SYBILLA is the infanta of Spanish fashion. A super-talent of chiffon, a perfectionist who chose gifted photographers to project her image. She designs pure forms, plain clothes, curvaceous with rounded hips, a flowing line that enhances the shape of the body. And funny, charming accessories. And household linen. Her whole world is gathered in a former saddler's workshop from the turn of the century: concrete floor and furniture made of untreated iron and rope. But there are also deep sofas, mirrors and bouquets of flowers.

SYBILLA 62, RUE JEAN-JACQUES-ROUSSEAU I – 42 36 03 63

LOEWE is pronounced 'louayvay' and is the most beautiful leather shop in Spain, founded in 1846. The equivalent of Hermès plus Vuitton from beyond the Pyrenees. They supply Princess Diana and Madonna, and generally use a fabulously soft Nappa leather. They sell clothes as well as bags, following the stylish guidance of the very French, very elegant Françoise Mohrt. The skirts with coloured panels are sublime and the gloves with their large cuffs are supremely elegant. There are very soft suede shirts and everything comes in a wide range of colours.

♡ LOEWE 57, AVENUE MONTAIGNE VIII – 45 63 73 38

ADOLFO DOMINGUEZ A designer from Galicia, he opened a shop in the Place des Victoires in 1985, with men's and women's collections. This exceptional colourist has another strength: beautiful materials, heavy silks, linen and light wool which he cuts with strength and precision.

ADOLFO DOMINGUEZ 2, RUE CATINAT I – 47 03 40 28

ROBERTO VERINNO is one of the great masters of the ready-to-wear world. Expensive and beautiful, his fashion seduces active women who like superb, comfortable materials and a certain classicism in the design. Despite the modest size of his Paris boutique, you will find almost all his designs there.

ROBERTO VERINNO 33, RUE DE GRENELLE VII – 45 44 57 35

GENE CABALEIRO Decorated by the Argentinian architect Haly Bonomo, the Parisian flagship of Cabaleiro is well aligned to the baroque style of the Spanish designer. Crazy décor and expensive materials characterize a world in which extravagance reigns supreme.

GENE CABALEIRO 6, RUE VIVIENNE II – 42 61 42 57

JESUS DEL POZO likes women to wear low-cut dresses, have rounded hips and amplify their shoulders. This highly seductive stylist remains faithful to his beloved beige, pink and pale yellow and can be bought at:

KASHIYAMA 147, BOULEVARD SAINT-GERMAIN VI – 46 34 18 45/ 46 34 11 50

ZARA is to Spain what Benetton is to Italy. You can get dressed from head to toe there, inexpensively, trendily and in a very friendly atmosphere. Better still, everything is arranged by theme, colour and style.

ZARA 2, RUE HALÉVY IX – 49 24 92 98

CASTANER is the king of the Spanish espadrille: he makes them for all the top people in the trade including Saint Laurent and Kenzo. You will find his original, inventive collection at:

STÉPHANE KÉLIAN 13 BIS, RUE DE GRENELLE VII – 42 22 93 03

PACO CHICANO is known for his message-bearing T-shirts with symbols dear to the Spanish: angels, roses, guitars and crosses. He also designs a very kitsch ready-to-wear collection.

PACO CHICANO at VICTOIRE 1, RUE MADAME VI – 45 44 28 14

CARTUJANO sew their shoes from the finest leather, following age-old traditional methods. Juan Carlos and Felipe Gonzales are regular customers. You have to try them.

CARTUJANO at L'ÉCLAIREUR 26, AVENUE DES CHAMPS-ÉLYSÉES VIII – 42 62 48 11

JOAQUIM BERAO works on his jewels like sculpture, which harmonizes the primitive with the avant-garde. He plays on the texture of shining bronze and silver with strength and simplicity. Emmanuelle Béart is a total devotee. And we are too.

♡ **JOAQUIM BERAO at MARIA LUISA** 2, RUE CAMBON I − 47 03 96 15

PALOMA PICASSO The dove has landed in Paris, in a wonderful shop. Bags, belts, scarves, glasses, everything is designed by Paloma with spirit and originality.

PALOMA PICASSO 5, RUE DE LA PAIX II − 42 86 02 21

LLONGUERAS is the only Spanish hairdresser in Paris. The stylists are trained in Barcelona, the director is Spanish and the style is international.

LLONGUERAS 229, RUE SAINT-HONORÉ I − 42 60 63 36

PASO DOBLE Because she has her shoes made for her in Spain, Claude Gallois, the stylist, has named both her shop and her trademark collection 'Paso Doble'. In a beige and red décor, the shoes are displayed on hanging trays. A sofa and a cast-iron stove create a homely atmosphere, reinforced by the vivacity of Claude, who greets the customers personally. Strong points: invention, classicism and low prices.

♣ **PASO DOBLE** 65, RUE DAGUERRE XIV − 43 27 28 94

LA LIBRAIRIE ESPAGNOLE offers bullfighting fans reproductions of paintings by Goya and Velázquez, and, also, wonderful art books.

LA LIBRAIRIE ESPAGNOLE 72, RUE DE SEINE VI − 43 54 56 26

PERSONA, NESTOR PERKAL and **MEUBLES ET FONCTIONS** have put the creations of the Catalonian designer Oscar Tusquets into their shop windows.

PERSONA 47, RUE DE L'UNIVERSITÉ VII − 45 48 85 83

NESTOR PERKAL 8, RUE DES QUATRE-FILS III − 42 77 46 80

MEUBLES ET FONCTIONS 135, BOULEVARD RASPAIL VI − 45 48 55 74

AXIS A long time has passed, already, since Axis led us to the discovery of the talents of Mariscal and his other pals from the Barcelona School.

AXIS 18, RUE GUÉNÉGAUD VI − 43 29 66 23

LORCA goes looking for ceramics beyond the Pyrenees and, to be precise, in Andalucia and the area around Murcia. They are perfect for country houses.

LORCA 42, RUE GRÉGOIRE-DE-TOURS VI − 40 46 02 55

C. M. DIFFUSION imports beautiful ceramic tiles from the Iberian peninsula. In the spirit of Valencia, there is semi-enamelled stoneware, stencilled with a frieze of winged lions interspersed with yellow flowers.

C. M. DIFFUSION   47–49, RUE SAINT-GEORGES IX – 48 78 39 32

SCANDINAVIAN COUNTRIES

To keep warm and still look delightful, try the Jacquards, leg-warmers and thick, woolly socks that come from the lands of the North. Barely off the boat from Norway or Iceland, and the women are already fighting over them in fashion shops.

KERSTIN ADOLPHSON is directed by Tordjön, a Swede and friend of the sculptor César. They sell work clothes and large postmen's sacks made of leather piled up around simple wooden clogs with no backs. They also sell wonderful jackets, cardigans and Jacquard pullovers.

KERSTIN   ADOLPHSON   157,   BOULEVARD   SAINT-GERMAIN   VI – 45 48 00 14

BREIZ NORWAY Almost 20 years ago, Marie and Francis Vatinel opened their charming shop, a bit of a jumble, a bit of a mess, but devoted to goods from Brittany and Scandinavia. On the Breton side there are reefer jackets, Quimper earthenware and 'chouchen', a kind of local mead. On the Norwegian side there are unvarnished Norway-spruce cradles, designed from a 100-year-old model, and traditional school satchels which you can use as backpacks, as well as all the really thick, warm Jacquard jumpers.

BREIZ NORWAY   33, RUE GAY-LUSSAC V – 43 29 47 82

TORVINOKA has been exhibiting an eclectic selection of furniture made of white wood, leather and canvas, designed by all the great names of the Norwegian design world. The collection is completed by beautiful tableware with floral and animal patterns.

TORVINOKA   4, RUE CARDINALE VI – 43 25 09 13

GEORG JENSEN is a silversmith and table artist. You will find a selection of the famous Royal Copenhagen china in his shop.

GEORG JENSEN   239, RUE SAINT-HONORÉ I – 42 60 07 89

FLORA DANICA with its 60s' décor is a tasty little stopping-place on the Champs-Elysées.

FLORA DANICA   142, AVENUE DES CHAMPS-ÉLYSÉES VIII – 43 59 20 41

LA BOUTIQUE DANOISE imports furniture and modern Scandinavian artwork.

LA BOUTIQUE DANOISE   42, AVENUE DE FRIEDLAND VIII – 42 27 02 92

And also:

FORUM   SCANDINAVE 43,   BOULEVARD   BEAUMARCHAIS   III – 40 27 00 12

LA BOUTIQUE SCANDINAVE   19, RUE DES PYRAMIDES I – 42 60 67 51

NETHERLANDS

DAMMANN'S is the name of a young man from Holland who sells delicious ice-creams in his charming tea room.

DAMMANN'S   20, RUE DU CARDINAL-LEMOINE V – 46 33 61 30

BELGIUM

DELVAUX is one of the oldest Belgian leather shops, supplier to high society and with a branch in Paris for a number of years now. It is wonderfully decorated and laid out on two floors. The leather is sumptuous and the patterns are original. Some are in two or three colours.

DELVAUX   18, RUE ROYALE VIII – 42 60 85 95

NATAN is the Belgian royal family's designer and specializes in jersey.

NATAN   8, RUE DU CHERCHE-MIDI VI – 45 44 54 18

POLAND

KSIEGARNIA POLSKA The Polish bookshop with the unpronounceable name. Of course they sell the original Polish editions of books, but they also sell beautiful works of art in popular prints, ceramics and recordings of folk and classical works.

KSIEGARNIA   POLSKA   123,   BOULEVARD   SAINT-GERMAIN   VI – 40 51 08 82

PORTUGAL

PORTO SANTO imports embroidery from Madeira, white and blue crockery from the Algarve and rugs from Alentejo.

♧ **PORTO SANTO   7, RUE DU VINGT-NEUF-JUILLET I – 42 86 97 81**

GREECE

ILIAS LALAOUNIS and **ZOLOTAS** translate the beauty of Ancient Greek jewelry into designs for our times.

ILIAS LALAOUNIS   364, RUE SAINT-HONORÉ I – 42 61 55 65

ZOLOTAS   318, RUE SAINT-HONORÉ I – 42 60 98 63

THE STATES ON THE SEINE

Discovering America without leaving Paris has now become easy. All you have to do is play cowboys and Indians, strike up a Dolly Parton pose and dress as if you're in Santa Fe.

RALPH LAUREN He has always taken the inspiration for his clothes from the Country and Western scene. Parisian Preppies, Yuppies and Nappies all swear by him. His 'total look' stretches from the nightdress to the jacket via trousers and suede jackets that have all become classics of the style. There is an impressive collection of polo-necks and pullovers made of Jacquard and ribbed cotton.

RALPH LAUREN   2, PLACE DE LA MADELEINE VIII – 44 77 53 50

RITA KIM set up a shop over ten years ago which is entirely devoted to gadgets marked 'Made in the USA'. Collectors, journalists, fans of American style and regular customers searching for an original gift all turn up to this funny jumble of a shop, to root out Americana. It may not all be original 50s' gear, but there are a lot of reproductions.

RITA KIM   79, QUAI DE VALMY X – 42 39 82 49

ESPRIT The famous 'wonder boys' from San Francisco launched their first collection made entirely of 100% natural fabrics. The jackets have recycled glass buttons or wooden ones, hand-painted by artisans from North Carolina. The shirts are cut in organically grown cotton containing no chemical fertilizers and using vegetable dyes. The concept stretches right down to the bags made of cactus fibre and woven by hand in a Mexican cooperative.

ESPRIT   9, PLACE DES VICTOIRES II – 40 39 00 95

LEVIS SHOP   The 501s are the archetype for all denim jeans everywhere, immortalized by James Dean. They are made of the famous indigo material which originated in Nîmes and the first pairs were produced in 1873 and still bear the number of that first lot of material. Real Levis have their tell-tale trademarks: copper rivets and a small red label sewn into the seams.

LEVIS SHOP   7, RUE PIERRE-LESCOT I – 45 08 19 19

RODSON   Completely smitten with the cinema of the 40s, he commissions replicas of Robert Mitchum's jackets, the trench-coat that Bogart wore in *Casablanca*, or the flying jacket that Cary Grant sported in *Only Angels Have Wings*. They also sell genuine stetsons.

RODSON   25, RUE DU LOUVRE I – 40 26 46 36

VENTILO   Navajo skirts with velvet panels, embroidered shirts and Santa Fe jackets, as well as the well-known brand of American loafers called 'Bass'.

VENTILO   3, RUE D'ARGOUT II – 42 21 39 83

ALLEN EDMONDS   In 1922, a young shoemaker in Milwaukee invented a new kind of ultra-strong shoe, made in the finest quality leather, without using nails to fasten the heels. In the Paris shop, there are brogues next to the style they call 'Strend', which are lace-ups with toe-caps.

ALLEN EDMONDS   115, AVENUE VICTOR-HUGO XVI – 47 27 56 10

COW BOY DREAM   collects American Indian clothes and Texan cowboy boots, not forgetting the original New York Police Department jackets.

COW BOY DREAM   16–21, RUE DE TURBIGO II – 42 36 30 05; 110, RUE SAINT-DENIS II – 42 36 38 15

EL PASO BOOTY   stocks up with American college rings, rockers' leather and bikers' Perfecto jackets and boots imported from across the Atlantic.

EL PASO BOOTY   79, RUE SAINT-DENIS I – 42 33 42 07

CHEVIGNON   sells a large selection of blankets, quilts and bedspreads in Navajo designs that girls wear as wraps like sarongs, around their waists, or generously belted with leather.

CHEVIGNON   49, RUE ÉTIENNE-MARCEL II – 42 36 10 16

WESTERN HOUSE has been causing the punters to dream about America for almost 30 years. From Hanes T-shirts to Harley Davidson jackets, from Reebok trainers to Cimarron's, Levis and other jeans. And, of course, they still sell the moccasin loafers designed by Penny Loafer and Clarks and the Converse All-Star or Top Sider basketball boots. There are numerous worked leather belts with heavy buckles, piles of coloured bandannas, jewelry from Santa Fe made of silver and turquoise and, for real James Dean fans, a cardboard, life-size, cut-out of the legendary actor!

WESTERN HOUSE   13, AVENUE DE LA GRANDE-ARMÉE XVI – 45 00 44 93; 23, RUE DES CANETTES VI – 43 54 71 17

The decorative feel of New England, California and New Mexico has seduced Parisians who no longer have to cross the Atlantic to furnish their houses in this way.

LE ROUVRAY 20 years ago they were the ones to introduce Parisians to the beauty of patchwork quilts, the bedspreads made by the first New World immigrants with all the odd pieces of material they could get their hands on. A poor man's skill became an art form. An American, Diane de Obaldia, used to buy them from the Amish, the Mennonite sect. She still brings them over to this day, but now also organizes classes and seminars so that you can learn the skill yourself. She sells all the necessary equipment to enable you to do so, as well as numerous books on the subject.

♡ LE ROUVRAY   1, RUE FRÉDÉRIC-SAUTON V – 43 25 00 45

RALPH LAUREN The cowboy fashion designer is also a decorator. In 1983 he added a Home section to his American stores and in 1990 he brought the idea across the Atlantic. 'I don't sell a jacket, a belt or crockery', he explains, 'I sell a way of life'. On the 'Home Collection' floor, you won't think you're in a shop, but in the private home of people who've been living there for years. You go through the scenery of a Hudson Bay fur-trapper to that of a New England mansion. You are sure to spend ages looking at the chambray and the dried-flower arrangements and then the cane furniture which would look just perfect on a Californian terrace. The owner of five mansions himself, Ralph Lauren has a wonderful eye for detail and we adore him.

♡ RALPH LAUREN   2, PLACE DE LA MADELEINE VIII – 44 77 53 50

AUTOUR DU MONDE-HOME COUNTRY Serge Bensi-mon has a passion for the States. Armchairs with lacquered wood-slats from upstate New York, patchwork and Santa Fe-style pottery are all displayed alongside one another in this very pretty shop.

AUTOUR DU MONDE-HOME COUNTRY   8, RUE DES FRANCS-BOURGEOIS III – 42 77 06 08

BAKER is located in the magnificent Grand Veneur building in the Marais district. You will find very beautiful American furniture, particularly from California and Florida. It's expensive but go there, even if it's just to have a look at the décor.

BAKER   60, RUE DE TURENNE III – 40 27 04 50

HARRY WINSTON is the jeweller whose praises Marilyn Monroe sang in that delightful film *Gentlemen Prefer Blondes*. As for Elizabeth Taylor, she's one of his numerous celebrity clients.

HARRY WINSTON   29, AVENUE MONTAIGNE VIII – 47 20 03 09

BRENTANO'S is the 'bilingual bookstore with an American accent', where you can buy the amazing Sunday editions of the *New York Times*, the *Village Voice* and the American edition of *Cosmopolitan*. They stock the novels of Ernest Hemmingway, F. Scott Fitzgerald and Robert Littell in English, and they always keep a copy of *Gone with the Wind*, as well as records, cassettes and videos in English.

BRENTANO'S   37, AVENUE DE L'OPÉRA I – 42 61 52 50

BLUE JEAN ATTITUDE 2,000 square metres devoted to jeans and everything you could ever wish to wear with them. A wonderful space, opened in April by Galeries Lafayette. On the floor there are natural wood floorboards and stencilled blue dinosaurs direct you round the shop. Every display area is highly accessible and tastefully decorated in a Cowboy or Santa Fe style. You will find all the well-known brands: Lee, Levis, Lee Cooper, Bensimon, etc., and, for the first time, Gap has crossed the Atlantic to Paris. They also sell Abaco leather and silver belts as well as Harpo silver and turquoise jewelry plus all the T-shirts, sweatshirts and jackets you could ever wish for. And even skirts to harmonize with jeans tops. In case you get a bit peckish, Lina has transported her delicious sandwiches and her distinctive décor from the Rue Etienne-Marcel (the pastrami is particularly good).

BLUE JEAN ATTITUDE   on the first floor of GALERIES LAFAYETTE BOULEVARD HAUSSMANN IX

COLLECTION PRIVÉE is run by Kim Benoit, the owner of a stand-ins and ticket agency. She has just opened a shop which is entirely devoted to jeans from floor to ceiling, with armchairs, luggage, studded skirts and breakfast trays.

COLLECTION PRIVÉE   15, AVENUE VICTOR-HUGO XVI – 44 17 91 85

JAPANESE, IF YOU PLEASE

In the wake of Kenzo and Miyaké (see THE CREATORS OF FASHION*), numerous Japanese stylists and designers have taken shops in Paris. Even if their sober, pure lines have been to some extent counter-pointed by the current baroque and 'urban street' trends, that doesn't make them any the less important.*

JUNKO SHIMADA Arrived in Paris to become an assistant at Cacharel and mastered the art of designing suits and little waisted dresses that give one a thin but spirited form. After having worked at the Mafia agency with Maimé Arnodin and Denise Fayolle, she launched her own label in 1981. Nothing is more up-to-the-minute than her 'princess' dresses and her little jersey sheath dresses.
JUNKO SHIMADA   54, RUE ÉTIENNE-MARCEL I — 42 36 36 97

ZUCCA In the shadow of Saint-Sulpice, you will come across a lacquered wood façade, two beautiful windows and a glass-roofed space. This is the kingdom of Zucca, the leader of simple, avant-garde style. The particular bonus extra of the 'princess' dresses and the navy-blue blazers is the sophistication of the finishing, executed just as if they were from top designer houses.
ZUCCA   34, RUE SAINT-SULPICE VI — 40 51 07 11

SHIHO A well-known name in the Empire of the Rising Sun for three generations and famous for the richness of its kimonos and its hand-embroidered silk fabrics. In the shop, which was styled by Wilmotte, Yuko Matsuo rolls back partitions to reveal sumptuously cut dresses in plain silks, printed silks, seersucker, streaked with gold thread or shaded with silver. These are small miracles, woven by hand, at prices that reflect all this.
SHIHO   17, RUE DE GRENELLE VII — 42 22 26 81

ATSURO TAYAMA has opened up in the Marais district, in a superb, light shop with a white marble floor and chrome-plated brass railings dating from the year 1910. A graduate of the Bunka Fashion College and Yohji Yamamoto's assistant in Tokyo, he exhibits his designs like works of art. Baggy, crocheted jumpers and masculine jackets – his speciality – with drawstring waists.

♡   **ATSURO TAYAMA   40, RUE DE SÉVIGNÉ III – 42 78 40 99**

L'EST ROSE A Japanese fashion label that set up in a former second-hand clothes store. Deliberately quaint décor, rococo and romantic in English Colonial style, shows off the work of the 15 designers from the Tokyo office, who collectively create pretty printed dresses, embroidered knitwear and retro-stitched outfits.

L'EST ROSE   9, RUE DE TURBIGO I – 40 39 07 00

SETSUKO Well-designed, inexpensive models, cut in the studio behind the shop: quilted jackets and kimono trenchcoats.

SETSUKO   17, RUE SAINTE-CROIX-DE-LA-BRETONNERIE I – 42 71 56 23

PACO FUNADA A former stylist at both Cacharel and Lassance, he now exhibits his own collection in an all-white setting (which Japanese dispassion requires). You should particularly look out for the pretty Scots-thread knitwear in pastel and acid colours.

PACO FUNADA   17, PLACE DES VOSGES IV – 40 27 94 29

MATSUDA His father sold kimonos in Tokyo. He came to Paris in the 80s, to study fashion and to preserve the memory of a famous French model, Nicole de Lamargé. His company, Nicole, now has more than 400 outlets throughout the world but it's under his own name that Matsuda exhibits his collection in Paris. They only sell refined goods here: meticulous, contrasting linings; hand-finishing; jewel-buttons made of mother-of-pearl and brass. There is a very beautiful, heavily worked and embroidered shirt collection, and pullovers made of guipure lace and macramé.

MATSUDA   26, BOULEVARD RASPAIL VII – 45 49 12 03

JUN ASHIDA This talented Japanese couturier has wanted to open a branch in Paris since the 60s. Now he has realized his dream with no expense spared: white marble staircase, dotted with decorative studs, which links the ground-floor, where the daywear is displayed, to the first floor, which is taken up with eveningwear.

ASHIDA   34, RUE DU FAUBOURG SAINT-HONORÉ VIII – 42 65 09 30

JIN ABE Japanese rigour of design, with brushed-metal bars suspended from the ceiling and from which the clothes hang, frosted-glass shelving and remarkable Jacquard knitwear executed with incredible technical skill.

JIN ABE 40, RUE DE GRENELLE VII – 45 44 37 02

CIEL DE VOSGES A funny name for a shop in Saint-Germain-des-Prés! Chosen by the Japanese, who were totally seduced by the sky above the Place des Vosges (since this is what the name means in translation)! Their specialities are the bags that they have made in France and Italy following patterns created by their style bureau.

CIEL DE VOSGES 25, RUE DU DRAGON VI – 45 44 35 32

YAMADA An important Japanese jewelry line set up in Paris with an objective in mind: to get its jewels known without the help of a middleman. Out of which emerge the seductive prices for their wonderful malachite, onyx and paste brooches and the ivory and ebony bracelets.

YAMADA 30, RUE DANIELLE-CASANOVA II – 42 86 94 81

HIDEO WAKAMATSU is the son of the president of the Japanese leather manufacturers' association. He opened a brushed-aluminium space with a cream-coloured gravel floor to highlight the modernity of his attaché-cases, briefcases and suitcases. All the designs are very Japanese with magnetic clasps, extension pouches, adjustable straps and integral umbrella-holders.

HIDEO WAKAMATSU 77, BOULEVARD SAINT-MICHEL VI – 43 54 71 63

YUKI TORII The textile prints and the embroidery are wonderful, charming and original and they change every season.

YUKI TORII 38–40, GALERIE VIVIENNE I – 42 96 64 66

And also:

KENZO, YOHJI YAMAMOTO, COMME DES GARÇONS and ISSEY MIYAKÉ

SHIRO KURAMATA was one of the greatest architect-designers in Japanese history. He died quite recently but his designs are still sold in France. The most famous is a tall chest of drawers he called 'Side One Side Two' with very curvaceous lines, which was, as he was wont to say with a trace of a smile, a tribute to the shape of Marilyn Monroe's behind!

SHIRO KURAMATA at GALERIE YVES GASTOU 12, RUE BONAPARTE VI – 46 34 72 17

SHIZUKA stands for serenity and harmony. In the Parisian shop that bears its name, you will find all the perfectly designed gadgets that friends once had to bring us back from trips to Tokyo. There are small matt vinyl, coloured bags, beautiful tool boxes, pencils and paper made from recycled goods, well-thought-out crockery and comfortingly heavy face towels.

SHIZUKA   49, AVENUE DE L'OPÉRA II – 42 81 54 61

DAÏMARU allows the mistresses of Japanese households to prepare dishes from their homeland by supplying them with the ingredients in this self-service grocery store. As a foreigner, however, you will simply have to guess what these ingredients are, since nothing is translated. They sell delicious little noodles artistically intermixed and that famous local delicacy – hot sake. They also astutely stock portable clothes pegs and kitchen utensils.

**DAÏMARU at PALAIS DES CONGRÈS, PLACE DE LA PORTE MAILLOT XVII –
40 68 21 05**

GISEH make kimonos, quilts, cushions and, particularly, futons, those Japanese mattresses that roll out in the evening and become beds. They are excellent if your kids have pals to stay the night.

GISEH   27, QUAI DE LA TOURNELLE V – 46 34 09 29

IKEBANA DÉCO designs Japanese gardens for his clients' terraces and little landscapes in glasshouses for the ones without gardens. They have an enormous selection of bonsai trees which will be diminutively to your taste.

IKEBANA DÉCO   70–72, BOULEVARD SAINT-GERMAIN VI – 43 26 69 56

KIMONOYA is one of the prettiest Japanese shops to have opened in Paris. Gérald Ménager and his wife, Machi Kojima, have gathered a collection of cedar combs and angora paint-brushes, tweezer-scissors and old and new kimonos. Everything is divinely displayed.

♡   KIMONOYA   11, RUE DU PONT-LOUIS-PHILLIPE IV – 48 87 30 24

MIKI HOUSE also belongs to Gérald Ménager and sells Japanese children's clothes. Bold colours, comfortable styles and rather expensive prices.

MIKI HOUSE   1, PLACE DES VICTOIRES I – 40 26 23 00

SHISEIDO One of the largest brands of beauty products in Japan, whose artistic director, Serge Lutens, is French!

SHISEIDO in the **PERFUMERY** departments of the big department stores

SHU UEMURA is also a substantial beauty product range. With an incredible palette of eyeshadows as creams (28 colours), as pencils (35 colours) or in powder compacts (90 colours). Eye pencils, lipstick, nail-varnish and blusher are also all there in plentiful supply. The make-up remover oil is perfect with its clever spill-proof pourer. They've just started selling eau-de-toilette and the application brushes in all shapes and colours are simply fab!

SHU UEMURA   176, BOULEVARD SAINT-GERMAIN VI – 45 48 02 55 and at GALERIES LAFAYETTE BOULEVARD HAUSSMANN IX

TOKYO-DO is the largest Japanese bookshop in Paris. Numerous Japanese tourists flock there to buy their daily papers and their favourite magazines. Western travellers on their way to the Land of the Rising Sun go there to find guide-books, dictionaries and various books on cooking and origami, that wonderful folding art.

TOKYO-DO   4, RUE SAINTE-ANNE I – 42 61 08 71

TORAYA has been supplying the Japanese Imperial Court with pastries for the last 11 centuries! They opened in Paris in 1980 and everyone's been going mad over their surprising little cakes that look like works of art.

TORAYA   10, RUE SAINT-FLORENTIN I – 42 60 13 00

MIKIMOTO is the name of the inventor of the cultured pearl and is still one of the biggest names in the Japanese jewelry world. In the Place Vendôme you will find the pearls exhibited in a pale wood décor, and you can go there to have your strings of pearls, your chokers and your dog-collars rethreaded.

MIKIMOTO   8, PLACE VENDÔME I – 42 60 33 55

ANSHINDO import their pearls from the Tsushima Islands. Round, oval or baroque, they come in all the colours of the rainbow and are threaded on to stainless steel, which is unbreakable but pliable as well.

ANSHINDO   8, RUE DE LA PAIX II – 40 20 07 65

JUNKO KOSHINO In her gallery she wants to combine the rich artistic traditions of Japan with modern industrial technology. She exhibits the work of her compatriots as well as that of French designers.

JUNKO KOSHINO   10, AVENUE MONTAIGNE VIII – 47 20 38 92

YAMAKADO is a young designer who now lives in France. Her designs are poetic and include chairs decorated with flowers and butterflies and 'Elfe' tables with feet in the shape of tree-trunks, as well as hunch-backed coat racks.

YAMAKADO at GALERIES LAFAYETTE   BOULEVARD HAUSSMANN IX

MOKUBA dresses the hair of many a Parisian lady with sublime organza ribbons, iridescent with colour. Or they are used to make beautiful gift-boxes. There are 21,999 other kinds of ribbon to chose from as well.

♡   **MOKUBA**   18, RUE MONTMARTRE I – 45 08 80 02

IRIS produces 5 million buttons a day in Japan. In the Paris shop you can spend hours just looking at them all. The big jewel-buttons are a must for the dressy suits of the great French couturiers.

IRIS   350, RUE SAINT-HONORÉ I — 42 61 53 75

A TASTE OF THE EXOTIC

You like it or you hate it, you might prefer the colonial look or the post-colonial return to a festoon of native colour. In whatever form, exoticism is here to stay. From India to Morocco, from Kenya, Guatemala and China, it's landed higgledy-piggledy and in every conceivable style – as we deliver it to you.

SIMRANE has soft, yielding bedcovers made in India as well as cushions, tablecloths and bedspreads from designs and colours inspired by the local culture. Embroidered with pearl pendants, there are big voile sarongs with matching scarves, which have been very successfully adapted to Western tastes.

♡ **SIMRANE   23–25, RUE BONAPARTE VI — 43 54 90 73**

LE JARDIN MOGHOL Via its textiles, this shop tells the story of the Moghul period of Indian history, from the beginning of the 16th century to the end of the 18th. Brigitte Singh has very beautiful prints made for her in Rajasthan, in cotton or silk-cotton mixes. Back in Paris, her friend Béatrice Jaunet sews them into clothes, tablecloths, and so on, and then adds material and antiques from the Far East to the collection. It's all very sophisticated.

♧ **LE JARDIN MOGHOL   53, RUE VIEILLE-DU-TEMPLE III — 48 87 41 32;**
33, QUAI DES GRANDS-AUGUSTINS VI — 44 07 09 42

DIWAN covers mattresses, cushions and bolsters with Oriental carpet, made of mohair velvet with Kashmiri or arabesque motifs, to make comfortable, low sofas. You can also furnish your entire living-room in an exquisite Oriental style and even hang dyed fabrics on your walls. These are made-to-measure by Jean Lillet.

DIWAN   10, RUE SAINTE-ANASTASE III – 42 78 99 94

LA DÉLÉGATION À L'ARTISANAT MAROCAIN stands next to the country's Tourist Board office – the eponymous country being, of course, Morocco. For those people who daydream about Morocco, they sell pretty leather bags, embroidered in matching colours or two contrasting colours. They also sell boxes made of worked thuja wood, soft stripy Arabic tunics, flower-pot holders and candlesticks made of hammered or chased copper. The white cotton tablecloths, which are very reasonably priced, are embroidered in Fez and the wonderful knotted woollen rugs originate in Rabat.

LA DÉLÉGATION À L'ARTISANAT MAROCAIN   161, RUE SAINT-HONORÉ I – 42 60 50 27

MICHÈLE BACONNIER is passionate about Morocco and every time she goes she brings back trunkfuls of local craftwork. There are ceramic vases from Fez, tin-plate and glass lanterns, hand-painted ceramic tiles of all sizes and tables made in traditional Arabic designs.

MICHÈLE BACONNIER   6, RUE DE VARENNE VII – 45 48 46 77

TISSUS CHARLES The Kissaria of Montmartre is the nickname of the Rue Pierre-Picard, which stands in the shadow of the Sacré-Coeur and where there are a large number of textile shops. This is because it reminds lovers of the Orient of the Kissaria or tents from which the local textile-merchants do their trade. You are just as likely to meet the most chic society ladies in the street as the beautiful exotic girls of Paris, who go there to kit themselves out in their traditional costumes. Each one uses the pools of colour in her own way – to make up traditional 'gandouras' or cushions. Or they use the batiquework to make long African-style tunics and tablecloths, or the broderie anglaise fabrics to make tops and table-covers, or the tie-dye textiles to make turbans and curtains. As for the embossed velvet and the sequinned muslins, they bring joy to the hearts of costume-designers and, occasionally, even the top couturiers of Paris. You have to hunt around and let your imagination run riot. The two best shops are:

♡ **TISSUS CHARLES   8, RUE PIERRE-PICARD XVIII – 46 06 63 08;**

TEX RECORD 14, RUE PIERRE-PICARD XVIII – 42 58 91 65

The **LIBRAIRIE BOUTIQUE DE L'INSTITUT DU MONDE ARABE** is on the ground floor of this wonderful building designed by the architect Jean Nouvel. They sell an eclectic assortment of wares and you will find jewelry and cookbooks side by side, muslin shawls from Aleppo and T-shirts printed with extracts from the Koran, Oriental music recordings and kilim bags.

LIBRAIRIE BOUTIQUE DE L'INSTITUT DU MONDE ARABE   23, QUAI SAINT-BERNARD V – 40 51 38 38

LE MONDE SAUVAGE takes us to strange climes in its four shops, located in the Les Halles area of Paris. Old material from the Hindu Kush, dhurries in gentle stone-washed colours, multi-coloured baskets from Kenya, Chinese suitcases.

LE MONDE SAUVAGE   86 and 101, RUE SAINT-DENIS I – 40 26 28 81; 82, RUE RAMBUTEAU I – 40 26 85 06;   20, RUE PIERRE-LESCOT I – 40 26 28 09

INNA KOBJA Loincloth material from Bouaké (on the Ivory Coast), fringed cotton from Mexico, Indonesian batiks . . . This casbah of a shop is more like an Oriental bazaar, strangely scattered with armchairs, pictures and pieces from the 40s that Inna Kobja (an anagram – almost – of Annie Jacob) has turned up from hunting round old junk shops.

INNA KOBJA   23, RUE DES FRANCS-BOURGEOIS IV – 42 77 41 20

Y'ATOUT is a vast emporium, specializing in leather. Bags, both for the city and the beach, fringed like rugs and photographed for magazines from all over the world, are imported from Kenya. Arlette Rosenfeld, the owner, has had leather handles added to them to make them look more Western. She has done the same with the Guatemalan bags, crocheted entirely out of cotton in cross-stitching. Her leather-goods department now holds pride of place.

Y'ATOUT   30, RUE DE BUCI VI – 43 26 96 98

AFRICA DESIGN wants to create a modern vision of African design by using precious wood from the regions and by taking up traditional designs. Ebony dishes from Togo, exotic wooden trays from the Central African Republic, bottle-openers made of thuja roots, lids made from Senegalese wood, office items in Moroccan thuja, brushed leather diaries from Burkina Faso, batiks from Burkina and Togo, dyed raffia panelling with decorative inserts from Zaïre, woven loincloths from the Niger, amber, silver and flecked pearl necklaces from the Niger and Zaïre. Real quality goods.

AFRICA DESIGN   155, QUAI DE VALMY X – 42 05 71 02

TOTO SOLDES There are great piles of batik lying around the shop. The cotton fabrics with the big patterns which African women like are made specially for them in China and the Netherlands.

♣ **TOTO SOLDES   25, AVENUE DE CLICHY XVII – 43 87 34 36; 7, PLACE DE LA MADELEINE VIII – 42 66 67 69**

You are bound to feel disorientated if you go for a walk around the 13th arrondissement of Paris. In other parts of Paris, too, there are numerous Asians, who have opened super little shops.

STASIA dresses little girls to look like Suzy Wong, with great slits up the sides of their skirts. For women there are embroidered tops made of polyester or silk, silk jackets either with embroidery or without, embroidered pullovers with sequins in matching tones, and pearl necklaces with mother-of-pearl, jade, coral and ivory insets, all at reasonable prices.

STASIA 14, RUE DES FRÈRES D'ASTIER-DE-LA-VIGERIE XIII – 45 86 26 16

ANNY designs swishing wedding-dresses for Oriental types. The very sexy little sheath-dress with a cute round collar is the thing to wear to ceremonies in pagodas – it's traditional.

ANNY   32, AVENUE DE CHOISY XIII – 45 70 80 89

WA QUAN is an expert on steamed food. You will find all the necessary equipment in the shop, including the china bowls and the right kind of chopsticks. There is a wonderful teapot made of lined wicker that you can use to keep tea warm. Wa Quan sells a special auto-cooker for rice and there is an impressive, permanent collection of teapots.

WA QUAN 15, RUE DES FRÈRES D'ASTIER-DE-LA-VIGERIE XIII – 45 83 33 02

KIM THANH The bazaar in which to find everything you wanted to buy but didn't have room to bring back from your trip: quilted jackets, embroidered tops, painted china, etc.

KIM THANH   69, AVENUE D'IVRY XIII – 45 83 62 00

TANG FRÈRES supplies the ingredients to the Asian community in the 13th arrondissement of Paris. In the supermarket they sell strange fruit and vegetables: ginger, sweet potato, tito, taro, banana leaves and packets of fine noodles, pork and cooked beef, dried black mushrooms and lotus plant roots.

TANG FRÈRES   48, AVENUE D'IVRY XIII – 45 70 80 00

KAWA Their regular customers are the owners of the Asian restaurants you find in Paris, but they sell to individuals as well. They stock white and blue china spoons, and some in pretty, pastel colours, little sake and soup bowls, plates and flowerpot holders. The décor is defined by sculpted wood screens and even pot-bellied Buddhas. They also sell all kinds of tea.

KAWA   3, PLACE DE STALINGRAD X – 40 37 96 03

COMPAGNIE FRANÇAISE DE L'ORIENT ET DE LA CHINE A Parisian businessman, François Dautresme, came home from China, more than 20 years ago, bowled over by the richness of their traditional art forms. He very rapidly opened a couple of shops that concentrate equally on clothes, materials and pieces of art. Their speciality is blue and white Chinese pottery but they also sell silk jersey T-shirts and frogged jackets.

COMPAGNIE FRANÇAISE DE L'ORIENT ET DE LA CHINE   163 and 167, BOULEVARD SAINT-GERMAIN VI – 45 48 00 18

LA ROUTE DU TIBET sells objects from that wonderful country (and other countries as well) that are made by exiles who now live in Nepal. There are carpets dyed with vegetable colourings, natural silk shirts woven by hand, traditional chiffon dolls and silver and turquoise jewelry.

LA ROUTE DU TIBET 3, RUE DES FOSSÉS SAINT-JACQUES V – 46 33 10 16

The **GALERIE URUBAMBA** has been selling old and modern high-class pieces for almost 20 years. They operate from inside an old half-timbered house in the Latin Quarter. Stern masks, feather headdresses, silver and turquoise jewelry, belts, blankets and strikingly embroidered fabrics are all exhibited under beautiful posters and photographs that make you want to pack your bags immediately. Sociology and ethnology books complete this beautiful collection of cultural objects.

♡   GALERIE URUBAMBA   4, RUE DE LA BÛCHERIE V – 43 54 08 24

ANDINES imports goods from Colombia and Ecuador. There are coloured toy trucks, embroidered clothes and carved animals, all at reasonable prices.

ANDINES   24, RUE ANDRÉ-DEL-SARTE XVIII – 42 59 87 19

LA PAMPA gathers together craftwork from Argentina, Peru, Colombia, Guatemala, Mexico and Chile. There's enough to make a grand tour of South America, just going round and admiring the palo-santo-wood birds and the Chuculanas and Nazca Indian pottery. They also sell wooden, bronze, horn and marble jewelry, and material from Guatemala, made up into bags, belts, shirts, cardigans, hats. And it's all pretty cheap.

♧ **LA PAMPA** 189, RUE LEGENDRE XVII – 42 29 53 71

CUMBIA exhibits objects from Colombia, a country that Renée Raymond particularly likes. There are black and red pots from La Chamba, and 'barniz', which are resin-covered painted wooden carvings from Pasto. They also sell 'chinas de Pitalito', which are exquisite little models of Colombian lorries, and some jewelry, reproducing the pieces exhibited in the Bogotá museum.

♡ **CUMBIA** 115, RUE DU CHERCHE-MIDI VI – 40 49 02 82

LA BOUTIQUE D'AMÉRIQUE LATINE is in the heart of Montparnasse and is stuffed full of toucans and exotic birds made of papier maché in bright colours or of very pale wood from the Amazonian rainforest. You can also find Peruvian and Colombian jewelry.

LA BOUTIQUE D'AMÉRIQUE LATINE 68, BOULEVARD PASTEUR XV – 43 20 91 91

EXPLORA sells a selection of decorative pieces from Mexico and Guatemala including: woollen rugs, emerald blown glassware, ceramic fruit, beaded coconuts and ikat patchworks.

EXPLORA 46, RUE TIQUETONNE II – 40 41 00 33

L'OEUF DE COLOMB sells goods from Mexico: papier maché monsters in bright colours, silver crosses, etc.

L'OEUF DE COLOMB 23, RUE DES BLANCS-MANTEAUX IV – 42 72 21 22

FRIDA is an Ali-Baba's cave of Latin American goods, with its naively designed terracotta and its little coaches that are painted to look just like the ones that go round the Colombian roads. There are also papier maché flowers and animals from Mexico, ceremonial masks from Guatemala, rain-wands from Peru and objects made of precious wood from Argentina.

FRIDA 9, RUE DU DRAGON VI – 42 22 57 02

MÉLO imports wonderful ikats, old and new, hand-woven by the Guatemalan and Mexican Indians. A joyful rainbow of colours.

MÉLO 46, RUE VIEILLE-DU-TEMPLE IV – 42 71 99 43

PACIFIC COMPAGNIE discovered Mexican painted furniture that reproduces the luxuriance of the native flowers and plants. They also import the ceramic blue and black dinner services and the wonderful cast-aluminium dishes that come in all sizes.

PACIFIC COMPAGNIE 63, AVENUE DE LA BOURDONNAIS VII – 47 53 83 99

CÔTÉ HACIENDA wants us all to discover the art of living on its large Mexican estates. Truly wonderful.

CÔTÉ HACIENDA   14, RUE DE BIRAGUE III − 42 77 99 97

PALENQUE also imports beautiful craft objects from Mexico: pottery, vases, jewelry, scarves and jackets. You are bound to feel as if you're on a journey to foreign shores.

PALENQUE   26, RUE DANIELLE-CASANOVA II − 42 96 23 59

LE COMPTOIR MEXICAIN has an impressive stock of terracotta tiles, enamelled ceramics, bricks, flowerpots and bowls, all made by hand. There are a large number of white and blue or white and green motifs but there are many other bright colours as well. And there are even some sculpted wooden doors and columns. It's wonderful.

LE COMPTOIR MEXICAIN   38 BIS, RUE RAPHAËL 92170 VANVES − 46 44 64 12

And also:

COCODY   1, RUE FERDINAND-DUVAL IV − 42 77 28 82

ARTISANS DU MONDE   20, RUE ROCHECHOUART IX − 48 78 55 54

MAAM SAMBA   14, RUE DU ROI-DE-SICILE IV − 42 77 40 11

MACHU PICHU   4, RUE DES PYRAMIDES I − 42 97 44 82

LIGHT LUNCH
AND A TEATIME TREAT

LIGHT LUNCH AND A TEATIME TREAT

Everyone knows that women like a light, quick lunch, rounded off, at teatime, with a delicious little pastry or an ice-cream to accompany their cup of Lapsang Souchong. Or, indeed, to make a special detour, in order to buy up a particular confectionery shop.

Light lunches

LINA'S is admirably well-placed, not a stone's throw from the Place des Victoires. Lina Ghosn and Noémie Ermelin make fabulous American-style sandwiches with pastrami, smoked salmon and cream cheese, and so on. The brownies melt in your mouth and the red-fruit juice is delicious. The queue between 1 pm and 2 pm can be pretty long, but it's sophisticated and they have two cafés in Paris. Our favourite is:

♡ LINA'S 50, RUE ÉTIENNE-MARCEL II – 42 21 16 14

LE CAFÉ DES LETTRES owes its name (the café of letters) to the fact that it's in the publishing area of Paris. It's decorated in blotting-paper green and Hermès red and they serve Swedish food. The atmosphere is designer-intellectual.

LE CAFÉ DES LETTRES   53, RUE DE VERNEUIL (in the courtyard on the left) VII – 42 22 52 17

VIRGIN CAFÉ is on the second floor of the Mecca of music. It is decorated in black, brown and beige, broken up by beautiful black and white photographs. Above one's head a wall of video screens transmits clips of singers, and newspapers are piled up on the grand piano. There is an uninterrupted view of the Champs-Elysées. It's all full of atmosphere.

VIRGIN CAFÉ   52, AVENUE DES CHAMPS-ÉLYSÉES VIII – 42 89 46 81

The **BAR DES THÉÂTRES** allows you to rub shoulders with all the top models and all the chicest fashion retailers in Paris.
BAR DES THÉÂTRES   6, AVENUE MONTAIGNE VIII – 47 23 34 63

LADURÉE In 1862 this was a bakery. The painted ceilings with their chubby cherubim and wood-panelling date from 1890 and you eat off marble and marquetry pedestal tables. The hot chocolate is sublime as are the bite-size sandwiches wrapped in greaseproof paper. The hippest place to eat in town! One of the writers of this guide is addicted to their macaroons.
LADURÉE   16, RUE ROYALE VIII – 42 60 21 79

DALLOYAU has had a shop in the Faubourg Saint-Honoré since 1802. The tea-shop in which the writer and photographer François-Marie Banier, as a young man, swallowed a dozen cakes in a few minutes is on the first floor and has recently been redecorated in sycamore panelling and shades of salmon-pink. Of course, you can also have lunch there and the other writer of this guide can't get enough of these macaroons.
DALLOYAU 99–101, RUE DU FAUBOURG SAINT-HONORÉ VIII – 43 59 18 10

MARIAGE FRÈRES has been importing tea since 1854 and now sells more than 400 flavours, displayed in large metal tins. You will find the wonderful tea-room in the Marais district at the back of the shop, where it is decorated in an old colonial style. There's also a cafe on the Left Bank, on the first floor of a building with a very 17th-century feel.
MARIAGE FRÈRES   30, RUE DU BOURG-TIBOURG IV – 42 72 28 11; 13, RUE DES GRANDS-AUGUSTINS VI – 40 51 82 50

FAUCHON A pleasant and convenient café for women who shop around the Rue Royale, the Madeleine, the Rue Tronchet and the department stores.
FAUCHON   26–30, PLACE DE LA MADELEINE VIII – 47 42 60 11

WILLI'S WINE BAR was the first wine bar in Paris around 15 years ago. It's a particular godsend for the women who like to have a single glass of wine with their lunch, and that's all. The pleasant tables are laid out at the back of the bar, near the windows.
WILLI'S WINE BAR   13, RUE DES PETITS-CHAMPS I – 42 61 05 09

The **BAR DE L'HÔTEL WESTMINSTER** is decorated in green with a wonderful chimney-piece. There are low armchairs on a level with pedestal tables and the atmosphere is quiet, while the little treats are delicious. It's terribly discreet.
   ♡ **BAR DE L'HÔTEL WESTMINSTER   13, RUE DE LA PAIX II – 42 61 57 46**

VERLET has been roasting since 1880. Caffeine addicts feed themselves here by snatching a *croque-monsieur* with a side-salad. The décor is sober but the smell divine.

VERLET   256, RUE SAINT-HONORÉ.I – 42 60 67 39

WEST SIDE CAFÉ has a very Manhattan feel to it. They serve clam chowder and combination sandwiches. For afters, they have brownies and cheesecake, which are both fab!

WEST SIDE CAFÉ   34, RUE SAINT-FERDINAND XVII – 40 68 75 05

ANGELINA is a regular haunt of the many chic people who are fans of that most melting of pastries, the Mont Blanc, a Parisian monument to chestnut purée and whipped cream. Gilded wood-panelling and little pedestal tables provide the setting, hot chocolate, so thick that your spoon will almost stand vertically, provides the refreshment. And there's a view of the Tuileries gardens. When the top designers and stars of the fashion world present their shows in the courtyard of the Louvre, journalists, buyers and models all run over to this very special café.

♡   ANGELINA   226, RUE DE RIVOLI I – 42 60 82 00

BOISSIER has, thank God, preserved its pretty, blue crackled metal tins of boiled sweets. The tea-room is comfortable and frequented by perfect people.

BOISSIER   184, AVENUE VICTOR-HUGO XVI – 45 04 87 88

COQUELIN specializes in a kind of chestnut ice-cream dessert, which should really be eaten at the right time of year, which happens to be winter. The tea-room only has a few tables but the service is fast at lunch-time. On holidays, this is the meeting-place for all the private-school kids in the area.

COQUELIN   67, RUE DE PASSY XVI – 45 24 44 00

A PRIORI THÉ has one of the prettiest terraces in Paris. Under the glass-roof of the Galerie Vivienne, you will find rattan tables and chairs. Passers-by stop and kiss their pals: stylists, designers, journalists, 'readers' from the nearby Bibliothèque Nationale and shoppers from the Place des Victoires. It's all very chic.

A PRIORI THÉ   35–37, GALERIE VIVIENNE II – 42 97 48 75

LE LOIR DANS LA THÉIÈRE (or 'the dormouse in the teapot') has preserved its Alice-in-Wonderland name throughout the years, as well as maintaining its divine atmosphere and its very tasty cakes.

LE LOIR DANS LA THÉIÈRE   3, RUE DES ROSIERS IV – 42 72 90 61

LES DEUX ABEILLES combines turn-of-the-century décor and a winter garden in the chicest part of Paris. The cakes and

AV. DES CHAM

AV MARCEA

AV. TR

ROOSEVELT

TSCHERRER

MUGLER

NINA RICCI

51

49

54

LAROCHE

39

AV. MONTAIGNE

VUITTO

HARRY WINSTON

40

34

CHANEL

29

THEATRE DES CHAMPS ELYSEES

32

CARON

DIOR

26

CHRISTIAN LACROIX

18

PORTHAULT

14

OIS 1er

600

INES DE LA FRESSANGE

6

BAR DES THEATRES

2

UNGARO

AV. DES CHAMPS-ELYSÉES

AVENUE MARCEAU

AV. GEORGE V

AV. MONTAIGNE

ROOSEVELT

AV. FR. D...

R. WASHIN...

R. PO...

R. DE LA BOET...

R. DE L'ANTH...

R. du COLISÉE

R. BASSANO

R. de... QUENT...

RUE FRANÇOIS

RUE CHARRON

R. CHARRON

RUE MARBEUF

RUE MARIGNAN

R. de Marignan

VELT

RUE de la TREMOILLE

RUE TREMOILLE

AV. PIERRE 1er

SERBIE

ILSON

ALMA MARCE...

1er

RUE JEAN GOUJON

COURS ALBERT 1er

PLACE DE L'ALMA

QUARTIER TRIANGLE D'OR

the clientèle are both way above average.

LES DEUX ABEILLES 189, RUE DE L'UNIVERSITÉ VII – 45 55 64 04

LES BOURGEOISES The customers in this tea-room in the Marais, with its beige façade, eat their sweet delights in a softly lit environment.

LES BOURGEOISES 12, RUE DES FRANCS-BOURGEOIS IV – 42 72 48 30

LES ENFANTS GÂTÉS have hung tasteful black and white photos of stars all over their ochre-coloured walls. There are rattan and old leather armchairs, piles of newspapers, and you can spend the whole afternoon just sitting around relaxing. There's also a painting gallery in the basement.

♡ **LES ENFANTS GÂTÉS** 43, RUE DES FRANCS-BOURGEOIS IV – 42 77 07 63

MARAIS PLUS is an art bookshop, as well as being a toyshop and a supplier of all kinds of teapots. There are two floors and you will receive a warm welcome.

MARAIS PLUS 20, RUE DES FRANCS-BOURGEOIS IV – 48 87 01 40

LA PALETTE GOURMANDE In a pink and green setting, on a mezzanine floor, you can partake of little savoury tartlets, brownies and cream cheese cakes.

LA PALETTE GOURMANDE 1, RUE SAINTE-ANASTASE III – 42 78 19 90

LES FOUS DE L'ÎLE are as mad about 'brunching' as they are about painting.

LES FOUS DE L'ÎLE 33, RUE DES DEUX-PONTS IV – 43 25 76 67

AU VIEUX CONTINENT has opened a special 'quick snack' corner (serving items like steak tartare, courgette tart and Mexican beer) on the mezzanine floor of this megastore.

AU VIEUX CONTINENT 5, RUE D'ARGOUT II – 40 39 94 94

L'ENTREPÔT has a charming bar they call Paris-Plage on a mezzanine floor at the back of this large store.

♡ **L'ENTREPÔT** 50, RUE DE PASSY XVI – 45 25 64 17

VENTILO has a tea-room upstairs. You will find the red-currant meringue utterly delicious.

VENTILO 27 BIS, RUE DU LOUVRE II – 45 08 49 00

CHEVIGNON TRADING POST has opened a coffee-shop in the basement, where you can have American-style snacks in a Western atmosphere.

CHEVIGNON TRADING POST 4, RUE DES ROSIERS IV – 42 72 42 40

L'HEURE GOURMANDE is hidden away in the Passage Dauphine. The mezzanine floor shelters the secret conversations of publishers and their authors. At tea-time, grandmothers go bananas over the buns and even buy more to take home for breakfast.

L'HEURE GOURMANDE   22, PASSAGE DAUPHINE VI − 46 34 00 40

FLORA DANICA has always retained its 60s décor. The Scandinavian platter with a light beer makes a perfect combination. The bilberry tart, topped with cream, is just delicious, but pay attention because the entrance is under the archway, on the right.

♡ ♧   **FLORA DANICA   142, AVENUE DES CHAMPS-ÉLYSÉES VIII − 43 59 20 41**

LE SALON DE THÉ DE LA MOSQUÉE is reserved for the nostalgic joys of mint tea and honey, almond and pistachio cakes. The atmosphere is altogether foreign and you will only emerge from this Turkish bath of an establishment when forced to, after a very pleasant stay indeed.

♡   **LE SALON DE THÉ DE LA MOSQUÉE   39, RUE GEOFFROY-SAINT-HILAIRE V − 43 31 18 14**

And also:

LA COUR DE ROHAN   61, RUE SAINT-ANDRÉ-DES-ARTS VI − 43 25 79 67

NOURA   27, AVENUE MARCEAU XVI − 47 23 02 20

LES DEUX MAGOTS   190, BOULEVARD SAINT-GERMAIN VI − 45 48 55 25

VALÉRIE TORTU   11, RUE DE LA GRANDE-CHAUMIÈRE VI − 46 34 07 58

L'ASSIETTE À PÂTES   50, RUE DE VERNEUIL VII − 47 03 91 10

LE BISTROT SAINT-JAMES   2, RUE DU GÉNÉRAL-HENRION-BERTHIER 92200 NEUILLY − 46 24 21 06

LA CRIÉE   10, AVENUE DE MADRID 92200 NEUILLY − 46 24 05 30

ROSE THÉ VILLAGE SAINT-HONORÉ   91, RUE SAINT-HONORÉ I − 42 36 97 18

L'ÉPICERIE RUSSE   3, RUE GUSTAVE-COURBET XVI − 45 53 46 46

LES ÉTAGES   35, RUE VIEILLE-DU-TEMPLE IV − 42 78 72 00

MUSCADE   36, RUE MONTPENSIER I − 42 97 49 59

CASTA DIVA   27, RUE CAMBACÉRÈS VIII − 42 66 46 53

LUNCHTIME   255, RUE SAINT-HONORÉ I − 42 60 80 40

CONCERTEA   3, RUE PAUL-LOUIS-COURIER VII − 45 49 27 59

LES NUITS DES THÉS   22, RUE DE BEAUNE VII − 47 03 92 07

BRÛLERIE DE L'ODÉON   6, RUE CRÉBILLON VI − 43 26 39 32

Confectionery

LE DUC DE PRASLIN The only sweetshop on the Avenue Montaigne. The boxes, designed by Christian Duc, are as sublime as the Amanda, Lyette, Mirabo and Passion bonbons that they contain. Once you've eaten the sweets, you are bound to want to keep the boxes, as well as the charmingly old-fashioned packaging that contains those classic pralines from Montargis.

♡ **LE DUC DE PRASLIN** 44, AVENUE MONTAIGNE VIII – 47 20 99 63

LA MÈRE MICHEL is actually called Christiane Simon and owns a delicious old-style confectionery shop. There are chocolates and really fresh crystallized fruit, Commercy madeleines, Nançay shortbread and sweeties from Rheims, all vying with each other for shelf-space.

LA MÈRE MICHEL 44, RUE OLIVIER-DE-SERRES XV – 42 50 46 91

À L'ÉTOILE D'OR is in the heart of the theatre and cabaret district. Denise Acabo, with her blond plaits and her tie, is mad about chocolate. For her, 'eating chocolate is, quite frankly, an orgasmic experience'!

À L'ÉTOILE D'OR 30, RUE FONTAINE IX – 48 74 59 55

FOUQUET The traditional delicatessen, with a quite exceptional selection of tea, jam, and chocolate in all possible variations. There are also old-fashioned sweets like sugar violets and poppies.

FOUQUET 22, RUE FRANÇOIS-Ier VIII – 47 23 30 46

LA MÈRE DE FAMILLE has seen generations of gourmets turn up at its doors since it opened in the 18th century. The décor only dates from 1900 (!), but, just for the hell of it, you can buy yourself a caramel-covered chocolate lollipop.

LA MÈRE DE FAMILLE 35, RUE DU FAUBOURG-MONTMARTRE IX – 47 70 83 69

LA CONFISERIE SAINT-PIERRE makes up charming baskets decoratively filled with things like red-fruit jam, China tea and honey from the Gâtinais region.

LA CONFISERIE SAINT-PIERRE 33, RUE DE CHAILLOT XVI – 47 20 39 28

AUX FRIANDISES DE FRANCE serves traditional specialities from the four corners of France: *calissons* from Aix, *négus* from Nevers, *forestines* from Bourges, *bêtises* from Cambrai and *berlingots* from Nantes. All packed in most original boxes.

AUX FRIANDISES DE FRANCE 44, AVENUE CHARLES-DE-GAULLE 92200 NEUILLY – 46 24 83 11

Pastry shops

LA VIEILLE FRANCE continues making your French grandmother's old cake recipes with delicacies like the Salammbô, the Sanflorain and the Religieuse (cream bun), to which the couturier Christian Lacroix is very partial.

LA VIEILLE FRANCE 14, RUE DE BUCI VI – 43 26 55 13

SALBRON On Saturdays and Sundays only, they make a famous speciality they call the 'kouglof', which is recommended by the Egon Ronay of French cuisine, Jean-Pierre Coffe.

SALBRON   4, PLACE BRANCUSI XIV − 43 21 76 18

MICHEL PLOUSSEAU is an expert on Chibouste tart, which is a kind of puff-pastry miracle made with apples, on to which you pour the light Chibouste cream sauce, caramelized over the heat. It's heavenly. But do raise your eyes to the ceiling to admire the pretty glass.

MICHEL PLOUSSEAU   208 BIS, RUE DE GRENELLE VII − 45 51 29 98

LE STÜBLI specializes in Viennese pastry with whipped cream. The *Käsesahnetorte* (made with cheese and whipped cream) is simply divine, as is the apple strudel and the nut shortbread.

♧ **LE STÜBLI   11, RUE PONCELET XVII − 42 27 81 86**

STOHRER arrived in France following the reign of Queen Marie Leszczynska (in the 18th century, for those who have temporarily forgotten the dates!), and opened a shop in the Rue Montorgueil where he invented rum-baba and the 'Alibaba'.

STOHRER   51, RUE MONTORGUEIL II − 42 33 38 20

GÉRARD MULOT The whole of Saint-Germain-des-Prés goes there for their lemon tart.

GÉRARD MULOT   76, RUE DE SEINE VI − 43 26 85 77

HELLEGOUARCH comes into its own in the soft-fruit season.

HELLEGOUARCH   185, RUE DE VAUGIRARD XV − 47 83 29 72

BOURDALOUE still drives us all crazy with its wells of love.

BOURDALOUE   7, RUE BOURDALOUE IX − 48 78 32 35

Chocolate-makers

LA MAISON DU CHOCOLAT of Monsieur Robert Linxe is considered the ultimate in the field by the real experts. The tea-room in the Rue François-Ier is very pleasant. Listen to the advice of the waitresses when they tell you to order the hot chocolate, of which there are several varieties: Caracas, Seville, Bacchus, Guayaquil, etc. And you don't just imbibe chocolate. In the summer, the chocolate sorbet is a real delight. You might meet Catherine Deneuve, Philippe Noiret or perhaps even the designer Angelo Tarlazzi. The parent shop is located in the Faubourg Saint-Honoré.

♡ **LA MAISON DU CHOCOLAT   56, RUE PIERRE-CHARRON VIII −
47 23 38 25; 225, RUE DU FAUBOURG SAINT-HONORÉ VIII − 42 27 39 44**

CHRISTIAN CONSTANT has written a book (published by Nathan) on the subject. The banana tart with a cream base is delicious and the hot chocolate is fit for the Aztec gods.

CHRISTIAN CONSTANT   26, RUE DU BAC VII – 47 03 30 00

DEBAUVE ET GALLAIS has existed since 1800 and has one of the prettiest shopfronts in Paris. Painted in green Louis XVI style with vaulted windows and fanlights, on the inside you would imagine that you're in a little temple. The traditionally made delicacies have names like Jacob, VII and Bonaparte, which is logical given the location. For legitimists and Orleanists (monarchists, in other words), there are chocolate bars with moulded fleur-de-lys (the traditional symbol of the French royal family). A suitable motif for the merchant who once supplied the kings of France.

DEBAUVE ET GALLAIS   30, RUE DES SAINTS-PÈRES VII – 45 48 54 67; 33, RUE VIVIENNE II – 40 39 05 50

WEISS They have been chocolate merchants in Saint-Etienne since 1882, and package their chocolates in aluminium foil, then in boxes the colour of jewels. This was the idea of the stylist Primrose Bordier, who is hooked on chocolate.

♡ ♧   WEISS at the PALAIS DES CONGRÈS   PLACE DE LA PORTE MAILLOT XVII – 40 68 21 55

JADIS ET GOURMANDE weaves chocolate plaits and then dots them with crystallized fruit and almonds. These taste as attractive as they look. For more literary types, there are letters you can buy individually so that you can make up your own name, message or motto.

♡ ♧   JADIS ET GOURMANDE   49 BIS, AVENUE FRANKLIN-D.-ROOSE-VELT VIII – 42 25 06 04; 88, BOULEVARD DE PORT-ROYAL V – 43 26 17 75; 27, RUE BOISSY-D'ANGLAS VIII – 42 65 23 23

RICHART has got rid of the customary gilded packaging and now surrounds himself with white. The advice of the management is to take careful note of the 'sell-by' date and then eat all the contents in less than ten days. Which is eminently possible!

RICHART   258, BOULEVARD SAINT-GERMAIN VII – 45 55 66 00

MICHEL CHAUDUN names his creations after the South American regions that supply the cocoa solids.

MICHEL CHAUDUN   149, RUE DE L'UNIVERSITÉ VII – 47 53 74 40

LA FONTAINE AU CHOCOLAT is normally reserved for fans of the strong sensation – digestively speaking, of course. One particular surprise is the dark chocolate that contains a white grape-seed coated with vintage marc.

LA FONTAINE AU CHOCOLAT   107, RUE JOUFFROY XVII – 47 63 15 15

Ice-cream shops

BERTHILLON, a café since 1954, offers 36 sorbets including a wonderful wild-strawberry flavour, 30 straight ice-creams including 7 different chocolate flavours, and 6 alcoholic sorbets. The chestnut ice-cream brings instant sunshine to a winter's day and is quite simply divine.

♡ **BERTHILLON   31, RUE SAINT-LOUIS-EN-L'ÎLE IV – 43 54 31 61**

BEZANÇON has devastated the population of Neuilly, and the Sainte-Croix school-children in particular, by moving to Boulogne. The ice-creams are still as good and the shop is much, much larger.

♡ **BEZANÇON   38, RUE JEAN-BAPTISTE-CLÉMENT 92100 BOULOGNE – 48 25 91 46**

RAIMO The house speciality is Peach Melba. This dessert was invented by the great chef Auguste Escoffier for the Australian singer Dame Nellie Melba, and celebrated its centenary in 1992. The cinnamon, honey and mint sorbets are just as delicious.

RAIMO   59–61, BOULEVARD DE REUILLY XII – 43 43 70 17

BAGGI has been making ice-cream since 1850. 'Chocolatine' is made of chocolate, caramel and orange, 'Brasilia' is a kind of iced coffee and 'Gourmet' is a coffee cream with added almond.

BAGGI   33, RUE CHAPTAL IX – 48 74 01 39

HÄAGEN DAZS is the Number One ice-cream maker on the other side of the Atlantic. Since they opened in Paris two years ago the shops have become favourite places for teenagers to meet and eat pecan ice-cream, chocolate brownie ice-cream and 25 other flavours.

HÄAGEN DAZS   1, RUE D'ARCOLE IV – 40 51 08 51; 3, PLACE DE LA CONTRESCARPE V – 40 51 03 51; 5, PLACE VICTOR-HUGO XVI – 45 00 95 65

BASKIN-ROBBINS was started in the United States 25 years ago and is as famous as McDonalds over there. They sell unusual blends of ice-cream.

BASKIN-ROBBINS   1, RUE DU FOUR VI – 43 25 10 63; 96, RUE RAMBUTEAU I – 42 21 18 19; 84, BOULEVARD DU MONTPARNASSE XIV – 43 21 47 56

DAMMANN'S sells a wonderful selection of ice-creams right in the middle of the Latin Quarter. And has the good taste not to drown its Peach Melba in fresh cream, which it serves on the side.

DAMMANN'S   20, RUE DU CARDINAL-LEMOINE V – 46 33 61 30

FASHION AND BEAUTY INDEX

*This is organized according to the initial letter of the first name of the company.
Christian Lacroix, for example, is listed under 'C' and Galeries Lafayette under 'G'.*

LIFESTYLE INDEX

This index includes luggage, country weekend, classics, the 'World in Paris' section and jewelry. It is organized according to the initial letter of the first name of the company; for example, Christian Dior under 'C' and Galeries Lafayette under 'G'.